AF540272

GROWING URBANIZATION
CHALLENGES AND STRATEGIES

GROWING URBANIZATION
CHALLENGES AND STRATEGIES

Edited by
Dr. (Mrs.) D. Sai Sujatha
Post-Graduate
Associate Professor
Deptt. of Population Studies & Social Work
Sri Venkateshwara University
Tirupati (Andhra Pradesh)
(INDIA)

DISCOVERY PUBLISHING HOUSE PVT. LTD.
NEW DELHI-110 002

Published by:
Tilak Wasan

DISCOVERY PUBLISHING HOUSE PVT. LTD.
4383/4B, Ansari Road, Darya Ganj
New Delhi-110 002 (India)
Phone : +91-11-23279245, 43596064-65
Fax : +91-11-23253475
E-mail : parul.wasan@gmail.com
discoverypublishinghouse@gmail.com
web : www.discoverypublishinggroup.com

***First Edition:* 2012**
ISBN: 978-93-5056-087-7

Growing Urbanization: ***Challenges and Strategies***

Printed at:
Shree Balaji Art Press
Delhi

PREFACE

India's urban population is second largest in the world after China. Barring China, America and Russia, in numerical terms India's urban population is higher than the total urban population of all countries of the world. 30 per cent of the India's population is living in urban areas and this 400 million people are generating two-thirds of the Gross Domestic Product (GDP) of our country and 90 per cent of the government's revenue. Five of the most densely populated cities in the world are in India. This rapid growth of urban areas is the result of two factors—natural increase in population (excess of births over deaths), and migration to urban areas. Today the movement of people from rural to urban areas (internal migration) is the most significant. It has been estimated by 2020, 140 million people will be migrating to the urban areas and it will reach to 700 million by 2050. Rapid urban growth is responsible for many environmental and societal changes in the urban areas and its effects are strongly related to global change issues. This, in fact, has become a threat to India. India has to improve its urban areas to achieve objectives of economic development. Keeping in view of the vital importance of growing urbanization and its effects on basic amenities, an attempt has been made to compile the papers presented in the National Seminar on "Growing Urbanization: Basic Amenities—Challenges and strategies" by the academicians of different universities and institutions, to examine the various challenges and to assess the strategies to provide basic amenities on par with growing urbanization.

The present volume contains 29 articles on various aspects Growing Urbanization in India, Causes and Consequences, Problems, Impact on Economic Development, Education, Role of Migration, Challenges of Urban Development with a Focus on Urban Community development and community participation. These articles can give an idea about the various issues that arised or likely to arise with increasing urbanization. It will be very helpful to the academicians of all the Social Sciences, NGOs, planners and policy-makers.

I am grateful to Andhra Pradesh State Council of Higher Education, Hyderabad, and the Indian Council of Social Science Research, New Delhi, for their financial support to organize the seminar. I convey my profound gratitude to all the contributors for their contribution to this volume. I am highly thankful to all those who helped me directly and indirectly in bringing out this volume.

D. SAI SUJATHA

CONTENTS

LIST OF CONTRIBUTORS

Dr. T. Sita Kumari, Associate Professor, P.G. Department of Law, S.V. University, Tirupati.

Mr. G. Adinarayana, Assistant Professor, P.G. Department of Law, S.V. University, Tirupati.

Dr. M. Reddi Ramu, Assistant Professor, Siddartha Institute of Engineering and Technology, Narayanavanam Road, Puttur, Chittoor (District).

Dr. C. Sujathamma, Department of Geography, S.P.W.D and P.G. College, Tirupati, A.P.

Dr. K. Mahadevamma, Head, Department of Social Work, S.P.W. College, Tirupati, A.P.

Dr. V. Venkateswarlu, Assistant Professor and Co-coordinator, Department of Sociology and Social Work, Acharya Nagarjuna University, Guntur.

Mrs. P. Hemalatha, Research Scholar, (FIP), Department of Sociology and Social Work, Acharya Nagarjuna University, Guntur.

Ms. K. Srivalli, Research Scholar, Department of Economics and Applied Economics, Acharya Nagarjuna University, Nagarjunanagar, Guntur.

Ms. M. Galaiah, Research Scholar, Department of Economics and Applied Economics, Acharya Nagarjuna University, Nagarjunanagar, Guntur.

Ms. N. Radha, Research Scholar, Department of Economics and Applied Economics, Acharya Nagarjuna University, Nagarjunanagar, Guntur.

Mrs V. Usha Reddy, Assistant Professor, Department of EEE, SV U College of Engineering, Tirupati, A.P.

Ms. S. Gouthami, Final Year B.Tech Student, Department of EEE, SV U College of Engineering, Tirupati, A.P.

Dr. T. Ramashri, Associate Professor, Department of EEE, SV U College of Engineering, Tirupati, A.P.

Dr. Allu Gowri Sankar Rao, Assistant Professor, Department of Sociology & Social Work, Acharya Nagarjuna University, Guntur.

Mr. G. Samba Siva Rao, Research Scholar, Department of Sociology and Social Work, Acharya Nagarjuna University, Guntur.

Mrs. M. Subhashini, Research Scholar, Department of Political Science and Public Administration, Acharya Nagarjuna University, Nagarjunanagar, Guntur.

Dr. K. Radhika, Associate Professor, Department of Economics, S.V. University, Tirupati.

Mr. A. Ramesh, Research Scholar, Department of Economics, S.V. University, Tirupati.

Dr. Naraginti Amareswaran, Researcher, Department of Education, Sri Venkateswara University, Tirupati, A.P.

Dr. T. Mallikarjuna Sharma, Principal, Satyam College of Education, Kodumur, Kurnool District.

Mr. P. Raju, Siddhartha Institute of Engg. and Technology, Puttur, Chittoor (District).

Dr. K. Ganesh Babu, Department of Political Science and Public Administration, S.V. University, Tirupati, A.P.

Dr. I. Narendra Kumar, Department of Econometrics, S.V. University, Tirupati, A.P.

Dr. G. Brahmanda Reddy, Department of Population Studies, S.V. University, Tirupati, A.P.

Mrs. B. Anupama Devi, Principal, Universal College of Education, Tirupati, A.P.

Dr. K. Dhanalakshmi, Assistant Professor, Department of Sociology & Social Work, Acharya Nagarjuna University, Guntur.

Mr. B. Ramesh, Research Associate, Council for Social Development, Southern Regional Centre, Rajendranagar, Hyderabad.

Ms. A. Mary Princess Lavanya, Research Scholar, Department of Sociology and Social Work, Acharya Nagarjuna University, Nagarjunanagar, Guntur.

Mr. N. Sagar, IIIrd B.Tech, Civil Engineering, S.I.E.T.K., Puttur.

Mr.V. Parameswar, IIIrd B.Tech, Civil Engineering, S.I.E.T.K., Puttur.

Mr. T. M. Prasad, Research Scholar, Department of Sociology, S.V. University, Tirupati, A.P.

Dr. K. Suneetha, Assistant Professor, Department of Social Work, Vikrama Simhapuri University, Nellore.

Mr. V. Yellappa, MSW Student, Department of Social Work, Vikrama Simhapuri University, Nellore.

Mr.G. Raveendra, MSW Student, Department of Social Work, Vikrama Simhapuri University, Nellore.

Dr. N. Rajani, Assistant Professor, Department of Home Science, SPMVV, Tirupati, A.P.

Mrs. Karima Ferhana, Doctoral Student, Department of Home Science, SPMVV, Tirupati, A.P.

Dr. A. Samanthakamani, Associate Professor, Department of Political Science and Public Administration, S.V. Arts College, Tirupati, A.P.

Dr. I.S. Kishore, Department of Political Science and Public Administration, S.V. University, Tirupati, A.P.

Dr. Reddi Bhaskara Reddy, Assistant Professor, Department of Geography, S.V. University, Tirupati, A.P.

Dr. S. Anil Kumar Reddy, Regional Co-coordinator, JKC (IEG), S.V. University Region, Tirupati, A.P.

Dr. C. Janardhan Reddy, Principal, Rama Raja B.Ed. College, Tirupati, A.P.

Mr. K.V. Sunil Kumar, Research Scholar, Department of Population Studies, S.V. University, Tirupati.

Mr. M.C. Sidda Reddy, Research Scholar, Department of Management Studies, S.V. University, Tirupati, A.P.

Dr. C.L. Chenna Reddy, Junior Lecturer (Contract) in Civics, S.V. Junior College, Tirupati, A.P.

Dr. P.B. Reddy, Department of Political Science and Public Administration, S.V. University, Tirupati, A.P.

Dr. P. Ganesh, District Coordinator, Family Health International, Kadapa and Anantapur Districts, A.P.

Dr. T. Chandrasekarayya, Assistant Professor, Department of Population Studies and Social Work, S.V. University, Tirupati, A.P.

Dr. D. Sai Sujatha, Associate Professor, Department of Population Studies and Social Work, S.V. University, Tirupati, A.P.

Mrs. V.T. Hinduja, Research Scholar, Department of Population Studies and Social Work, S.V. University, Tirupati, A.P.

Dr. A. Kusuma, Academic Consultant, Department of Population Studies and Social Work, S.V. University, Tirupati, A.P.

Ms. B. Ereesha, MSW Student, Department of Population Studies and Social Work, S.V. University, Tirupati, A.P.

Urbanization in India

A Study

Dr. T. Sita Kumari,
Mr. G. Adinarayana

Urbanization in General

Urbanization is a process indicating growth of urban centers in number as well as in the population occupying these centers. It specifically means a process involving an increase in the proportion of the population, that is urban in relation to the increase in the proportion of the total population as in relation to the proportion of non-urban population of a region. Generally, urban phenomenon is supposed to be the consequence of economic growth. But the bases which are responsible for urbanization vary from time to time. In recent years industrialization and economic development are found predominantly responsible for urbanization. But the historical context, of the problem reveals that social, cultural and political forces have their impact in the process of urban growth.

Urbanization in India

India, at present is under the pressure of two forces:

- Rapid rate of population growth.
- Rapid rate of urbanization.

This pressure has created a number of problems like the lack of essential amenities of life. The acute among the various problems is water which is very serious in nature. Water is one of the major problems of urbanization. No town can exist without it. Both its quality and quantity are important and it has no substitute. Water is necessary both for human consumption and for industrial use. The other problems are, urban transport, problems of housing, sanitation, public health, communication and electricity. Cities are seen as 'engines of economic growth', are invention and innovation nodes where new technologies are developed and taken into productive use. In order to be competitive and stay profitable, there is a continuous sniggle to improve the productivity by increasing the machine and knowledge intensity of production. The best examples are industrial districts of the north and Bangalore which is a high-tech region.

Migration is the other side of urbanization. In a country like India, urban poverty and rural urban migration are closely related. The cities as compared to villages, promise more convenient work, and steadier and higher wages. Many or most migrants see urban earnings as supplementing the rural, their urban stay as temporary and their places of origin as their permanent homes. Migration is a strategy on the part of the peasant families to bring some of the city's wealth to the village. Urban exploitation of rural resources, through many of the development process, directly or indirectly forcing rural populations to migrate to nearly towns.

Urbanization is both demographic and sociological, thereby sometimes used interchangeable demographic urbanization is physical urbanization, where people live and sociological urbanization is the provision of appropriate amenities for urban life. Thus urbanization is a social process like of becoming urban, moving to cities, changing from agriculture to other pursuits common to cities and corresponding changes of behaviour patterns.

The changing character and the role of the city in consequence of growth of urbanization are of prime significance as objectives of the urban studies. Recent growth of urbanization in the developing countries has given rise to a giant urban area where the great majority of people depend on urban jobs and urban services. This radical change has brought about the change in urban environment, the impact of which, in terms of measurements like commuter zones, service areas and the exchange of goods and information, expands to involve each part of the city areas in complex services of interactions with other parts. The objective is not only to study attitudes to the city which are common within the prevailing culture, but also and at the same time, the new trends and fashions manifest themselves. Urbanization as phenomena is not static but changing overtime—being dynamic.

So urban environment is the composite effect of city terrain, drainage including water bodies, modes of transport and movement within the city as well as firm and to the city. Population of the residential areas, density of buildings, industries and commercial areas, alignment of roads and streets, workplaces and institutions of economy, health and education, and also cultural, all what is that form urban infrastructure give rise to the concept of urban environment. From times immemorial cities have compacted for influence, power and commerce. In the 21st century cities will compete to attract talent and human capital. More than half the world's population now lives in urban areas. There is a need to consider the environmental costs and benefits of this shift. So the government goal is shifting to the concept of city with security, with safety and a need for self-discipline.

Policies for Urban Governance

The policy and strategy of urban development have undergone major changes during the past two and a half decades. This has resulted in transformation of the organizational structure for managing urban sector schemes and the supporting financing system that need to be analyzed. A review of the evolution of the policy perceptive on urban development indicates that until the Sixth Plan (1980-85) the policies addressed largely the problems of housing, slums and provision of civic amenities. It did some times put forward vision of Master plans for large cities and development of small and medium towns in the context of regional development but did not propose specific programmes or projects to move towards the vision at national level. The Seventh Plan explicitly recognized the problems of urban poor but the issues of employment generation, pro-poor growth strategy, infrastructural requirement etc., did not figure in the strategy for this sector. The Eighth Plan (1992-97) for the first time talked of urban policies that could directly contribute to the goals of employment generation and poverty reduction by directing growth in certain directions. It envisaged a role for the local bodies in city development and stipulated cost recovery to be built into the municipal finance system. This perspective has further been reinforced in the Ninth Plan period (1997-2002) which talks of cities as engines of growth. It also puts forward a vision of market-oriented growth with substantial reduction in budgetary allocations for development of urban infrastructure.

The Tenth Plan document expressed concern regarding decline in the rate of growth of urban population during nineties but failed to mention that this was primarily due to decline in the absolute number of census towns and significantly higher decline in demographic growth of small and medium towns compared to average urban growth in the country. It recognized the need to address the disparity in the availability of infrastructure and services across different size class of urban centers underlining the fact that very small towns with extremely limited resources rarely see any improvement. It noted that larger cities generally have the capacity to raise resources from domestic as well as international. Unfortunately the plan proposed very little to address the problems of serious deficiency in infrastructure and basic amenities in small towns.

The Eleventh Plan like its predecessor, regarded deteriorating infrastructural situation in cities and to 'provide large economies of agglomeration' and are absorbing large proportions of the incremental urban population. It lays major emphasis on Jawaharlal Nehru National Urban Renewal Mission launched in the fourth year of the Last Plan 'in a 'mission mode'. This mission has succeeded to a large extent in getting the state and city governments to commit themselves to structural reforms which the central government had failed to achieve despite adopting several measures and incentive schemes since early nineties.

The Eleventh Plan talks of bringing about spatially balanced urbanization through development of new townships and growth centers. The taskforce for slum development for the plan proposes improving the level of basic services for non-mission cities through Integrated Housing and Slum Development Programme (IHSDP) which would replace National Slum Development Programme and Valmiki Ambedkar Awas Yojna. The mission is not for large cities alone but for promoting balanced urbanization in the country.

The mission besides attempting infrastructural development with market reforms is to provide the poor access to basic services and land with tenurial security. Unfortunately the component of infrastructure and reform in governance is being looked after by the ministry of urban development while provision of shelter, basic services and slum development are the responsibilities of a separate submission administered by the Ministry of Housing and Urban Development. It is noted that the milestones for implementation of reform agenda are unambiguous and easy to monitor as these can be ascertained based on an overview of the legislative charges, administrative orders etc., but the indicators for ensuring access to basic amenities and land to the poor are too complicated and difficult to construct.

Constitutional Provisions

In recent years, governments in most of the developing countries have come to appreciate that one of the primary obstacles in meeting the challenge of urbanization and implementation of national development policies and programmes has been the absence of capacity and skills, whether financial, local government level, i.e. at the municipal government level, urban local government is an integral part of the system of government of a country. As such, it is subordinate to the central and state governments with respect to legislation, policies and other matters of national interest there is optimum need to balance the distribution of functions and powers between various levels of government.

After independence the Indian Constitution was framed in federal principles, wherein it was assumed that the provision need be made only regarding the structure, functions and powers of the state and the union government. As far as municipal government is concerned it was assumed to be state function. Entry 5 of state list in the seventh schedule of the Constitution of India gives power to the state to legislate on the municipal laws, establishment, constitution and power of local governments.[1] Except for recognizing local self-government as an essential part of the system of government of the country, the Constitution does not confer any independent status or powers on the local government bodies. The urban local bodies are created by a statue passed by a state legislature and by the union parliament in the case of such bodies in union territories. The organization power and functions of these municipal bodies are dependent on this statute.[2] There are two kinds of statutory provisions for creating a municipal authority. Either the Statute itself may establish a municipal authority (like the Bombay Municipal Corporation Act (1888); Delhi Municipal Corporation Act (1957), or it may empower the state government concerned to create a Municipal Corporation (municipality, municipal authority, municipal council or a board) for a particular area. The extent of the municipality's power and the government power depends on the statute enacted for its creation. The state government exercised control over the appointments to superior posts, expenditure, budgets, accounts, audit, taxation and municipal borrowing. Besides these they exercised administrative functions like right to be informed, the power to sanction, inspection and action in case of default, the right to suspend the execution of orders of the municipal body etc. But the activities and functions of the local government bodies have vastly changed under the impact of urbanization. The local governments no longer remained as mere instruments of political education and civic conscience, but became institutions for promotion of social and economic development of the local community as an integral part of the national government.

73rd Amendment Act and Urbanization

Though the Panchayati Raj Institutions have been in existence for a long time, it has been observed that these institutions have not been able to acquire the status and dignity of viable and responsive peoples bodies due to a number of reasons including absence of regular elections, prolonged supersession's, insufficient representation of weaker sections like Scheduled Casts, Scheduled Tribes and women, inadequate devolution of powers and lack of financial resources.

Article 40 of the Constitution which enshrines one of the directive principles of State Policy lays down that the state shall take steps to organize village panchayats and endow them with such powers and authority as may be necessary to enable them to function as units of self-government. In the light of the experience in the last forty years and in view of the short comings which have been observed, it is considered that there is an imperative need to enshrine in the Constitution certain basic and essential features of Panchayat Raj Institutions to impart certainty, continuity and strength to them. Accordingly it is proposed to add a new part relating to panchayats in the Constitution to provide for among other things, Gram Sabha in a village or group of villages, Constitution of panchayats at village and other level or levels, direct elections to all seats in panchayats at the village and intermediate level, reservation of not less than one third of the seats for women, fixing tenure of five years for panchayats and holding elections within a period of six months in the event of super session of any panchayat, disqualifications for membership of panchayat.

Legislations Relating to Urbanizations

Land is an important resource but since it is privately owned, it can become available for housing at the market price. Market prices escalate simply because of scarcity. As land is primary input in urbanization and as long as land prices are high no housing programme can really be undertaken. The rich people buy vacant lands in undeveloped stage or sometimes agricultural lands (which afterwards are converted into non-agricultural land) by investing surplus money. Records of rights of landed property are not in order and no modernization in this respect has taken place. Because of absence of records over land, land deals absorb a lot of black money. People invest in land because it is the only commodity the price of which goes up to neutralize inflation to the fullest extent. Even in the wake of the growth of computer technology. It should not be difficult to organize record of rights in land on a scientific basic. The law in this regard is very primitive. Land grabbing by the rich is taking place constantly though unlike that of the poor, it is not visible.

Since land is so costly, housing is bound to be expensive. When the cases of land grabbing come before the court, the court persistently held that compensation payable on acquisition of property must be equivalent of the value of property. The Constitution was amended several times to overcome such judicial view resulting in total deletion of the right to property from part III of the Constitution and its reincarnation.

Land Policy and Urbanization

Land is an important input for producing goods and services for urban development. Under the conventional analysis factors of production, i.e. land, labour and capital flow to make goods and services but the social and environmental consequences are not reflected in such analysis. Sustainable urban development does take account of social and environmental effects and means balance between the development of areas and protection of the environment with an eye to equity in employment, shelter, basic services, Social infrastructure and transportation in the urban areas. One has to ensure that land is properly used to meet these objectives. Urban India is plagued by shortage of housing facilities and scarcity of land for social overheads like roads, footpaths, parks, schools and so on. The roots of these problems can be found in the inadequate and inefficient land policy of the country. So it is important to have an effective and appropriate land policy that would promote sustainable urbanization.

National Commission on Urbanization of India (NCU, 1988) recognized the need for adequate supply of land, efficiency and equity in allocation of land and promotion of flexibility in land use. Thus it mentioned that the objectives of urban land policy should be

1. To achieve an optimum social use of urban land.
2. To make land available in adequate quantity to both public authorities and individuals at reasonable prices.
3. To encourage co-operative community effort as well as individual builders to develop land construct houses.
4. To use land to finance urban development.
5. To prevent concentration of land in few hands.
6. To encourage socially and economically efficient allocation of land so that land development conserves resources and land utilization is optional.[3]

Also the Eleventh Five Year Plan (2007-12) of India emphasizes that governments at appropriate levels including local authorities have to strive to remove all possible obstacles that may hamper equitable access to land. It identifies failure to adopt appropriate urban policies and land management practices as the primary cause of inequity and poverty. Thus, the Eleventh Five Year plan calls for a flexible land policy which will make conversion from one use to another, cost-efficient and promote equity. It judges that urban planning tools like master planning, zoning and regulations are not enough for the requirement of land supply for rapid urbanization. The problem has been addressed by Jawaharlal Nehru Urban Renewal Mission in India.

Conclusion

The most important component in urbanization is land management for sustainable urban development. but equally important are the environmental friendly management of basic services like water supply, sanitation and also of energy. The issue of equity in delivery of services is one important requirement of sustainable urban development.

The great centers of civilization, commerce and administration have been urban—from Mohenjo-Daro and Rome to Constantinople and London. Thus in a fast urbanizing country such as India it is imperative to understand city growth in order to track the centers of value addition. Isolating the fastest growing cities has enormous significance in understanding investment opportunities, in terms of demand growth, industrial activity, real estate, but also in infrastructure and its financing policies regarding urbanization in India have received relatively less attention than accorded.

Notes

1. Entry 5: Local government, that is to say, the constitution and powers of municipal corporations, improvement trusts, distract boards, mining settlement authorities and other local authorities for the purpose of local self government or village administration.
2. Bidyut Mohanty, *Urbanisation in developing countries: basic services and community participation,* Indian Institute of Social Sciences, New Delhi.
3. Basudha Chattopadhyaya, 'Sustainable Urban Development in India, Some Issues', Urbanisation.pdf.

References

1. Kenneth Little, *Urbanization as a Social Process: An Essay on Movement and Change in Contemporary Africa,* Routhedge and Kegan Paul, London.
2. Jan Hesselberg, *'Issues in Urbanization',* Rawat Publications, New Delhi.
3. L.N. Verma, *'Urban Geography',* Rawat Publications, New Delhi (2006).
4. http://www.networkideas.org/
5. Amitabh Kunde, *Migration and Urbanization in India, in the Context of Poverty Alleviation.*

Urbanization in India
A Study on Causes and Consequences

Dr. M. Reddi Ramu

Introduction

Urbanization is a part of the development process. In backward stagnant societies the process of urbanization is rather slow, because cities fail to offer employment opportunities to people living in the countryside. Those who migrate to cities in such societies are, in fact, pushed out of villages due to economic and social purposes; they are rarely pulled by the so-called attractions of the urban life. In contrast to stagnant backward societies, urbanization process is fast in rapidly growing economies where newly established industries and ancillary activities continuously provide jobs to people who wish to migrate to cities. The economic pull of cities in this phase of development becomes particularly strong if industrial growth is fast, and in spite of high capital intensity industries offer jobs in increasingly large number. The process of urbanization slows down only when the proportion of urban population to total population in a country becomes very high. This stage has been reached in some 30-odd countries, which are characterized as developed industrialized countries.

- According to Louis Wirth it is "Way of Life". He identified population size, density and heterogeneity as the basic determinants of urbanization.
- Eldridge defines "Urbanization as a process of concentration of population and multiplication of points of such concentration".

Urbanization is a part of the development process. In backward stagnant societies the process of urbanization is rather slow; cities fail to offer employment opportunities to people living in the countryside. Those who migrate to cities in such societies are, in fact, pushed out of villages due to economic and social pressures; they are rarely pulled by the so-called attractions of the urban life.

The development strategy perceived many developed countries consequent to political inter-dependence appears to have developed urban areas and large cities. But the growth of towns and cities (urbanization) will be possible if it is backed by prosperity in rural areas. "Location of industries, expansion of government administration, educational institutions, commercial centers etc has played a major role in the urbanization process"[1].

In contrast the stagnant backward societies, urbanization process is fast in rapidly growing economic where newly established industries and ancillary activities continuously provide jobs to people who wish to migrate to cities.

The main objective of this paper is to analyze the urbanization in India and briefly discussed about difference between the main causes and consequences in urbanization.

The present paper covers first aspect of urbanization procedure, features, factors affecting to Indian urbanization, and the second aspect covers causes and consequences of urbanization in the present scenario in India.

Urbanization Across the World

Urbanization rates vary across the world. US, UK have a far higher urbanization level than China, India, Switzerland, but a far slower annual urbanization rate since much less of the population is living in rural areas.

Urbanization in US never affected the Rocky Mountains in locations such as Colorado, New Mexico, Jackson Hok, Douglas country. The lake districts of Northern Minnesota has also been affected as has verdant the cost of Florida and the barrier islands of North Carolina.

In UK two major examples of new urbanization can be seen in Swindon, Wiltshire and Milton Keynes, Berkinghumshire. These two towns show some of the quickest growth rates in Europe.

In general the countries of Europe, Anglo America, Australia, Newzeland, Japan, Singapore, Hong Kong, Israel, Bahrain, and South Korea are more urbanized. The proportion of urban population to total population in 2001 was 73 per cent, in Russia 77 per cent, in USA 79 per cent, in Japan 91 per cent, in Australia and 89 per cent in UK. Compared to them the Indian percentage of 27.78 in 2001 was too low.[2]

Urbanization in India

According to the 2001 census, India's urban population bears 285 million. India's level of urbanization at 27.78 per cent is lower than the level of urbanization of developed countries. India's level of urbanization is also lower than that prevailing in some of the developing countries of Asia and Africa, such as Pakistan 37 per cent, China 32 per cent, and Nigeria 44 per cent.

There is a great deal of variation in the level of urbanization between states. A high level of urbanization of above the national average (27.78%) is observed in Mizoram, Goa, Maharashtra, Gujarat, Tamilnadu and Karnataka while low levels of urbanization of less than 15 per cent characterize in Himachal Pradesh, Sikkim, Assam, Arunachal Pradesh, Bihar and Orissa. An important aspect of urbanization in India is the tendency towards concentration population in larger urban centers. According to 2001 census class I cities having one lakh or more population account for 9 per cent of the total urban centers and over 68 per cent of the urban population lives in these centers. These cities are growing rapidly and the services can never keep up with the pressure of population. Women are the worst affected, especially poor women. Both the economic and social conditions limit their access to various urban amenities. Added to this is the overcrowding, long queues and long distance to be traveled, all of which involve time and money, both scarce commodities. High concentration of urban population also puts severe strain on the job opportunities available in a labour surplus situation and new streams of migrants are forced to take up whatever jobs available. Here again poor women with their lack of education and skill are most constraint. Economic necessity and the need to better the lot of the younger generation force women to take up the residual jobs which are normally tedious extensions of house work and pay very poorly.

Features of Indian Urbanization

1. The Indian urbanization is of substance type whereby rural illiterate workers swarm into the cities to seek employment. This badly affects the quality of the urban life creating slums and squatter settlements.
2. The Indian urbanization has poly-metropolitan effect in which four premier cities—Mumbai, Kolkata, Delhi and Chennai—play dominant role.
3. The big cities of India are experiencing explosive population growth while the small towns are stagnating.
4. The Indian urban systems are not integrated both functionally and spatially. Hence there are breaks and imbalance in urban hierarchy and rural-urban profile.
5. Indian urban centers are growing more on the basis of tertiary sector rather than on the basis of secondary sector. It is only in recent years that some efforts are being made to create proper industrial base at the district level.
6. The western and southern parts of the country are more urbanized than their eastern and northern counterparts due to differential resource potential and history of urban development.
7. Urbanization in India during the 20th century is associated with a particular theme in each decade as given below:

Factors Affecting Urbanization in India

1901 — 1911 — Famine and Plague

1911 — 1921 — Influenza epidemics

1921 — 1931 — Agricultural depression

1931 — 1941 — World War

1941 — 1951 — Partition and after effects

1951 — 1961 — Planned development

1961 — 1971 — Urbanization in backward areas and concentrated urban growth around big cities.

1971 — 1981 — Decentralized urban growth

1981 — 1991 — Decelerated rural-urban migration and declining rate of natural increase

1991 — 2001 — Metropolitanisation.

Table 2.1: Patterns of urban population by size class of town—1901 to 2001

Size Class	CENSUS YEAR										
	1901	1911	1921	1931	1941	1951	1961	1971	1981	1991	2001
I	22.9	24.2	25.3	27.4	35.4	41.8	48.4	52.4	60.4	65.2	68.6
II	11.8	10.9	12.4	12.0	11.8	11.1	11.9	12.2	11.7	11.0	9.7
III	16.5	17.7	16.9	18.8	17.7	16.7	18.5	17.4	14.3	13.2	12.2
IV	22.1	20.5	18.9	19.0	16.3	14.0	13.0	12.0	9.5	7.8	6.8
V	20.4	19.8	19.0	17.3	15.4	13.2	7.2	5.2	3.6	2.6	2.3
VI	6.03	7.00	7.4	5.6	3.5	3.2	3.2	0.8	0.5	0.3	0.2
Total	100.00	100.00	100.00	100.00	100.00	100.00	100.00	100.00	100.00	100.00	100.00

Source: Several Census Reports.

The most important index in this study of urbanization is distribution of population by different size classes, over time which reveals the population concentration. Urban units in India are classified into six classes. Proportion of urban population by class, given in Table 2.1. It is evident that 22.9 per cent of the Indian urban population was inhabited in class I town in 1901, while it was 65.2 per cent in 1991 and reached 68.6 per cent in 2001. Over the years, the share of the class I towns in the Indian urban population has been tremendous. evidence indicates that, about two-thirds of increase in the urban population of the large cities as result of natural increase (Singh,1992) and remaining as the consequences of migration (Oberoi,1993). While in class II and III towns, the growth of population has more or less constant. On the other hand, the percentage share of urban population of small towns (IV to VI) had shown a steady decline, which results transfer of those towns to the higher categories. In these context, Shish Bose (1978) explained reasons such as declassification of the towns and changes in the definition of urban in

1961 census. Thus, Indian urbanization scenario shows a high concentration of population in large cities/towns, signals the economy of the urban problem such as socio-economic, environmental and administrative etc.[3]

Table 2.2: Pattern of urbanization and growth of urban population across major states in india —1971 to 2001

S.No	Name of the State	Percentage of Urban Population				Annual Exponential Growth Rate		
		1971	1981	1991	2001	1971-1981	1981-1991	1991-2001
1.	Andhra Pradesh	19.31	28.25	26.84	27.08	3.94	3.55	1.37
2.	Bihar	07.97	09.84	10.40	10.47	4.27	2.66	2.57
3.	Gujarath	28.08	31.06	34.40	37.35	3.42	2.90	2.50
4.	Haryana	17.06	21.96	24.79	29.00	4.65	3.56	4.11
5.	Himachal Pradesh	06.99	7.72	8.70	9.79	3.02	3.11	2.01
6.	Karnataka	24.31	28.91	30.91	33.98	4.08	2.55	2.53
7.	Krerala	16.24	18.78	26.44	25.97	3.19	4.76	0.74
8.	Madhya Pradesh	18.58	22.34	25.27	26.67	4.25	3.63	2.71
9.	Maharashtra	31.17	36.03	38.73	42.40	3.35	3.27	2.95
10.	Manipur	13.17	26.44	27.69	23.88	9.70	2.98	1.21
11.	Meghalaya	14.55	18.03	18.69	19.63	4.87	3.10	3.16
12.	Orissa	8.41	11.82	13.43	14.97	5.21	3.08	2.61
13.	Punjab	23.73	27.72	29.72	33.95	3.62	2.55	3.19
14.	Rajasthan	17.63	20.93	22.88	23.38	4.52	3.31	2.71
15.	Tamilnadu	30.25	32.98	34.20	43.86	2.45	1.76	3.56
16.	Tripura	10.43	10.98	15.26	17.02	3.26	6.19	2.53
17.	Uttar Pradesh	14.02	18.01	19.89	20.78	4.78	3.27	2.84
18.	West Bengal	24.75	26.49	27.39	28.03	2.75	2.54	1.84
INDIA		**19.91**	**23.33**	**25.72**	**27.78**	**3.79**	**3.09**	**2.73**

Source: Census of India 1981, 1991 and 2001 Reports.

Patterns of Urbanization by States

Analysis of pattern of urbanization by states provides an idea of change in the population overtime and indicates the pace of economic development. Table 2.2 provides the trends of urbanization by states during 1971-2001. Among major states, some developed states viz. Tamilnadu, Maharashtra, Punjab, Gujarat, Karnataka and West Bengal have registered higher proportion of urban population than the national level. These states attracted population in urban areas due to industrialization and infrastructure investment (Kunda, 2006). Moreover, the process of urbanization in Andhra

Pradesh, Haryana, Kerala and Madhya Pradesh have more or less equal to national average, may be due to differentials in industrialization and predominance of agriculture. In contrast the backward states like Bihar, Himachal Pradesh, Manipur, Meghalaya, Orissa, Rajasthan, Tripura and Uttar Pradesh have recorded below that the national average, indicating thereby the backward regions have continued to be backward or lagging in the industrial development with having agrarian sector.[4]

Analysis further reveals that decadal growth during 1971 to 1991 for developed states have recorded medium or low growth of population than some under-developed state viz., Haryana, Meghalaya, Orissa, and Uttar Pradesh showing alarming situation. In general, the speed of urbanization have declined during 1901 and 2001 than earlier decades, which reflects overall slowdown of economic development apart from low natural growth in urbanization.

Table 2.3: Rural and urban population in India

Year	Total Population (in millions)	Rural Population		Urban Population		Annual Percentage increase in population		
		Millions	Per cent	Millions	%	Total	Rural	Urban
1901	232.9	207.3	89.0	25.6	11.0	—	—	—
1911	246.0	220.4	89.6	25.6	10.4	0.56	0.63	0.00
1921	244.3	216.6	88.7	27.7	11.3	–0.07	–0.17	0.82
1931	270.8	237.8	87.8	33.0	12.2	1.08	0.98	1.91
1941	309.0	265.5	85.9	43.5	14.1	1.41	1.16	3.18
1951	361.1	298.7	82.7	62.4	17.3	1.69	1.25	4.34
1961	439.2	360.3	82.0	78.9	18.0	2.16	2.06	2.64
1971	548.2	439.1	80.1	109.1	19.9	2.48	2.19	3.82
1981	685.2	525.7	76.7	159.5	23.3	2.50	1.97	4.62
1991	844.3	627.1	74.3	217.2	25.7	2.32	1.93	3.61
2001	1027.0	742.0	72.2	285.0	27.8	2.16	1.83	3.12

Source: Registrar General & Census Commissioner of India, Census of India.

For measuring urbanization a number of measures are being used. One very simple method is to examine the changes in the level of urban population. From the data provided in Table 2.3, urban population increased from about 26 million in 1901 to 62 million in 1951, an increase of only 36 million in 50 years. But, thereafter, the absolute increase during the next three decades (1951-1981), was of the order of 98 millions. This indicates that programmes of industrialization did not make an impact in terms of population absorption in urban areas, though this impact is not very discernible. During the decade 1981-1991, urban population increased by 57 million which indicates growing trend towards urbanization. Urban population, in absolute terms, reached the figure of 285 million accounting for 27.8 per cent of total population in 2001. Presently India's urban population is larger than the urban population of all countries except China. Thus in absolute terms India's urban population is quite large and its significance must be clearly appreciated for the future development in this country.[5]

Urbanization Projections

According to UN Habitat 2006 Annual Report some time in the middle of 2007, the majority of people worldwide will be living in towns and cities for the first time in history, this is referred to as the arrival of "Urban Million". In regard to future trends, it is estimated, 93 per cent of urban growth will be occurring in Asia and Africa and to a smaller extent in Latin America and Caribbean, by 2050 over 6 billion people, 2/3 of humanity, will be living in towns and cities.[6]

The total urban population in India has increased 11 fold from 25.85 million in 1901 to 285.35 million in 2001. Relative growth of urban and rural populations can be seen from table 2.4.

Table 2.4: Relative Growth of Urban and Rural Population

Year	Population in million			% of total population		Urban and Rural Ratio
	Total	Rural	Urban	Rural	Urban	
1901	232.9	207.3	25.6	89.0	11.0	1: 8.1
1911	246.0	220.4	25.6	89.6	10.4	1: 8.6
1921	244.3	216.6	27.7	88.7	11.3	1: 7.8
1931	270.8	237.8	33.0	87.8	12.2	1: 7.2
1941	309.0	265.8	43.5	85.9	14.1	1: 6.1
1951	361.1	298.7	62.4	82.7	17.3	1: 4.7
1961	439.2	360.3	78.9	52.0	18.0	1: 4.5
1971	548.2	439.1	109.1	80.1	19.9	1: 3.7
1981	685.2	525.7	159.5	76.7	23.3	1: 3.3
1991	844.3	627.1	217.2	74.3	25.7	1: 2.9
2001	1027.0	742.0	285.0	72.2	27.8	1: 2.6

Source: Census Reports 1901 and 2001, Government of India.

Causes of Urbanization

The three main causes of urbanisation in LEDCs (Less Economically Developed Countries) since 1950 are:

1. Rural to urban migration is happening on a massive scale due to population pressure and lack of resources in rural areas. This is a 'push' factors.

Table 2.5: Levels of urbanization in India—1981, 1991 and 2001

India/ State/ Union Territory	Urban Population as percentage of Total Population		
	1981	1991	2001
India	23.34	25.72	27.78
Andhra Pradesh	23.32	26.84	27.07
Arunachal Pradesh	6.56	12.21	20.41
Assam	9.88	11.08	12.72
Bihar	12.47	13.17	13.36
Goa	32.03	41.02	49.77
Gujarat	31.10	34.40	37.35
Haryana	21.88	24.79	29.00
Himachal Pradesh	7.61	8.70	9.79
Jammu & Kashmir	21.05	23.83	24.88
Karnataka	28.89	30.91	33.98
Kerala	18.74	26.44	25.96
Madhya Pradesh	20.29	23.21	24.98
Maharashtra	35.03	38.73	42.40
Manipur	26.42	27.69	23.88
Meghalaya	18.07	18.69	19.62
Mizoram	24.67	46.20	49.49
Nagaland	15.52	17.28	17.74
Orissa	11.79	13.43	14.97
Punjab	27.68	29.72	33.95
Rajasthan	21.05	22.88	23.38
Sikkim	16.15	9.12	11.10
Tamilnadu	32.95	34.20	43.86
Tripura	10.99	15.26	17.02
Uttar Pradesh	17.95	19.89	21.02
West Bengal	26.47	27.39	28.03
Andaman & Nicobar Island	26.30	26.80	32.67
Chandigarh	93.63	89.69	89.77
Dadra & Nagar Haveli	6.67	8.47	22.89
Daman & Diu	36.75	46.86	36.26
Delhi	92.73	89.93	93.02
Lakshadweep	46.28	56.29	44.47
Pondicherry	52.28	64.05	66.56

Source: Census of India, 1981, 1991 and 2001.

2. People living in rural areas are 'pulled' to the city. Often they believe that the standard of living in urban areas will be much better than in rural areas. They are usually wrong. People also hope for well paid jobs, the greater opportunities to find casual or 'informal' work, better health care and education.
3. Natural increase caused by a decrease in death rates while birth rates remain high.

Drought

Drought is the classic pull affecting thousands of people especially in Telangana and some parts of Rayalaseema in Andhra Pradesh.

Water logging

Water can also be bigger factor for migration; the uncontrolled use of irrigation water has resulted in the water logging and salivation of lands. This has led to falling crop yields, which in turn has led to migration by poor families.

Population pressure and land fragmentation

Having little access to land in a predominantly agrarian society leaves the landless with few alternatives to migration. In some states access to land is so limited that nearly all poor young people view migration as their main and perhaps only livelihood option. Most of the studies opined that "The voices of poor people on the move, traveling to new places in hope of improving their circumstances". Majority of the migrants have been working temporarily or permanently to work in factories, farms, as domestics or selling handicrafts. The situation of the parts in A.P and India is the same where there are reports of "a new and growing breed of landless workers which has led to increased migration from rural areas to cities and other states.

Globalization affect to urbanization

The most recent push factors appears to be a fall in agricultural commodity prices brought about by macro-economic reforms linked with liberalization and globalization policies.

Other pull factors

Apart from environmental push factors is the downsizing of public sector jobs creation. Migration has been triggered by a rapid growth of their labour forces, high rate of unemployment and a heavy reliance on the public sector for job creation.

Consequences of Urbanization

- Dwyer points out "As ever larger of people try to make a living in cities unable offer either jobs or shelter, new forms of urbanization are emerging out of necessity—cities built substantially by the poor, for the poor".[7]

- Third world cities have performed the function of attracting large number of migrants but failed to create employment opportunities and so instead of becoming "Generative" the third world cities have largely remained "Parasitic", Siphoning away resources from other areas.
- Rapid growth of third world cities is generally interpreted as "Over Urbanization". Singh in 1993 argues in the countries of the third world, urbanization has not been accompanied by modernization as well as industrialization, i.e., a case of pseudo urbanization or over urbanization–which results in low labour absorption capacity.[8]
- The other consequences of urbanization have been the growth of the service sector, growth of slums squatter settlements, varying affects on productivity and manufacturing and increased demands on infrastructure.
- Traditional local services and small-scale industry give way to modern industry, widening the area for its own sustenance and goods to be traded or processed into manufactures.
- Research in urban ecology finds that larger cities provide more specialized goods and services to the local market and surrounding areas, function as a transportation and whole sale hub for smaller places and accumulate more capital, financial service provision and an educated labour force as well as often concentrating administrative functions for the area in which they lie.
- As the cities develop, effects can include a dramatic increase in rents often pricing the local working class out of the market including such functionaries as employees of local municipalities.

Above all these problems lies the problem of urban poverty, starkly visible and manifesting in the mass of beggars, petty hawkers and causal workers struggling to eke out a living for themselves. Gradually the urban centre became just merely large size villages and incorporates many characteristics of a peasant economy and this process is often termed as "Urban involution".[9]

Thus according to Harold Lubell, the informal constitutes the residual labour market of the last resort characterized by self-employment and low income procedures of marginal goods and services for lack of any other means of earning a livelihood.[10]

Urbanization has led to increased productivity and economic diversification but also deprivation, poverty and marginalization. 20-25 per cent of total population living slums often located near factories, power stations, garbage dumps and busy roads. The increased demand for services and infrastructure has depleted natural resources and caused environmental problems. Environmental problems are also caused by poverty and those caused by industrialization and change in consumption pattern.

Children in slums are more vulnerable to diseases and deficiencies than their natural and urban counterparts. Adult supervision of children is rare.

Thus to solve the above mentioned problems there is the necessity of planning for urbanization. Urbanization can be planned, pooped or organic. Planned urbanization, i.e. new town or the garden city is based on an advance plan which can be prepared for military, aesthetic, economic or urban design reasons. New urbanization is an amalgamation of old-world design patterns, marred with present day demands.

Conclusion

The urbanization in India due to migration of people from rural areas has not gathered enough momentum so as to enable to absorb a significant chunk of the rural population by simultaneously going for industrialization. So there is a need to settle that labour in the urban areas by providing enough work to stay back. If that is not possible, there is a severe economic impact not only on the rural economy but also on the total economy.

Thus to solve the above mentioned problems there is the necessity of planning for urbanization. Urbanization can be planned, organic. Planned urbanization, i.e. new town or the garden city movement is based on an advance plan which can be prepared for military, aesthetic, economic or urban design reasons. New Urbanization is an amalgamation of old-world design patterns, merged with present day demands.

References

1. Andhra Pradesh Economic Association, Annual Conference, 2008: Urbanization and Economic Development in A.P, February 9th and 10th 2008, S V University, Tirupathi, p. 297.
2. Dwyer D.J: 1975, *People and Housing in the Third World Cities*, Longman, London.
3. Census Reports 1901 and 2001, Government of India.
4. Census of India, Provisional Population Totals Paper-2 of 2001. Rural, Urban Population, Series 29, Registrar General of India, New Delhi, 2001.
5. Geertzcliffirt: Pedders 2001 and Princes *Social Change and Economic Modernization in Indonesian Towns*, Chicago and London.
6. Lubel Harold: July 1973,"Under Development and Employment in Calcutta", *International Labour Review*, Volume-XIX, No.1, p. 28.
7. Census of India, 1981, 1991 and 2001 Reports, Government of India.
8. Ms. Bharka Tondon and Dr. D.K Singh: June 2007, Rural Urban Migration in India, *Status* and *Kurukshetra*.
9. Registrar General and Census Commissioner of India, Census of Various Issues.
10. Sing Ram Bali: 1993, "Process of Urbanisation in the Third World" in Jayamala Deede and Vimala Rangaswami (Ed) *Urbanisation Trends, Perspective and Challenges*, Rawat Publications, Jaipur p. 57.

Migrant Tribal Women

Dr. I. Narendra Kumar,
Dr. G. Brahmanda Reddy

India has the largest concentration of tribal people anywhere in the world except perhaps in Africa. The tribal's live mostly in isolated villages or hamlets. A smaller portion of their population has now settled in permanent villages as well as in town and cities. The prominent tribal areas constitute about 15 per cent of the tribal geographical area of the country. The tribal population of India continues to suffer from discrimination, low education, marginalization, extreme poverty and conflict. They are being deprived of adequate access to the basic needs of life such as health, education, housing, food, security, employment justice and equity.

There are approximately 200 million tribal people in the entire globe, which constitute about 4 per cent of the global population. They are 533 tribes as per notified schedule under Article 342 of the Constitution of India in different states and union territories of the country. Nearly 50 per cent tribal population of the country is concentrated in the states like Madhya Pradesh, Chhattisgarh, Jharkhand, Bihar, Orissa, Maharashtra, Gujarat, Rajasthan and West Bengal. According to 2001 census, the population of ST in the country was 84.3 million constituting about 8.19 per cent of total Indian population (1028.6), the sex ratio among the ST is more towards female (972 female per 1000 males).

The tribal women migrate from tribal areas to urban areas mainly for employment. In urban areas they face number of problems. In urban areas due to lifestyle and environment they find it difficult to make adjustment with the changed situation and environment. In the above context we examine the socio-economic conditions and to the problems faced by the of migrant tribal women in Andhra Pradesh.

Objectives of the study were under

1. To study the socio-economic status of migrant tribal women in Andhra Pradesh.
2. To analyze the dynamics of social adjustment tribal women make in Andhra Pradesh in relation to employment and residential facilities.
3. To develop a system of help and rehabilitation of migrant tribal women, so that they can achieve the goals of their life and to suggest remedial measures of discouraging tribal migration to urban areas.

Methodology

The present study was conducted in Andhra Pradesh, physiographically in to Andhra Pradesh is divided: three regions Coastal Andhra, Rayalaseema and Telangana. In each region one district selected at randomly. The districts are Visakhapatnam, Kadapa and Warangal. A sample of 600 respondents was drawn from the universe. The migrant tribal women living in the urban area constituted the universe of the present study. The method of stratified sampling was used for selection of localities and families of migrant tribal women in the study area. Interview schedule was used as the main information of data collection. The primary data was collected in the urban areas and secondary data was collected by the Project Director, Project Officer and from other reports.

Findings

The tribal women migrated to urban areas, covered by the study, were found to have migrated from different tribal areas, far away from the towns in which they have settled. It is observed that in the process of migration of tribal women the *push-pull* factors have played an important role. The significant push factors found during investigation were very low rates of wages, unemployment, along with poverty and indebtedness. Marriage was found to be the single most important reason for the migration of female members of tribal communities in Andhra Pradesh. The reasons for migration of tribal women in Andhra Pradesh are presented in Table 3.1.

Table 3.1: Reason for migration of tribal women in Andhra Pradesh

S.No.	Reasons	No. of Respondents
1.	Employment	199 (33.16)
2.	Marriage	131 (21.83)
3.	Education	28 (4.66)
4.	Security	125 (20.83)
5.	Other	117 (19.5)
Total		600 (100.00)

Source: Field Data.

The in-depth analysis of reason for migration disclosed that out of 600 tribal women a majority of about 33.16 per cent of the women migrated to towns (urban and cities) reported lack of employment opportunities in the native places. Marriage was the main reason for migration to towns as reported by 21.83 per cent of the migrant women. For 4.66 per cent migrant women education was reason for migration to urban areas. Security (20.83 per cent) and other (19.5 per cent) reasons included acquisition of land/house for development project, repeated natural calamities like flood and famine and attraction of urban life. Age wise distribution of migrant tribal women is presented— Table 3.2.

Table 15.2: Distribution of age level of migrant tribal women in Andhra Pradesh

S.No.	Size of the Age	No. of Respondents
1.	15-25	194 (32.33)
2.	25-35	182 (30.33)
3.	35-45	146 (24.33)
4.	Above 45	78 (13.00
Total		600 (100.00)

Source: Field Data.

In table 3.2 examined the personal and family background of migrant tribal women and majority of migrant tribal women (32.33 per cent) were in the age group of 15-25 years, 30.33 per cent in the age group of 25-35 years, 24.33 per cent in the age group of 35-45 years and only 13 per cent of the migrant tribal women were in the age group of above 45 years. The education levels of respondents are presented in Table 3.3.

Table 3.3: Distribution of education level of migrant tribal women in Andhra Pradesh

S.No.	Level of Education	No. of Respondents
1.	Illiterates	265 (44.16)
2.	Primary	232 (38.66)
3.	Secondary	64 (10.67)
4.	Higher	25 (4.16)
5.	Technical	14 (2.33)
Total		600 (100.00)

Source: Field Data.

In table 3.3 shows that 44.16 per cent of women were illiterates, 38.66 per cent of women were primary, 10.67 per cent of women were secondary, 4.16 per cent of woman were higher and 2.33 per cent of women had technical qualifications in the study area of Andhra Pradesh. The sizes of the family of migrant tribal women are presented in Table 3.4.

Table 3.4: Distribution of size of the family of migrant tribal women in Andhra Pradesh

S.No.	Size of the family	No. of Respondents
1.	Small	173 (28.83)
2.	Marginal	206 (34.33)
3.	Large	221 (36.83)
Total		600 (100.00)

Source: Field Data.

From table 3.4 it is observed that only 28.83 per cent were from small families, 34.33 per cent were from marginal families and 36.83 per cent migrated tribal women had large families in the study area of Andhra Pradesh. The occupational levels of Tribal women are presented in Table 3.5.

Table 3.5: Occupational level of the tribal women in Andhra Pradesh

S.No.	Before migration of the occupation level	No. of Respondents
1.	Agriculture labour	241 (40.16)
3.	Produce the forest products	266 (44.33)
4.	Traditionally family occupation	93 (15.5)
Total		600 (100.00)

Source: Field Data.

Table 3.5 reveals that about 40.16 per cent of migrated women reported to be agriculture labour, 44.33 per cent reported collection and sale of forest products and 15.5 per cent of women reported traditional family occupation in the study area of Andhra Pradesh. Farming played important role in the generation of income. The member of earning members in the family are presented in Table 3.6.

Table 3.6: Distribution of earning member in the family of tribal women in Andhra Pradesh

S.No.	Earning member of the family	No. of Respondents
1.	0 – 2	165 (27.5)
2.	2 – 4	213 (35.5)
3.	Above 4	222 (37)
Total		600 (100.00)

Source: Field Data.

Table 3.6 shows that a large majority of 37 per cent migrant tribal women reported above 4 earning members in the family, 35.5 per cent of tribal women reported 2–4 earning members and 27.5 per cent of the tribal women reported 0–2 earning members in the study area of Andhra Pradesh. The distribution on the basis of ownership of houses of tribal women is presented in Table 3.7.

Table 3.7: Ownership of houses of tribal women in Andhra Pradesh

S.No.	Ownership of Houses	Before Migration	After Migration
1.	Own	418 (69.66)	165 (27.5)
2.	Rented	182 (30.33)	435 (72.5)
Total		600 (100.00)	600 (100.00)

Source: Field Data.

Table 3.7 reveals the ownership of houses in which the tribal women were living before and after migration to urban areas. The present study revealed that a majority of tribal women had their own houses (69.66 per cent) and rented houses (30.33 per cent) before migration. After migration to urban areas 27.5 per cent own houses and 72.5 per cent were living in rented houses in the study area of Andhra Pradesh. The types of houses are presented in Table 3.8.

Table 3.8: Type of houses of tribal women in Andhra Pradesh

S.No.	Type of Houses	No. of Respondents
1.	Hut	263 (43.83)
2.	Kutcha	184 (30.66)
3.	Pucca	65 (10.83)
4.	Mixed	88 (14.66)
Total		600 (100.00)

Source: Field Data.

Table 3.8 shows that most of the tribal in India live in huts made by local available materials like grass, bamboo, wooden logs and mud. Especially they have only one room in the house which is used for all purposes. The type of houses of tribal women found that 43.83 per cent migrated women reported huts, 30.66 per cent reported kutcha houses, 10.83 per cent reported pucca houses and 14.66 per cent reported mixed houses. The housing facilities are presented in Table 3.9.

Table 3.9: Housing facilities of tribal women in Andhra Pradesh

S.No.	Facilities	Before Migration	After Migration
1.	Water	—	101 (16.83)
2.	Electricity	—	248 (41.33)
3.	Toilets	—	66 (11.00)
4.	Bath room	—	185 (30.83)
Total			600 (100.00)

Source: Field Data.

From table 3.9 it is observed that housing facilities include all civic amenities such as water, electricity, latrine and bath room etc. Before migration there were no such facilities in the areas migrated tribal women ere living.

After migration they reported about the civic amenities like water facilities 16.83 per cent, 41.33 per cent electricity, 11 per cent toilets and 30.83 per cent bath room facilities in the living houses of the study area of Andhra Pradesh. The social adjustments of migrant tribal women are presented in Table 3.10.

Table 3.10: Distribution of social adjustments of migrant tribal women in Andhra Pradesh

S.No.	Social Adjustments	Before Migration	After Migration
1.	Food habits	381 (63.5)	488 (81.33)
2.	Pattern of clothing	373 (62.16)	468 (78)
3.	Standard of living	389 (64.83)	497 (82.83)
4.	Social behavior	393 (65.5)	389 (64.83)
5.	Communication (Local language to urban language)	374 (62.33)	515 (85.83)
Total		600 (100.00)	600 (100.00)

Source: Field Data.

Table 3.10 reveals the social adjustments of migrant tribal women like lifestyle in the urban areas, food habits, pattern of clothing, standard of living, social behaviour and language problems. Particularly the tribal women migrated to urban areas belonged to different tribal regions of the Andhra Pradesh and such they had different pattern of lifestyle. They gradually shifted from their traditional lifestyle to the urban lifestyles, and adjusted themselves in the urban of lifestyle. Especially 81.33 per cent of the migrant tribal women changed their food habits, 78 per cent changed their pattern of clothing, 82.83 per cent of positive changed standard of living, 64.83 per cent have changed their social behaviour and 85.83 per cent changed communication to speak in urban language (local language to urban language). The migrant tribal women faced a number of problems. The main problems are presented in Table 3.11.

Table 3.11: Problems faced by migrant tribal women in Andhra Pradesh

S.No.	Problems	No. of Respondents
1.	City life	176 (29.33)
2.	Employment	116 (19.33)
3.	Irregular employment	86 (14.33)
4.	Very low rates of wages	103 (17.16)
5.	Absence of medical facilities	119 (19.83)
Total		600 (100.00)

Source: Field data.

Table 3.11 shows that the tribal women faced a number of problems immediately after their migration to urban areas which included difficulty of communication in local language, employment, education of children and local contacts, adjustment with urban life and environment etc. The most serious problems were adjustment with changed environment of city life (29.33%), employment (19.33%), irregular employment (14.33%), very low rates of wages (17.16) and absence of medical facilities in or nearby the locality (19.83%). The status of employment of migrant tribal women is presented in Table 3.12.

Table 3.12: Employment status of migrant tribal women in Andhra Pradesh

S.No.	Employment status	No. of Respondents
1.	Domestic servants	261 (43.5)
2.	Construction labour	95 (15.83)
3.	Industrial worker	83 (13.83)
4.	Self employment	27 (4.5)
5.	Private jobs	134 (22.33)
Total		600 (100.00)

Source: Field Data.

Table 3.12 reveals the employment status of migrant tribal women in the urban areas. About 43.5 per cent of tribal women were working as domestic servants, 15.83 per cent were working as construction labourer, 13.83 per cent were as industrial labourer, 4.5 per cent were self employ and 22.33 per cent were in private jobs in the study area of Andhra Pradesh. The awareness about the welfare programmes among the migrated tribal women is presented in Table 3.13.

Table 3.13: Awareness programmes of the migrant tribal women in Andhra Pradesh

S.No.	Programmes	No. of Respondents
1.	Benefit of free education	165 (27.5)
2.	Benefit of scholarships	105 (17.5)
3.	Benefit of employment due to reservation policy	159 (26.5)
4.	Benefit the ITDP	171 (28.5)
Total		600 (100.00)

Source: Field Data.

Table 3.13 examine the role played by central and state governments in socio-economic development of tribal women in urban areas. As a result only 27.5 per cent of them could take the benefit of free education, 17.5 per cent get scholarships, 26.5 per cent get employment due to reservation policy and 28.5 covered under ITDP. The tribal associations formed by the tribal people in urban areas undertook some activities of socio-economic development. It is conclude that to improve the socio-economic status of migrant tribal women in urban areas certain suggestions can be made.

Suggestions

The tribals in India have inherited a rich culture from their ancestors. However, with the onslaught of industrialization, urbanization and modernization and the resultant migration of tribal men and women to urban centers the age-old culture of these primitive human societies is on the verge of extinction. It is suggested that all-out efforts must be made to make the tribal realize the importance of their culture and to motivate them for preserving their unique culture at any cost. The greater responsibility in this respect rests with the migrant tribal women and girls who lost contacts with the tribal people in their hinterlands.

The growing trend of migration of tribal to cities must be arrested by providing ample employment opportunities to them in tribal areas so that they do not think of running to the urban areas in search of employment. Monetary support required for this purpose should be provided to the State governments having sizable tribal population from the President of India's special fund. Majority of the migrant tribal women are reported to be illiterate. This situation is due to lack of awareness among the tribal communities about the schemes of state and central governments for providing free education to the tribal boys and girls. As such, it is necessary to create awareness on mass scale by involving NGOs working in the tribal areas. It is also necessary to provide facilities of primary and secondary education in the tribal localities and slum areas in the cities where migrant tribal women have settled themselves.

The migrant tribal women should be motivated to adopt the family planning methods to limit the size of their families. It is very difficult to have a reasonable standard of living with a large number of members in the family having only one or two earning members. It is suggested that sufficient number of Family Welfare and Guidance Centers should be opened in or nearby the localities where migrant tribal women are living.

Most of the tribal women are living in slum areas surrounded by unhealthy environment. Moreover, about half of them do not have their own houses and are living in rented accommodation. With a view to provide them better houses the Tribal Development Boards in the states should undertake construction of Housing Complex for migrant tribal families settled in big cities. The migrant tribal women in big cities are living in acute poverty because they themselves or other earning members in their families are either unemployed or under-employed. To overcome this problem it is necessary to provide basic educational facilities along with hectic efforts of vocational guidance and training for development of their skills with a view to improve their potential for employment in public and private sector organizations.

The average monthly income of tribal women in cities is very low, i.e. below the minimum wage, as most of them are employed as domestic workers and in private establishments. Becouse the minimum wage is not effectively implemented, in these sector, it is, therefore, suggested that the minimum wage should be strictly implemented in all the sectors of employment including domestic work. Moreover, to reduce the exploitation by moneylenders SHGs of migrant tribal women should be formed for providing micro-credit facilities to them. The local NGOs should be motivated to take lead in forming such SHGs.

It was observed during the investigation that a large majority of tribal women is unaware of the Tribal Development Programmes of the union and state governments. It is, therefore, suggested that these programmes should be given wide publicity through visual and written media. In addition, the educated youths from tribal areas should be trained and employed for door-to-door publicity of Tribal Development Schemes of the union and state governments and for giving them proper guidance in seeking benefits from those schemes.

To solve the problems faced by migrant tribal women in Andhra Pradesh, the government should involve the local NGOs and provide such organizations sufficient funds for effective work. These NGOs should, first of all undertake tracer-studies for identification and rehabilitation of migrant tribal women in urban areas. There should be an integrated programme offering a package of services simultaneously from normal social, economic and educational fronts. No fruitful solution is likely to emerge without striking at the deep roots into the tentacles of the problem faces by migrant tribal women in the study area. It will be possible to bring out a total transformation in the lives of this most deprived section of India population which has been the victim of atrocities, exploitation and social injustice.

The development process initiated by the government and voluntary agencies among the tribal have, on one hand, created situations for restructuration of the tribal society and on the other, given rise to some structural problems. The formulations of specific plans for their social and economic upliftment have surely brought about some favourable changes in the quality of life of the tribal communities. However, new problems emerging from these changes are, nonetheless, minor ones. Moreover, the migrant tribal women could not be covered under the Tribal Development Projects because the same are being implemented in rural areas of tribal regions. We, therefore, would like to suggest that the union and state governments should design special programmes for the development of tribal in the urban areas and more specifically for migrant tribal women in urban areas.

The analysis of educational levels of migrant tribal women in the urban areas revealed that about 44.16 per cent of women were illiterate. Out of literate the concentration is more at primary and middle school level and as such a large majority is deprived of higher education. As a result they are unable to take advantage of the seats reserved for them in technical and professional courses. They are also losing the chances of getting employment in state and central government services against the seats reserved for them. The employment opportunities thrown up by industrialization and modernization are also beyond their reach. This is all due to low education levels of tribal women, it is only a massive education programme which can develop a forceful leadership from tribal women which can stand against and fight the entrenched forces of exploitation of tribal women in the study area of Andhra Pradesh.

Urbanization: Is It a Rural Push or Urban Pull

Dr. K. Mahadevamma

Introduction

Urbanization is an index of transformation from traditional rural economies to modern industrial one. It is progressive concentration of population in urban unit. Quantification of urbanization is very difficult. It is a long term process. Kingsley Davis has explained urbanization as process of switch from spread out pattern of human settlements to one of concentration in urban centers. It is a finite process—a cycle through which a nation pass as they evolve from agrarian to industrial society. He has mentioned three stages in the process of urbanization. *Stage one* is the initial stage characterized by rural traditional society with predominance in agriculture and dispersed pattern of settlements. *Stage two* refers to acceleration stage where basic restructuring of the economy and investments in social overhead capitals including transportation, communication take place. Proportion of urban population gradually increases from 25 per cent to 40 per cent, 50 per cent, 60 per cent and so on. Dependence on primary sector gradually dwindles. *Third stage* is known as terminal stage where urban population exceeds 70 per cent or more. At this stage level of urbanization remains more or less same or constant. Rate of growth of urban population and total population becomes same at this terminal stage.

Concept of Urbanization

Urbanization refers to general increase in population and the amount of industrialization of a settlement. It includes increase in the number and extent of cities. It symbolizes the movement of people from rural to urban areas. Urbanization happens because of the increase in the extent and density of urban areas. The density of population in urban areas increases because of the migration of people from less industrialized regions to more industrialized areas.

Causes of Urbanization

Urbanization usually occurs when people move from villages to cities to settle, in hope of a higher standard of living. This usually takes place in developing countries. In rural areas, people become victims of unpredictable weather conditions such as drought and floods, which can adversely affect their livelihood. Consequently many farmers move to cities in search of a better life. This can be seen in Karnataka as well where farmers from Raichur, Gulbarga districts, which are drought-stricken areas, migrate to Bangalore to escape poverty. Cities in contrast, offer opportunities of high living and are known to be places where wealth and money are centralized. Most industries and educational institutions are located in cities whereas there are limited opportunities within rural areas. This further contributes to migration to cities.

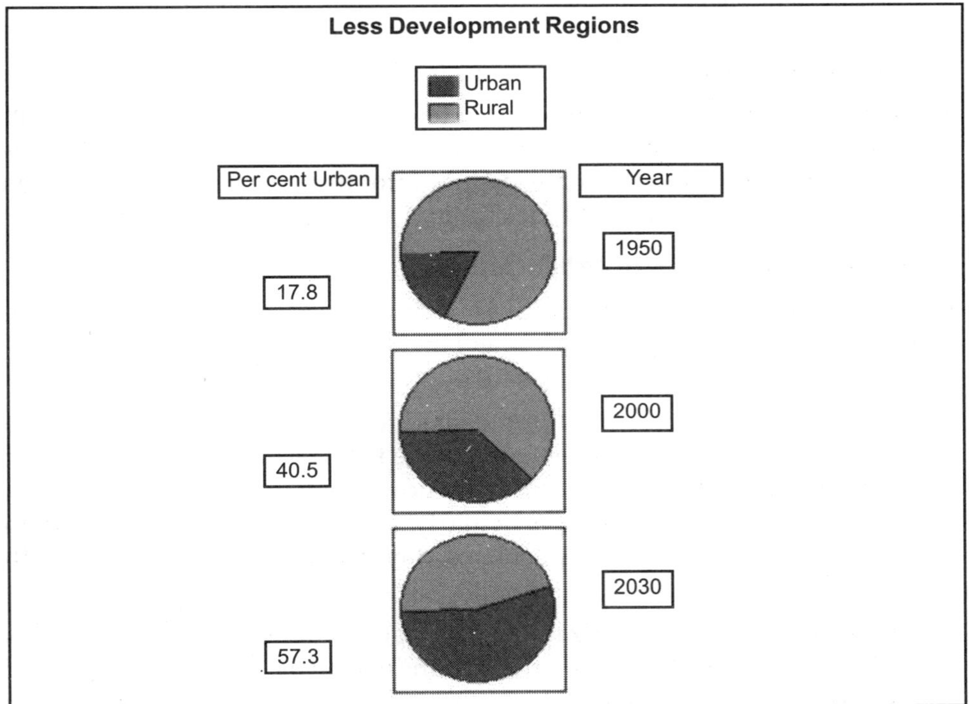

Fig. 4.1: Shift of population from rural areas to urban areas.

Effects of Urbanization

Urbanization brings with it several consequences—both adverse and beneficial. They impact on social and environmental areas.

Adverse Effects of Urbanization

There is increasing competition for facilities due to the high standard of living in urban areas, which has triggered several negative effects. Many people including farmers who move to cities in search of a better life end up as casual laborers, as they lack adequate education. This leads to one of the worst problems of urbanization — the growth of slums.

Slums

They are urban areas that are heavily populated with substandard housing and very poor living conditions. As a result several problems arise.

- *Land insecurity*: Slums are usually located on land, which are not owned by the slum dwellers. They can be evicted at any time by the landowners.
- *Poor living conditions*: Crowding and lack of sanitation are main problems. This contributes to outbreak of diseases. Utilities such as water, electricity and sewage disposal are also scarce.
- *Unemployment*: Since the number of people competing for jobs is more than jobs available, unemployment is an inevitable problem.
- *Crime*: Slum conditions make maintenance of law and order difficult. Patrolling of slums is not a priority of law enforcing officers. Unemployment and poverty force people into anti-social activities. Slums become a breeding ground for criminal activities.

Environmental Impacts of Urbanization

- *Temperature*: Due to factors such as paving over formerly vegetated land, increasing number of residences and high-rise apartments and industries, temperature increases drastically.
- *Air pollution*: Factories and automobiles are symbols of urbanization. Due to harmful emissions of gases and smoke from factories and vehicles, air pollution occurs. Current research shows high amount of suspended particulate matter in air, particularly in cities, which contributes to allergies and respiratory problems thereby becoming a huge health hazard.
- *Water issues*: When urbanization takes place, water cycle changes as cities have more precipitation than surrounding areas. Due to dumping of sewage from factories in water bodies, water pollution occur which can lead to outbreaks of epidemics.
- *Destruction of habitats*: To make an area urbanized, a lot of forested areas are destroyed. Usually these areas would have been habitats to many birds and animals.

Benefits of Urbanization

Though urbanization has drawbacks, it has its benefits:

- *Efficiency:* Cities are extremely efficient. Less effort is needed to supply basic amenities such as fresh water and electricity. Research and recycling programs are possible only in cities. In most cities flats are in vogue today. Many people can be accommodated within a small land area.
- *Convenience*: Access to education, health, social services and cultural activities is readily available to people in cities than in villages. Life in cities is much more advanced, sophisticated and comfortable, compared to life in villages. Cities have advanced communication and transport networks.
- *Concentration of resources*: Since major human settlements were established near natural resources from ancient times, a lot of resources are available in and around cities. A lot of facilities to exploit these resources also exist only in cities.
- *Educational facilities:* Schools, colleges and universities are established in cities to develop human resources. A variety of educational courses and fields are available offering students a wide choice for their future careers.
- *Social integration*: People of many castes and religions live and work together in cities, which creates better understanding and harmony and helps breakdown social and cultural barriers.
- *Improvements in economy*: High-tech industries earn valuable foreign exchange and lot of money for a country in the stock markets.

Component of Urban Growth

Urban growth (Bhagat, 1992) can be attributed to mainly three components:

1. Natural increase
2. Net migration
3. Areal reclassification

These components have been estimated using residual method. Since separate information in wake of change in the area and population due to extension of municipal boundaries during the inter-censal period is not available either for total or for migrant population it is difficult to estimate decadal migration to urban areas. Besides migration data for new and declassified towns are not available separately and so there is a possibility of error in estimating contribution of migration in the share of urban growth. During 1971-81 about 41 per cent of urban growth (estimated by Jain, RG, 1991 census) can be attributed to natural increase which reflects the role of demographic momentum, 36 per cent due to net migration and municipal boundary changes and 19 per cent due to reclassification of area. But urban growth due to natural increase has increased from 42 per cent in 1971-81 to about 60 per cent during 1981-91. Urban growth due to migration and changes in municipal boundaries has reduced from 39 per cent in 1971-81 to 22 per cent in 1981-91. But estimates by Pathak and Mehta for these components of urban growth reflects slightly different results (Pathak and Mehta, 1995). It is clear that urbanization process in India is not mainly "migration lead" but a product of demographic explosion due to natural increase. People migrate to cities not due to urban pull but due to rural push. Poverty led migration (Sen and Ghosh, 1993) has induced very poor quality of urbanization followed by misery, poverty, unemployment, exploitation, rapid growth of slum, inequalities, degradation in the quality of urban life.

Basic Feature and Pattern of India's Urbanisation

Basic feature of urbanization in India can be highlighted as:

1. Lopsided urbanization induces growth of class I cities.
2. Urbanization occurs without industrialization and strong economic base.
3. Urbanization is mainly a product of demographic explosion and poverty induced rural-urban migration.
4. Rapid urbanization leads to massive growth of slum followed by misery, poverty, unemployment, exploitation, inequalities, degradation in the quality of urban life.
5. Urbanization occurs not due to urban pull but due to rural push.
6. Poor quality of rural-urban migration leads to poor quality of urbanization (Bhagat, 1992).
7. Distress migration initiates urban decay.

The pattern of urbanization in India is characterized by continuous concentration of population and activities in large cities. Kingsley Davis used the term "over-urbanization where in urban misery and and rural poverty exist side by side with the result that city can hardly be called dynamic" and where inefficient, unproductive informal sector (Kundu and Basu, 1998) becomes increasingly apparent. Breese depicts urbanization in India as pseudo-urbanization where in people arrive in cities not due to urban pull but due to rural push.

This paper investigates the shortcomings and potentials of the current governance structure to mainstream risk reduction and prevention in urbanization as well as to sustain the rural environment. This paper discusses some issues relating to rural push towards urban and its impact on urban development.

The present study is also an effort to examine between the knowledge, attitude and utilization of primary health services and some socio-economic factors. The findings of the study would help to identify the women who have poor knowledge, who do not have positive attitude towards primary health services and who are not utilizing the primary health services. The main objective of the study is to assess the level of knowledge, attitude and utilization of Primary Health Services among rural women.

The locale of the study is the Chittoor district in Rayalaseema region of Andhra Pradesh was purposely selected. A random of 600 married women in the age group of 15 to 45 years with at least one child was selected for the present study by using "Three stage random sampling technique" and simple random sampling. In the study it was found that women who have crossed 25 have poor knowledge and are not favourably disposed towards PHC services and they are not properly utilizing the services. The reason came out from this study is one distance whoever is nearer to the centre is prevailing the services and who are far are not utilizing it. Secondly, as they travel to that distance which takes to spend whole day so they will loose one day income or one day wage. Thirdly, the attitude towards PHC makes them not to utilize the services. Here comes the play of rural push towards urban community. Another finding is that there is association between the knowledge of PHC and education and frequency of visits to urban community. Whoever is visiting frequently they are very well aware about the services of Primary Health Centers. So here plays the role of urban pull. As they are aware about the different comforts and services people are pulled towards that community. It is clear that if there is any discomfort it is not accepted and pushed towards the other end. Not only in the health services it is one of the area where clearly gives an indication how the people are pushed and pulled towards their fulfillment of the needs.

Another fair example is of education. There is trend changing and attracting the parents to give or provide English medium education where they are attracted towards urban schools. Opportunities can be created within rural areas to reduce stress on cities. This also results in a higher standard of living for the people of the country as a whole. Some of the villages in South Kanara district of Karnataka set a good example for this. They have efficient transport and communication system and electricity. Co-operatives have been set up to provide financial aid to peasants. The rural people have been encouraged to engage in cottage industries and commercial activities such as making pickles, handicrafts, sweets and savories. Through cooperative agencies, marketing of these goods also has become easy. This is an efficient method of curbing urbanization, by creating opportunities for people in villages. This reduces the rate of migration.

References

1. Bhagat, R.B. (1992), "Components of Urban Growth in India with Reference to Haryana: Findings from Recent Censuses", *Nagarlok*, Vol. 25, No. 3, pp. 10-14.
2. Pathak, P and Mehta, D. (1995), "Recent Trend in Urbanisation and Rural-Urban Migration in India: Some Explanations and Projections", Urban India, Vol. 15, No.1, pp. 1-17.
3. Sen, A. and Ghosh, J. (1993), "Trends in Rural Employment and Poverty Employment Linkage", ILO-ARTEP Working Paper, New Delhi.
4. Kundu, A. and Gupta, S. (2000),"Declining Population Mobility, Liberalisation and Growing Regional Imbalances—The Indian Case", in Kundu, A. (ed), *Inequality, Mobility and Urbanization*, Indian Council of Social Science Research, Manak Publications, New Delhi.
5. www38.homepage.villanova.edu/jameson.chace/.../melville.htm.

Urbanization in India
Challenges and Strategies

Dr. V. Venkateswarlu,
Mrs. P. Hemalatha

Introduction

Urbanization is not a product, but is a process by which rural areas become transformed into urban areas, whereby people instead of living in predominantly dispersed agricultural villages start living in towns and cities dominated by industrial and service functions. Historical evidence suggests that urbanization process is inevitable and universal. A majority of the developing countries, on the other hand, started experiencing urbanization only since the middle of 20th century.

There are three stages in the process of urbanization. *Initial stage* characterized by rural traditional society with predominance in agriculture and dispersed pattern of settlements. *Acceleration stage*—where basic restructuring of economy and investments in social capital take place (transportation, communication). *Terminal stage*—here urban population exceeds 70 per cent or more. Level of urbanization remains more or less constant. Rate of growth of urban population and total population becomes same.

India's urbanization is often termed as over-urbanization, pseudo-urbanization. The big cities attained inordinately large population size leading to virtual collapse in the urban services and followed by basic problems in the field of housing, slum, water, infrastructure, quality of life etc. According to the United Nations—state of the world population 2007 report, the urbanization of India is taking place at a faster rate than in the rest of the world. By 2030, 40.76 per cent of India's population will be living in urban areas compared to about 28.4 per cent now.

The metropolitan cities like Mumbai and Kolkata have a far greater number of people moving out than coming in. Urbanization is a sign of liberalization but the condition of slum dwellers was even worse than that of the poor in villages. The population of towns and cities in developing countries like India is set to double in the space of a generation, while the urban population in the developed world is expected to grow relatively lower. In comparison to the urban population growth rate, the world's rural population is expected to decrease by some 28 million between 2005 and 2030.

Scenario of Urban Slums

The nature, intensity and gravity of urban problems are exponentially related to the degree of urbanization. This is more so in the developing and underdeveloped countries. Urbanization expectedly serves three basic functions in developing and developed countries.

1. Specialized processing and service activities.
2. Provision of transport facility, albeit expensive.
3. Meeting the physical and service requirements of international trade in India.

It cannot be denied that urbanization has paved the way for social and economic mobility of a vast majority of underprivileged and poorer sections of rural areas. In spite of a steady urban growth, present a picture of underdevelopment due to paucity of funds and matched by lethargic and indifferent response of the urban administration. The development in class I cities is again not even. Slums suffer from a plethora of problems: non-availability of affordable land, illegal land tenure, deficient environment, *kutcha* shelter, multiple deprivations. Add to them absence or inadequacy of basic amenities like provision of drinking water, sanitation, electrical lighting, *pakka* roads and others and that is the general scenario in almost all towns and cities.

Causative Factors

This is in spite of the fact of specific focus of each plan on different issues of urban problems and development. The urban local bodies are unable to cope with the problems due to the absence of sufficient statutory power in their hands and indifferent response of the respective government which hold the reins of financial power. The struggle for one upmanship between politicians of different hues in the elected bodies, which often witness unruly scenes, hampers decisions over important matters and speedy solution. Thus, it can be stated that the urban local bodies are structurally, politically and financially weak. Their domain and powers are eroded further while the urban problems keep mounting.

Considering the estimation that more than 50 per cent of India's population is expected to. live in urban areas by 2020, the urban situation will only be bleak, gloomy and beyond control unless corrective steps like strong political will to control, to mitigate urban problems, to empower the urban local bodies are taken as early as possible.

Impact of Urbanization on Women

Urbanization has enhanced the stress on women in terms of inadequate supply of basic urban services, forcing them to spend more time and undergo greater physical strain which entails further subordination of women. Increasing degree of industrialization has resulted in intolerable levels of pollution and irreparable damage to the environment affecting the quality of living of people directly or indirectly. Marginalized groups such as EBCs, SCs and STs who are residing in slums are most adversely effected due to urban crisis than others. The incidence of crime is positively correlated with the degree of urbanization.

Table 5.1: Patterns and trends of urbanization in India

Census years	Number of towns	Urban population (in millions)	% urban	Annual exponential growth rate	Rate of urbanization
1901	1,916	25.9	10.8	—	—
1911	1,908	25.9	10.3	0.0	-0.46
1921	2,048	28.1	11.2	0.8	0.87
1931	2,220	33.5	12.0	1.7	0.71
1941	2,422	44.2	13.8	2.8	1.50
1951	3,060	62.4	17.3	3.5	2.54
1961	2,700	78.9	18.0	2.3	0.40
1971	3,126	109.1	19.9	3.2	1.06
1981	4,029	159.5	23.3	3.8	1.72
1991	4,689	217.6	25.7	3.1	1.02
2001	5,161	284.5	27.8	2.7	0.82

Source: Census of India, 1991, 2001.

The patterns and trends of urban population and the number of towns in India during 1901 to 2001 show that the total urban population has increased more than ten times from 26 million in 1901 to 285 million in 2001, whereas total population has increased less than five times from 238 million to 1,027 million during the same period. A continuous increase has been noticed in the percentage of urban population from 11 per cent in 1901 to 17 per cent in 1951 to further 28 per cent in 2001. In the same fashion, the number of towns has also increased from 1,916 in 1901 to 2,422 in 1951 and then to 5,161 in 2001. This reveals the process of rapid urbanization in India.

According to 2001 census of India out of total population of 1027 million about 285 million live in urban areas and 742 million live in rural areas. Sex ratio, defined as number of female per 1000 male, for urban, rural and total India are 900, 945, 933 respectively.

Table 5.2: Population of India by residence

Census years	Number of urban agglomeration/town	Total population	Urban population	Rural population
1901	1,827	23,83,96,327	2,58,51,873	2,12,54,44,54
1911	1,825	25,20,93,390	2,59,41,633	22,61,51,757
1921	1,949	25,13,21,213	2,80,86,167	22,32,35,046
1931	2,072	27,89,77,238	3,34,55,989	24,55,21,249
1941	2,250	31,86,60,580	4,41,53,297	27,45,07,283
1951	2,843	36,10,88,090	6,24,43,709	29,86,44,381
1961	2,363	43,92,34,771	7,89,36,603	36,02,98,168
1971	2,590	59,81,59,652	10,91,13,977	48,90,45,675
1981	3,378	68,33,29,097	15,94,62,547	52,38,66,550
1991	3,768	84,43,24,222	21,71,77,625	62,71,46,597
2001	5,161	10,27,015,247	28,53,54,954	74,16,60,293

Sources: Various Census Reports.

Table 5.3: Population of India by sex and residence, 2001

India	Male	Female	Total Person	Sex ratio
Urban	15,01,35,894	13,52,19,060	28,53,54,954	900
Rural	38,11,41,184	36,05,19,109	74,16,60,293	945
Total	**53,12,77,078**	**49,57,38,169**	**1,02,70,15,247**	**933**

Source: IND_CEN01, Census 2001, Office of the Registrar General

Objectives

The present paper attempts to study the following objectives:

1. To observe the challenges of urbanization in selected colonies.
2. To analyse the factors responsible for the challenges as perceived by respondents.
3. To suggest strategies to cope up with the challenges.

Methodology

Two slums in Guntur town namely Swarnabharathi Nagar and Swarnandhra Nagar colony were selected. A group of 50 persons, 25 from each colony comprised the sample for present study through random sampling method from the voters list. They were divided into groups as per their convenience to conduct focus group discussions. Unstructured interviews are also used to elicit the needed information from the respondents.

Findings

The table 5.4 clearly shows that the majority of the respondents hail from the age group of 41 to 60 years followed by 38 per cent with the age group of 21-40 years.

Table 5.4: Age wise distribution of the respondents

Age	No. of respondents
Below 20 years	02
21–40 years	19
41–60 years	23
60 & above years	06
Total	**50**

Source: Primary data.

Table 5.5: Caste-wise distribution of respondents

Caste	No. of Respondents
OC	09
BC	13
SC	17
ST	11
Total	**50**

Source: Primary data.

It is evident from the table 5.5 that the selected colonies are a mixture of all the castes with little variations, i.e. 34 per cent of SCs, 26 per cent of BCs followed by 22 per cent ST's and the remaining 18 per cent with OCs.

Table 5.6: Distribution of respondents by their educational status

Status	No.of respondents
Illiterate	19
Low	18
Medium	10
High	03
Total	**50**

Source: Primary data.

The above table 5.6 clearly indicates that 38 per cent of the respondents are illiterates and 36 per cent are with low literacy level, i.e below primary education. 20 per cent completed upto upper primary and high school. Only 6 per cent are with college education.

Table 5.7: Distribution of respondents by their income

Income	No. of Respondents
Below poverty line	24
Poor	16
Middle income group	10
Total	**50**

Source: Primary data.

Data in the above table clearly shows that 48 per cent of the respondents are below poverty line and 32 per cent are with low economic status. Only 20 per cent are having comfortable income and livelihoods.

Table 5.8: Distribution of respondents by occupation category

Labour category	No. of Respondents
Manual labour	18
Hawkers and vendors	13
Rickshaw pullers	08
Artisans	04
Pvt. employees	03
Petty business	04
Total	**50**

Source: Primary data.

The table 5.8 clearly reveals that majority of the respondents (18) are working as manual labourers followed by hawkers and vendors (13) while the others are engaged in various activities. Thus, it shows that the respondents living in urban colonies are heterogeneous in character with regard to their occupational background.

Table 5.9: Distribution of respondents by type of family

Type of family	No. of Respondents
Joint /extended	19
Nuclear	31
Total	50

Source: Primary data.

From table 5.9 it is clearly seen that nuclear family system is predominant (62%) in these colonies and only 38 per cent of the respondents are living in joint/extended families.

The table 5.10 reveals the perception of the respondents regarding the problems of urbanization as per their personal experiences. Majority of them (42) felt that transport is the major problem in the newly established colonies which are the part of urbanization scenario and followed by inadequate provision for social infrastructure like roads, hospitals and schools (41). This might be the main reason for non occupation of allotted houses built by the government under various schemes. The other problems observed are water supply (39) and sanitation is also bigger problem as no one cares about these dwellers (38). (35) Members expressed that urbanization leads to increased social conflicts, crimes and anti-social activities. The other problems are low wage rates (34) followed by housing (31), overcrowding (29).

Table 5.10: Challenges of urbanization N = 50

Problems as expressed by the respondents	Yes	No
Housing	31	19
Crowding	29	21
Transport	42	08
Water supply	39	11
Sanitation	38	12
Inadequate provision for social infrastructure, proper roads, hospital, school etc.	41	09
Saturation level of employment generating capacity.	28	22
Increased social conflicts, crimes and anti social activities.	35	15
Environmental degradation with all sorts of pollution.	29	21
Inefficient and unproductive informal sector with low wage rates.	34	16

Source: Primary data

Table 5.11: Causative factors for rapid urbanization as perceived by the respondents N =50

Factor	Yes	No
Increased migration into the towns	39	11
Lack of industrial development in rural areas	28	22
Unplanned urban settlements	26	24
More employment potential in urban areas	39	11
Non-profitable agricultural occupations	42	08
Attraction towards ways and means for easy income	35	15
Increased real estate business, decreased land for agriculture	41	09
Political involvement in government policies for their selfish activities	27	23
Lack of awareness regarding health, sanitation in Public	26	24
Lack of supervision and sincerity in officials	38	12
Lack of will to serve the people in public servants	34	16
Increased corruption at all levels of life	33	17

Source: Primary data.

The table 5.11 shows the results of the focused group discussions on the causes of rapid urbanization as expressed by the respondent's majority (42) felt that non-profitable agricultural occupations are forcing the rural folk to migrate to towns and 41 are of the opinion that real estate business, decreased land for agriculture are the other reasons. They 39 felt that in urban areas more avenues for employment are available. 38 felt that lack of sincerity and supervision in the government officials is another cause for uncontrollable urban growth. 35 stated that youth are attracting towards ways of easy income like anti-social activities. 34 are of the opinion that lack of will to serve in the public servants is creating unplanned colonies without basic amenities. Lack of opportunities in rural areas for industrial development is another cause of urbanisation as perceived by the (28) respondents. The other causes are increased corruption (33) political involvement (27), lack of awareness in public about health etc. (26) which affects the lives of urban people.

Strategies to combat the challenges of urbanization:

1. Developing strong economic base for strong and medium cities.
2. Re-direction of migration flows.
3. Directing growth efforts and investments towards small cities.
4. Strengthening the functional base of urban economy.
5. Policy should relate to proper operational, developmental and restorative planning.
6. Emphasizing on agro-based industries.
7. Integrating rural and urban economy.
8. Planning housing for slum dwellers with human face.
9. Arranging free transportation to slum dwellers to access social infrastructural facilities like schools, hospitals etc. so that they accustom to newly settlements.
10. Proper care in planning new urban settlements.

Conclusion

Unplanned urban areas given rise to combination of problems. The government is allotting residential areas to poorer sections of the country without establishing basic amenities like roads, drainage, drinking water, street lighting, schools, health centers etc. So the dwellers are not willing to settle in their allotted spaces. Moreover they are selling them for less prices through illegal dealings and still continuing to settle in the middle of the towns, creating problems of crowding and insufficient basic amenities.

The government is indifferent to retain the heritage and culture of old historical towns. Heavy influxes of migrants are changing the nature of towns and cities. Local bodies are unable to cope up with the demands of the people. The urbanization policy needs to be changed to prescribe policy perspective in each area to combat the undesirable consequences of the urbanization processes. Specific interventions have to be undertaken to bridge the gaps in policies and programs. Urbanization is creating tremendous pressure on the housing situations. Government should build housing complexes with the contribution of private bodies and make them available for nominal rents.

In India, unprecedented population growth coupled with unplanned developmental activities has resulted in urbanization that lack infrastructure facilities. The squatter settlements are the examples for this. Large chunks of urban space and population lie outside the purview of official development planning, civic infrastructure provision and frameworks of law and order. Thus a residual social policy separates the elite from the poor. Our urban problems are not the result of any one single issue. A confluence of political, economic and socio-cultural forces have created the current urban crisis of incapacity. A collaborative, problem-solving and action-oriented approach is needed to bring fruitful results of urbanization.

References

1. Gokhale, N.A., (2003), "Tick-tock of Doom", *Outlook* (September 22).
2. Kalpana Markandey and S. Simhadri, (2009), *Urban Environment and Geoinformatics,* Rawat Publications.
3. D.Venkateswarlu, M. Hanumantha Rao, S. Bhaskar (2006), *Facets of Urban Society in India: Processes, Problems And Development,* Serials Publications, New Delhi.
4. Participative Development: "A Special Issue on Women Empowerment" Vol. 7 No. 1: Centre for Social Research and Development, Pune.
5. Pranathi Data (2006), "Urbanization in India", research article presented at European Population Conference:
6. Thor, J.T., (2002), Pollution (Monograph), Pune: Department of Adult Continuing Education and Extension, University of Pune.
7. Padhya, Bhagavati Prasad, (2001), "Health Issues of Women and Children, A Case Study of the Beedi Industry", Issues in Women's Health, A Human Rights Perspective in *Women's Link,* 7(2).
8. Sobha (2001), "Figurative Challenges in National Health Issues, Women and Culture", *Women Link,* 7(3).
9. Verghese, Susan and P.V.L. Rama, (1999), "Women and Human Rights: Case Study of a Slum in Visakhapatnam", Indian *Journal of Human Rights,* 3 (182), *Women Speak-Unite Against Globalization, Poverty and Violence in India* (2000) Delhi: Progressive Printers.

Urbanization and Problems

Ms. K. Srivalli, Ms. M. Galaiah,
Ms. N. Radha

Urbanization and Urban Growth

Urbanization has been one of the most significant vehicles for the transformation of the societies over the last century. All the countries to a greater or lesser extent have gone through this process.

Urbanization is a global phenomenon experienced by economically advanced as well as developing countries. As countries place emphasis on industrial development. There is exodus of people from villages, town, cities and an impetus to the growth of metropolitan areas. Cities provide a variety of facilities such as educational facilities; health care services, entertainment pleasures and even friends to people that are not available in small towns. People migrate to cities for employment opportunities, to improve economic status and urban lifestyles. Even the anonymity that an urban area provides can be an attraction to some.

Although urbanization brings about development in the social, economical and cultural spheres of life, it disturbs ecological systems. The increase in urban population results in asymmetric patterns in resource utilization, land use and transportation. Rapid and uncontrolled growth of urban agglomerations generates a series of negative environmental and social effects. These include lack of infrastructure and basic services, housing problems, congestion, health problems etc.

Urbanization is an indicator of modernization, the sign of growth and economic progress. It is a natural consequence of economic changes that take place, as the nation develops. It is indispensable to economic growth and leads to social equally. Urbanization is the result of more avenues of industrialization but it is not matched to a commensurate degree of energy and transportation. "The most distinctive feature of the twentieth century has been the rapid and massive urbanization taking place everywhere in the world as a consequence of process of modernization. Migration from rural areas into towns is not peculiar to developing countries alone, but is a worldwide phenomenon". In the 21st century, the rate of urbanization is much more in developing countries than in developed countries.

The extraordinary growth of population taking place is generally made up of two processes namely urban growth and urbanization. And it is essential to distinguish them. Urban growth is the enormous and absolute increase in the numbers of people living in the urban areas. Urbanization, on the other hand, is the relative shift of population from the countryside to the towns and cities. Urbanization refers to the concentration of population at a center. It may be defined in a crude form, as the proportion of population residing in urban centers and in a sophisticated way refers to the proportion of population are engaged in secondary sector of economy in urban places. When the rates of increase in an urban population are equal to or less than the rate of increase of the total population of the region of which the urban population is a part, the condition of urban growth exists. In case where the rate of increase in the urban population, exceeds the rate of increase of total regional population especially by a considerable margin, that is the condition of urbanization. So long as there is an increase in this proportion of urban population to total·population there is urbanization.

Urbanized Area

An 'urbanized area' includes territory encompassing an urban area, its suburbs, and urban extensions such as airport, parks and stadium including undeveloped land on a way to 'urbanisation', which indicates transformation of land from rural to urban use, as a consequence of how far 'urbanization' spreads over the space as an instrument of 'social' and 'economic' change and of community's efforts to corresponding urban development. The urban extensions of an urbanized area may include 'new towns', satellite towns dormitory towns, sub-urban towns, shanty towns within the 'urban complex' from the hub of a metropolitan estuary.

New Town

In urban planning theory 'new town' is an urban entity created on a virgin site or by expanding a small nucleated settlement. The main characteristic is that it is a newly created urban area where its population earns its livelihood and also has an independent local government.

Satellite Town

A 'Satellite' town is a specific type of new or existing township, distinctively self-contained in itself, but at the same time, has a degree of dependency on the mother city (to which it acts as a satellite) and interaction with it. It is usually in close proximity to the mother city and yet at such a distance that it may not coalesce with the mother city in foreseeable future. The concept was developed after the First World War as an alternative to 'garden city'.

Dormitory Town

A 'Dormitory town' is an independent urban and semi-urban entity closely located nearby the mother city having an independent urban government but without its own economic base, essentially it is a place where people live but they do not earn their livelihood there. It is a part and parcel of an 'urban-complex' or metropolitan area.

Sub-urban Town

A 'Sub-urban town' is an integral part of and an extension of existing urban center, generally located at the periphery, having no local government and administrative organization of its town, but unlike 'dormitory town' a sub-urban town may have a certain measure of self-sufficiency.

Shanty Town

A 'shanty town' is an 'informal' and spontaneous growth of a settlement pattern, sometimes quit extensive, with minimum public services and unsanitary shaks, constructed with temporary material, most often built and occupied by squatters (who live on unauthorized public or private land) of rural migrants within or at the fringe of a town.

Metropolitan Area

A 'metropolitan area' is derived from Greek term 'metropolis', 'meaning' 'mother city'. Initially the term was used for the capital city of the state but, of late, it is now being used with reference to all important cities irrespective of their being a capital city or not. 'Metropolitan area', applies to settlements with over 100,000 inhabitants that include within it a contiguous urban area consisting of a more than one urban center with independent local government.

Slum Squatters' and 'Relocation' Area

Slum is an area declared 'dangerous or injurious to the health of the inhabitants' of that area by reasons of the absence of basic facilities and amenities, the narrowness or bad arrangement of streets.

It is different from 'relocation' area, "continuous by-product of planning and renewal is the enforced displacement of non-conforming uses-usually commercial undertakings of one sort or another." There may be a number of reasons for disturbance viz. for defence needs, construction of roads or vacation of land meant for other beneficial public uses.

Thus the urbanization is result of three components: *(i)* natural increase, *(ii)* increase due to migration, *(iii)* Appearance of new urban centers, Rural to urban migration is the moving force behind the progress of urbanization. Hence, urbanization is now a shift of people from low productive agricultural employment to another section of employment marked by low productivity as handicraft production, retail trading, and domestic services in urban areas.

Characteristics of Urbanization in Developing Countries

Among the specific features of the developing countries, the following of them have the strongest effect on the character and scope of urbanization. Beire and his associates have pointed out the following distinguishing features of urbanization in developing countries.

Rapid population growth

In the period of rapid urbanization the rates of urbanization for developing countries have been above two per cent per year. These much of high rates of population growth have resulted in both larger absolute population movements to cities and natural increase in population within the cities.

In some countries decline of available agricultural land area per capita at low levels of rural income

The ratio of population to agricultural land in most less developed countries (LDCs) far exceed those found in Europe or North America during their period of rapid urbanization and many countries have reached the practical limits.

Decline in cost of transportation and communication

In the least developed countries, the widespread diffusion of modern communications and transport which, in the first instance, encourages population movement by providing information concerning urban opportunities, and in the second, permits relatively cheap movements from the place of origin to the city, has also been contributing to the urbanization process.

Fixed territorial boundaries and barriers to international migrants

Another factor is distinguishing the urbanization in the least developed countries is the effect of relatively fixed territorial boundaries which do not allow, on any realistic short- or medium-term political assumptions, for major adjustments in national living space, natural resources, or the free migration of surplus populations.

Process of urbanization has shown an increasing trend in terms of spatial and population development

The urban population growth has been characterized by an uneven distribution between the different regions or states and also as between cities and towns of different population ranges.

Challenges of Urbanization

The gap between demand and supply in infrastructural service has been continuously widening. Increasing pressure of population, particularly concentration of urban population in larger cities and metros and escalating per capita cost of providing urban services account for deterioration of infrastructure services and amenities. The worst suffers are the poor, whose access to the basic services like drinking water, sanitation, education and basic health services is shrinking.

"Rapid population growth in cities often exerts pressure on the existing infrastructure, housing and other basic amenities". The services required to support large concentrations of population are lagging behind the pace of urbanization. Even the infrastructural facilities are not proper. All cities in the country have severe shortage of housing, water supply, sewerage, transportation, communication and other facilities. Haphazard growth of city leads to chaos, disorder and conflicts. Urban areas particularly metropolitan and large cities symbolize poverty slums and polluted environment.

The growth of urban agglomeration creates several problems of over concentration of population, problems of planning, co-ordination and development of civic amenities. Urbanization requires a healthy local government but it is made difficult by the explosive problems of urban areas. The unplanned and unbalanced urban growth is leading to inter-regional imbalances, rural-urban division, springing up of large slums and environmental pollution. It is also leading to social tension, depletion of resources etc. The process of urban development has been a big challenge to planners and administrators in India.

Urbanization poses several problems of multi-dimensional nature such as slums, insanitation, and environment pollution, scarcity of housing, water, electricity, transport and medical aid. The speed with which the urban population is rising has created difficulties for urban governments. The failure of the urban governments to meet the aspirations of the people can be attributed to unprecedented increase in population, inadequate finances, inefficient personnel management, rampant corruption, indifferent attitude of bureaucrats, excessive stage of government control, establishment of multitude of special purpose agencies, absence of political will, lack of able and inspiring leadership etc. The nature of challenge is such that some writers suggested that urban governments require total over-hauling, restructuring and revamping in order to remove the deficiencies and inadequacies they have been suffering from the past.

Urbanization brings demographic, social, economic and physical changes, which generate problems relating to civic urban services, planning, land use, policing and law and order managements. The growth of rich agglomeration creates several problems of over-concentrations of population, problems of planning, coordination and development of civic amenities. Urbanization leads to social problems which affect mutual relationship among the people. The main problem of urbanization in India is that there is no inter-dependence between the process of urbanization and social development.

Slums

Slums punctuate every city of the world. The phenomena of slums has come to be regarded as a major problem of urbanization. While no Indian city is free from slums, the problem appears to be more acute in metropolitan cities. Slum, in fact, is a worldwide phenomenon. Few countries deny their existence, they can be found in the Casba of Tunis or the resort centers of Havana and Bermuda. In some places, a whole city may be a slum. Types of slums vary from place to place. They include metropolitan and rural slums, new slums and hand-me-downs, hand-made and prefabricated slums. Some are in shack towns, other are found in back alleys of mansions. Some are made of scrap, other are put together with mud, adobe, thatch, or wood findings. Many are one storey high, but there are also six-storey slums. Even caves are in use in parts of Europe and Africa.

Slums are found in various parts of the world but their nomenclature is not uniform. In Kolkata they are known as *Bustees*, in Mumbai, in Chennai *Cherrys* and in Delhi, *Khatras*. Slum situation and cluster, like any other phenomenon, vary from country to country mainly in details. The slums all over the world, however exhibit fundamental similarities. Poverty, overcrowding, insanitation and ill-health etc., are some of the common but significant characteristics. It is the slum dwellers that most attracts the attention of the social scientists. The slum dweller has some unique and special pattern of life as reflected in this attitudes and values indicative of social alienation, indifference to sanitation, lack of interest in development and crisis in self–confidence.

The slum is something like an infectious skin disease. Unless and until proper diagnosis is made, slum expands sin size and spreads into new locations. Consequently, slums have become the hotbeds for many of present day urban ills. And yet the remedies to check them are not fool-proof.

However, today the word slum bears a negative connotation. It implies something evil, strange, to be shunned and avoided. In short, slums today stand for a street, or an alley, etc., situated in a crowded district of a town or city where people of a low class live, forming a thickly populated neighborhood.

Sociologically slums stand for a sub-culture with a set of norms and values reflected in poor sanitation and health practices, deviant behaviour and attributes of apathy and social isolation. People who live in slums are regarded as interior, isolated and suspicious of the outside world.

General conditions in slums

There are certain general conditions in slums which concern all. Crowded, neglected, deteriorated and often obsolete housing are some of the common characteristics which prevail in slums. Poorly arranged structure, inadequate light and circulation of fresh air, poor design and lack of sanitary facilities are also common to find in slums. Limited availability of running water, flush toilets, electricity and cooking facilities are some other prevalent conditions.

Environmental conditions in slums

In a place where there is shabbiness and dilapidation, where public facilities are insufficient, where streets and sidewalks often go unrepaired. Where rubbish and garbage are infrequently collected and to top it all, where educational institutions either non-existent or are of very poor quality, what else one can expect but an undesirable environment. In short, slum dwellers are the victims of biological, physiological and social consequences of the physical and social environment.

Shortage of water and sanitary facilities are common site. Where several hundred people share one water tap, where the water obtained from such a source is to be carried long distances and kept for hours or days in exposed tubs or cans, it is impossible to keep such water clean. Sanitation, the less said the better. The disposal of human feces is enough to boggle any mind. Latrines used by hundreds of families are rarely cleaned and the collection accumulates for weeks and this pollution is accepted as way of life. It is common to find children infected with intestinal parasites, round worm and hookworm and suffering from dysentery and diarrhea. Presence of rats, cockroaches and other pests complicate the problems further.

Embarrassingly, well laid out and clean residential colonies, and even highrise buildings, shoot up side by side the slum colonies. Astonishingly, most of these environmentally insulted individuals in the slums regularly go for work (full time or part time) in most of these better equipped houses nearby. Some of them go to work in the hotels and restaurants (a few located in the highrise buildings) of the city as well.

Types of Slums

There are three main types of slums.

One is the 'original' slum, an area, which, from the beginning, consisted of unsuitable buildings; these sections are beyond recovery and need to be razed.

The second type consists of slums created by the departure of middle and upper class families to other sections and subsequent deterioration of the area.

The third and the most unpleasant type of slum is mainly a phenomenon of transition. Once the area around a main business district has become blighted, physical and social deterioration spreads rapidly. This kind of slum teems with flophouses, overnight accommodation for the destitute, houses of prostitution and speak-easies.

Slum: A slum is a compact area with a collection of poorly built tenements of at least 20 households, mostly of temporary nature, crowded together usually with inadequate sanitary and drinking water facilities in unhygienic conditions. Such area will be considered as 'Slum'.

Pucca structure: A pucca structure is one of which walls and roofs (at least) are made of pucca materials such as cement, concrete, oven burnt bricks, stone blocks, jack boards (cement plastered reeds), iron, zink or other metal sheets, asbestos cement sheets etc.

Katcha structure: A structure which has walls and roof made of non-*pucca* materials is regarded as a *katcha* structure. Non-*pucca* materials include unburnt bricks, bamboo, mud, grass, leaves, reeds and or other thatch.

Un–serviceable katcha: Which includes all structures with thatched walls and thatched roof, i.e., walls made of grass, leaves, reeds etc., and roof of a similar material.

Serviceable katcha: This includes all *katch*a structures other than unserviceable *katcha* structures.

Semi-pucca structure: A structure which cannot be classified as a *pucca* or a *katcha* structure as per definition of semi-*pucc*a structure. Such a structure will have either the walls or the roof but not both, made of *pucca* materials, walls/ roof made partially of *pucca* materials are regarded as *katcha* walls/roof.

Causes for Formation of Slums

Regarding causes of slum formation, it has been often contended that rural urban migration has been responsible for it because rural poor migrate to the cities through casts, kinship and social network and are initially adjusted in slum areas. But of late, it has been observed that though migration plays a dominant role in the formation and growth of slums, it may be erroneous to uphold that the entire process slum expansion is due to fresh inflow of migrants to the cities. The failure of India's family planning programme, especially, in urban areas had led to raid natural growth that has also contributed to the growth of slums. Some other factors which have been held responsible for the emergence of slums include, highly inadequate housing stock, distortions in the urban land market which inhabit the legal assess of the urban poor to a site for the construction of shelter and obsolescence in the old parts of the cities and moreover, being vote banks, slums get strong support for their survival by local politicians.

Problems of Slums

Slums are found in all cities, they are a product of the urban poor, in the metropolitan areas, and they create major problems of public health, law and order and of locking up land which may be more useful for other community purposes.

Vices like drug addiction, gambling, prostitution and alcoholism are urban vices. In the absence of the protection of intimate groups, the urban man has to inevitably resort to these vices to get relaxation from unnecessary tensions and anxieties. These vices disorganize individuals, localities in an urban society. Every modern city has its implicated crime area, i.e., the zone in transition. White collar crime is realized into the city culture. Juvenile delinquency develops largely in urban areas because of the structure of its social life and conflicting value conditions.

Slums are a major factor in urban pathology. It affects the physical and mental health of the urban community.

- It is a constant eye-sore and area of social disorganization.
- It is an inhabited uninhabited habitation.
- Economic differentiation is the chief factor for its development.
- It is a congested area of poor housing.
- It prevents both public and private decency.
- It results in personal and family disorganization.
- It is a area which houses the criminal and the delinquent. Urban pathology is the result of loose social control and the lack of a stable value system.
- Health hazard remains a typical slum problem.
- Further, the slum affects the physical and mental health of its neighborhood.
- It is the reservoir and hiding group for all urban vices such as gambling, dope peddling, prostitution and so on.
- It promotes the lawlessness and social disorganization of the city.
- It is a disorganized residential area.

Earth clearance is a costly affair and faces the fury of slum dwellers to vacate their slums. Slums increase with the increase in the city and its population and with the growth of factories. The areas of slums reflect upon the urban community's inability to provide housing to all its inhabitants and poor town planning. However, the creation of a social consciousness among slum areas about the harms of the existence of a slum is the duty of every street.

To clear and develop a slum will mean removing the existing strictures and putting up in their place decent houses; laying sewage, drainage and water supply. Providing civic amenities like education, health and cultural activities and last, but not the means of livelihood by setting up industries in the nearby areas. Removal of slum is not only a matter of demolishing and insanity structures and putting up new and ordinary ones. It is a very difficult and complicated operation involving measurement in the living conditions of the individuals and their families with unfortunately have to inhabit these areas by force of circumstances.

These conditions must necessary include provision of employment, elementary education, basic sanitary needs, medical, environmental hygiene and the minimum of standards, according to which any civilized government may expect its citizens to live and work spheres, all these elementary but basic needs of this community of the slum dwellers can be met, no scheme of slum clearance or slum improvement are ever be successful.

References

1. Desai, A.R. and Devadas Pillai, S. (1990), "Introduction", in Desai, A.R. and Devadas Pillai, S. (ed.) *Slums and Urbanization,* Bombay: Popular Prakashan.
2. Dubey, V.P. (1990), "Urbanization: A Conceptual Framework", in Debey, V.P. (ed.), *Urban Development Administration,* New Delhi: Deep and Deep Publications.
3. Edwin, S. Mills, Charles, M. Becker (1986), "The Relationship between Urbanization and Economic Development", in Edwin S. Mills, Charles M. Becker (ed.) *Studies in Indian Urban Development,* The World Bank, Washington: Oxford University Press, p. 18.
4. Gupte, C.S. (1981), "Urban Development: Planning and Policy Issues", in Gopal Bhargava (ed.) *Urban Problems and Policy Perspectives,* New Delhi: Abhinav Publications, p. 25.
5. Inderjeet Singh Sodhi (2004), "Challenges and Prospects of Urabanization–Need for Better Approach and Strategy", *Nagarlok,* Vol. XXXVI, No. 2, June-April 2004, p. 21.
6. Joop, W. De. Wit (1996), "Policy Politics and the Urban Poor: Theoretical and General Perspective", in Joop W. Dewit (ed.) *Poverty Policy and of Survival, Gender and Leadership,* New Delhi: Sage Publications, p. 33.

Growing Urbanization Trends and Pattern in India

Mrs. V. Usha Reddy, Ms. S. Gouthami,
Dr. T. Ramashri

Introduction

Urbanization is progressive concentration of population in urban unit.

Quantification of urbanization is very difficult. It is a finite process—a cycle through which a nation pass as they evolve from agrarian to industrial society. There are three stages in the process of urbanization:

Stage One

It is the initial stage characterized by rural traditional society with predominance in agriculture and dispersed pattern of settlements.

Stage Two

It refers to acceleration stage where basic restructuring of the economy and investments in social overhead capitals including transportation, communication take place. Proportion of urban population gradually increases from 25 per cent to 40 per cent, 50 per cent, 60 per cent and so on. Dependence on primary sector gradually dwindles.

Stage Third

It is known as terminal stage where urban population exceeds 70 per cent or more. At this stage level of urbanization remains more or less the same or constant. Rate of growth of urban population and total population becomes the same at this terminal stage. The onset of modern and universal process of urbanization is relatively a recent phenomenon and is closely related with industrial revolution and associated economic development. As industrial revolution started in Western Europe, United Kingdom was the initiator of industrial revolution. Historical evidence suggests that urbanization process is inevitable and universal.

Currently developed countries are characterized by high level of urbanization and some of them are in final stage of urbanization process and experiencing slowing down of urbanization due to host of factors. A majority of the developing countries, on the other hand started experiencing urbanization only since the middle of 20th century.

Definition

Indian Census Definition of Urban Area:

In Census of India, 2001 two types of town were identified:

- *Statutory towns:* All places with a municipality, corporation, Cantonment board or notified town area committee, etc. so declared by state law.
- *Census towns:* Places which satisfy following criteria:
  - *(i)* A minimum population of 5000.
  - *(ii)* At least 75 per cent of male working population engaged in non-agricultural pursuits.
  - *(iii)* A density of population of at least 400 persons per sq km.

Urban Agglomeration

The following are the possible different situations in which urban agglomerations could be constituted:

- A city or town with one or more contiguous outgrowths.
- Two or more adjoining towns with or without their outgrowths.
- A city or one or more adjoining towns with their outgrowths all of which form a continuous spread.

Volume and Trend of Urbanization in India

India shares most characteristic features of urbanization in the developing countries. Number of urban agglomeration/town has grown from 1827 in 1901 to 5161 in 2001. Number of total population has increased from 23.84 crores in 1901 to 102.7 crores in 2001 whereas number of population residing in urban areas has increased from 2.58 crores in 1901 to 28.53 crore in 2001.

According to 2001 census (Table 7.1), in India out of total population of 1027 million about 285 million live in urban areas and 742 million live in rural areas. Sex ratio, defined as number of female per 1000 male, for urban, rural and total India are 900, 945, 933 respectively.

Table 7.1 Population of India by sex and residence: 2001

India	Male	Female	Total Person	Sex ratio
Urban	150135894	135219060	285354954	900
Rural	381141184	360519109	741660293	945
Total	531277078	495738169	1027015247	933

Source: IND-CEN01, Census 2001, Office of the Register General.

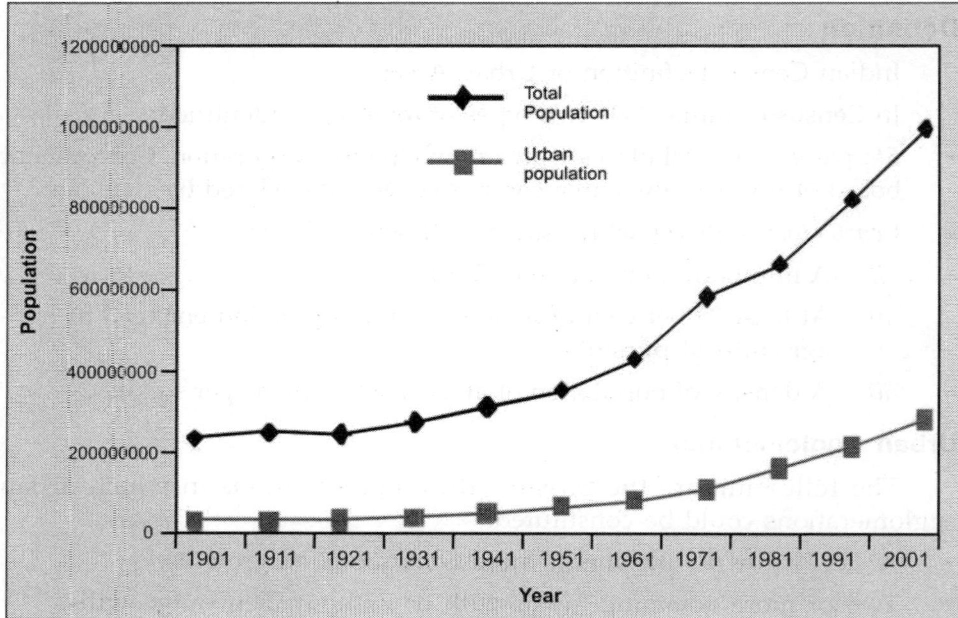

Fig. 7.1: Process of Urbanization in India

Degree of Urbanisation

The degree or level of urbanization is defined as relative number of people who live in urban areas. Per cent urban [(u/p)*100] and per cent rural [(r/p)*100] are commonly used for measuring the degree of urbanization. The ratio U/P has lower limit 0 and upper limit 11 i.e. 0< U/ P < 1. The index is 0 for total population equal to rural population. When whole population is urban, this index is one. The urban-rural ratio has a lower limit of zero and upper limit?, i.e. 0<U/R<?. Theoretically upper limit will be infinite when there is no rural population (R = 0) but this is impossible. From table 7.2 it is clear that per cent urban has increased from 11 per cent in 1901 to 28 per cent in 2011.

Table 7.2: Degree/index of urbanisation 1901-2001

Census year	% Urban	% Rural	Urban-Rural Ratio (%)
1901	10.84	89.15	12.16
1911	10.29	89.71	11.47
1921	11.18	88.82	12.58
1931	11.99	88.01	13.63
1941	13.86	86.14	16.08
1951	17.29	82.71	20.91
1961	17.97	82.03	21.91
1971	18.24	81.76	22.31
1981	23.33	76.66	30.44
1991	25.72	74.28	34.63
2001	27.78	72.22	38.47

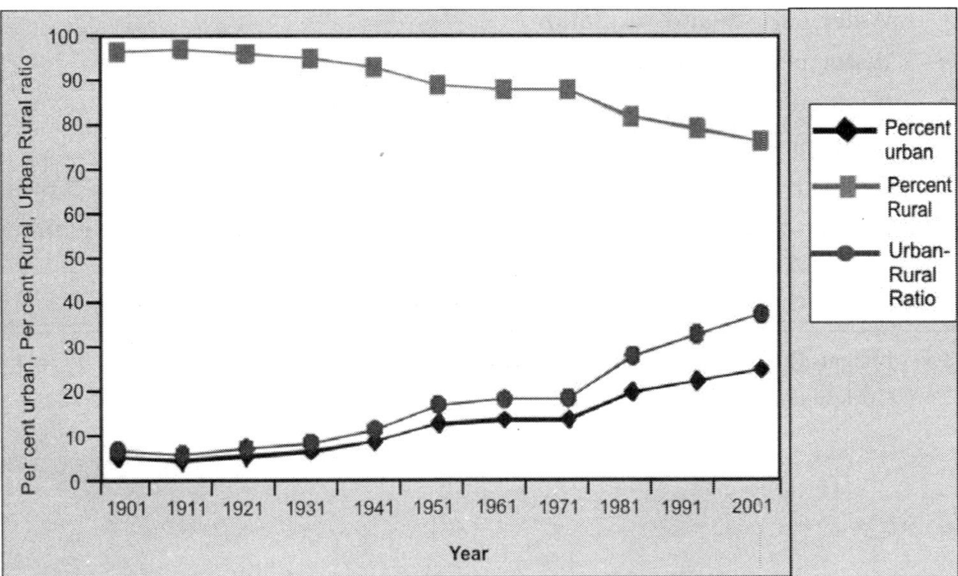

Fig. 7.2: Degree of Urbanization in India, 1901-2001

Basic Feature and Pattern of India's Urbanisation

Basic feature of urbanization in India can be highlighted as:

- Lopsided urbanization induces growth of class I cities.
- Urbanisation occurs without industrialization and strong economic base.

- Urbanisation is mainly a product of demographic explosion and poverty induced rural-urban migration.
- Rapid urbanization leads to massive growth of slum followed by misery, poverty, unemployment, exploitation, inequalities, degradation in the quality of urban life.
- Urbanisation occurs not due to urban pull but due to rural push.
- Poor quality of rural-urban migration leads to poor quality of Urbanisation.
- Distree migration initiates urban decay.

Problems of Urbanization

India's urbanization is followed by some basic problems in the field of:

- Housing.
- Slums.
- Transport.
- Water supply and sanitation.
- Water pollution and air pollution.
- Inadequate provision for social infrastructure (school, hospital, etc).
- Unemployment.
- Urban poverty.
- Drinking water, electricity, degenerating social and economic inequalities

References

1. Bhagat, R.B. (1992), *Components of Urban Growth in India with Reference to Haryana.*
2. Google.com

Practice of Social Work in Rapid Urbanization

Dr. Allu Gowri Sankar Rao,
Mr. G. Samba Siva Rao

Introduction

India has shared the growth pattern with some of the fastest growing regions in Asia. The country has witnessed around 8 per cent growth in GDP in the last couple of years. India's urban population is increasing at a faster rate than its total population. Urbanization has been recognized as an important component of economic growth. At 28 per cent, the pace of urbanization, however, has been slow and lower than the average for Asia. The absolute number of people in urban cities and towns, however, has gone up substantially. The researchers expect rate of urbanization to also increase in the coming years. With over 575 million people, India will have 41 per cent of its population living in cities and towns by 2030 from the present level of 286 million.

As per 2001 census report the slum population of India in cities and towns with a population of 50,000 and above was 42.6 million, which is 22.6 per cent of the urban population of the state/union territories reporting slums. This could also roughly be the size of Spain or Colombia. 11.2 million of the total slum population of the country is in Maharashtra followed by Andhra Pradesh (5.2 million), and Uttar Pradesh (4.4 million). Although the slum population has increased, the number of slums is lower (National Sample Survey Organization's 58th Round), which makes them more dense. There is higher concentration of slum population in the large urban centers (Census, 2001).

URBANISM AS WAY OF LIFE

Louis Wirth's classic essay on urbanism as a way of lie, published in 1938, influenced generation of sociologists in their approach to life in the city. He argued that size, density, and heterogeneity of the urban population paved the way for impersonal, transitory, and secondary social relationship based on anonymity, formality, and rational interest.

Urban life promotes sophistication and rationality, and all social relationship are considered mean to other ends. Thus, the urban way of life loses spontaneous self-expression. The segmented character and utilitarian accent of interpersonal relations in the city find their institutional expression in the proliferation of specialized tasks. The city also accentuates division of labour and specialization of occupations. The urban man tends to acquire and develop sensitivity to a world of artifacts, and becomes progressively farther removed from the world of nature. Since a transitory habitat does not generate binding traditions, the city-dweller is not a true neighbour. The pecuniary nexus which implies the purchasability of services and things has displaced personal relations as the basis of association. Therefore, personal disorganization, mental breakdown, suicide, delinquency, crime, corruption, and disorder might be more prevalent in the urban than in the rural community.

However, recent scholarship indicates that the view that modern urban societies constitute a mass of uprooted, impersonal individuals, disconnected with one another, unloved and alienated, is an exaggeration. There are hundreds of neighborhoods and little community's right in the heart of the city where people know and relate to one another. New in-migrants to the city also tend to gravitate to neighborhoods where people from their villages or regions live. Caste groups, religious communities, and linguistic groups provide effective personal networks and supports systems. Members of the same caste, people who speak the same language or hail from the same state or members of extended families and clans continue to maintain close social relationships.

Problems of Urbanisation

As per the 2001 census, the total urban homeless population is 7,78,599 people. Delhi had 3.1 per cent of the national level, and Bihar and Tamilnadu had 1.6 per cent and 7.3 per cent respectively. Many people interviewed chose the streets because paying rent would mean no savings and therefore no money sent back home and hence the street was the only option for them. Their condition is chiefly linked to their lack of adequate shelter. In Delhi, for over a 100,000 homeless people, the government runs 14 night shelters with a maximum capacity of 2,937 people, which is only 3 per cent of the homeless people in the city. Outside in the walled city of Delhi, private contractors called Thijawalahs rent out quilts (winter) and plastic sheets (monsoon) for five rupees a night. Iron cots are rented for 15 rupees a night. 71 per cent said that they had no friends. In a study of homeless populations, homeless men, women and children in four cities represented that they were beaten by the police at night and driven away from their make-shift homes/shelters.

Urban poverty in India remains high, at over 25 per cent. Over 80 million poor people live in the cities and towns of India. National Sample Survey Organization's survey report). This is roughly equal to the population of Egypt. A large number of states report poverty figures in urban areas much above that in rural areas. At the national level, rural poverty is higher than poverty in urban areas but the gap between the two has decreased over the last couple of decades. The incidence of decline of urban poverty has not accelerated with GDP growth. As the urban population in the country is growing, so is urban poverty. Urban poverty poses the problems of housing and shelter, water, sanitation, health, education, social security and livelihoods along with special needs of vulnerable groups like women, children and aged people.

Migration and Urbanisation

The report finds that the incidence of migration in India has shown an increase in 2001 as compared to consistent decline during 1961-1991. The economic motive remains the main reason for migration among male inter-state migrants. Economically backward states keep losing people to developed states. Poverty incidence was found less among migrates as compared to non-migrants, but it was higher among rural to urban migrants. Middle and higher income groups show higher propensity to move. The most successful group of migrants is urban to urban migrants in terms of type of occupation they have and their income levels due to better education and skills they possessed. Influx of migration towards metropolitan cities indicates that economic reforms have not been able to create much employment opportunities in small and medium towns and in rural areas.

Rapid Growth of Urbanisation

As the world moves into the year 2008, there will be more number of people living in urban areas than rural areas. In fact, the 20th century witnessed a rapid growth in urban population. The next few decades will see unprecedented scale of urban growth in the developing world including those in Asia and Africa continents. The urban population in these two continents will double in a period of 30 years. Asia has been witnessing the triple dynamics of growth, rapid urbanization and growing poverty. While many Asian countries witnessed highly economic growth, the growth pattern brought about enormous disparities across and within the nation.

India has shared the growth pattern and rapid urbanization with some of the fastest growing region in Asia. The country has witnessed around 8 per cent growth in GDP in the last couple of years and has planned to achieve a target of over 9 per cent growth by the end of 11th plan period. India's urban population is also increasing at a faster rate than its total population living in cities and towns by AD 2030 from the present level of 286 million and 28 per cent.

Consequences of Urbanisation

Economic development and urbanization are closely linked. In India, cities contribute over 55 per cent to country's GDP and urbanization has been recognized as an important component of economic growth. With India becoming increasingly globalized and urbanized, there is also an increase in the number of poor people living here. As per the latest NSSO survey reports there are over 80 million poor people living in the cities and towns of India. The slum population is also increasing and as per TCPO estimates, 2001, over 61.80 million people were living in slums. As a result of urbanization, the urban poverty poses the problems of housing and shelter, water, sanitation, health, education, social security and livelihoods along with special needs of vulnerable groups like women, children and aged people. To tackle these problems a social work professional approach needed to prevent, to slow or to minimize to the above mentioned problems.

Concept of Social Work

At the joint congress of the International School of Social Work and the International Federation of Social Workers in 2000, the following universal definition was adopted. "The Social Work profession promotes social change, problem solving in human relationships and the empowerment and liberation of people to enhance well-being. Utilizing theories of human behaviour and social systems, social work intervenes at the point where people interact with their environments, principles of human rights and social justice is fundamental to Social Work". Definition of social work in the earlier decades had focused on helping individuals to lead personally satisfying and socially useful lives through differential approaches. This also applied to groups and communities.

Practice is the hallmark of any profession which includes interventions in the domains of social and human development services. Depending upon the new concerns, reflections on one's experiences during practice, scientific and technological advances, institutional reorientation or reorganization, prioritization of societal concerns and allocation of resources, professions continuously examine the structure of their practice and its impact on society. Social work as a profession emerged in response to the urban crises and societal dislocations in the west to bridge social divides, rebuild interpersonal, social and community relationships, and to enhance social functioning of individuals as well as their contribution to society.

If one looks at the growth of the profession of medicine, several fields and sub-fields, specialties and super-specialties have come into existence in order to respond to individual and community needs. In the recent trends the professional approach of Social Work is very much needed like medicine, especially in the growing urban scenario.

Emerging Problems of Urbanisation

It is interesting to note that the ratio of urban in some of the larger states in higher than that of rural poverty leading to the phenomenon of "Urbanization of poverty". Urban poverty poses the problems of housing and shelter, water, sanitation, health, education, social security and livelihoods along with special needs of vulnerable groups like women, children and aged people. Poor people live in slums which are overcrowded, often polluted and lack of basic civic amenities like clean drinking water, sanitation and health facilities. Most of them are involved in informal sector activities where there is constant threat of eviction social security cover.

With growing poverty and slums, Indian cities have been grappling with the challenges of making the cities sustainable, i.e. inclusive, productive, efficient and manageable. The sustainability of urban development in India is seen in the context of shelter and slums. Basic urban services, financing urban development and governance and planning.

Social Work Intervention in Overcoming Urban Problems

India has entered the Eleventh Plan period with an impressive record of economic growth. However, the incidence of decline of urban poverty has not accelerated with GDP growth. In fact urban poverty will become a major challenge for policy-makers in our country as the urban population in the country is growing, so as urban poverty. Therefore, a need has arisen to develop new poverty reduction tools and approaches to attack the multi-dimensional issues of urban poverty. For this, policy-makers at the national and local levels should have a good understanding of the nature of urban poverty as well as accurate data on various issues relating to it, in order to develop programme/policies to manage urban poverty in systematic manner.

As a social worker he can play different roles by intervening in their social life. As a social actionist he can play a role in between the slum people, concerned authorities and planners to develop a healthy environment in their living area. The social worker also educate the slum dwellers regarding facilities provided by the government for the proper living and also motivate them to shift to the healthy environment, proper education, and for keeping good health. The social worker will also involve in the proper planning of sanitation, drinking water and in creating healthy housing for their reside acne. He works as a catalyst, organizer, advocate, enabler and therapist to all slum problems by intervening all aspects of their life and he wants to make them healthy one. The social worker works out for the financial development of women in slums by promoting SHGs and making linkage with the National Banks. He also creates awareness on population education and their school education for their better living.

References

1. Francis Abraham, "Contemporary Sociology–An Introduction to Concepts and Theories", *'Urbanization'* pp. 231-232, New Delhi, Oxford University Press.
2. Higgins, Benjamin, 1967, 'Urbanization, Industrialization, and Economic Development', in Glenn Beyer (ed.), *The Urban Explosion in Latin America,* Ithaca: Cornel University Press.
3. Herbert Hewitt Stroup, 1969, "Social Work—An Introduction to the Field" , Second Edition Surjeet Publications, New Delhi-110 007, pp. 308-309.
4. National Sample Survey Organisation's, 58th Round.
5. Simmel, Georg, 'The Metropolis and Menatal Life', in Richard Sennet (ed.), *Classic Essays on the Cultural of Cities,* pp. 47-60.
6. Indian–Urban Poverty Report 2009.
7. 2001 Census Report the Slum Population of India.
8. Paul Chowdhary, D. *'Introduction to Social Work'- History, Concept, Methods and Fields,* Atma Ram and Sons, Delhi, pp. 31-32.

Urbanization and Urban Problems

Ms. M. Subhashini

In the process of social evolution urbanization is an inextricable phenomenon. Urbanization exercises a growing influence on all aspects of human's life affecting the nature of economic development and social change. It is an indication of modernization, the sign of growth and economic progress. Urbanization is a natural consequence of economic change that take place, as the nation develops. It is indispensable to economic growth and leads to social equity. Urbanization is the result of more avenues of industrialization but it is not matched by a commensurate degree of energy and transportation. The most distinctive feature of the twentieth century has been the rapid and massive urbanization taking place everywhere in the world as a consequence of process of modernization (Inderjeet Singh Sodhi, 2004).

Urbanization is a global phenomenon experienced by economically advanced as well as developing countries. As countries place emphasis on industrial development, there is movement of people from villages to towns and cities. Cities provide a variety of facilities such as educational facilities, health care services, entertainment pleasures that are not available in small towns. People migrate to cities for employment opportunities to improve economic status and urban lifestyles. Even the anonymity that an urban area provides can be an attraction to some (B.Sudhakara Reddy, 2002).

There is a curious relation between rapid urbanization and growing population. The rising aspirations of people for better living standards, which also directly or indirectly draw upon the country's natural resources thereby affecting the overall environment both qualitatively and quantitatively. It has been noticed that India is gradually changing its socio-economic pattern from an agrarian to an industrial society. Large areas of land which were earlier cropland forests, are now being used for urbanization and industrialization (Pradeep Sachadeva, 1995). Urbanization and its consequence are worldwide phenomena and the increasing size and scale of urban settlements is a characteristic of the contemporary era. The urbanization process denotes a complex interplay of social, economic, political, technological, geographical and cultural factors (Michael Pacion, 1981).

Meaning and Definition

The term urban is usually applied to a spatial or a real unit having certain specific characteristics which differentiate it from the rural unit. An urban unit may take the form of a town, city or metropolis, while a rural unit is a village administratively defined as a *mouza* in India. Urbanism is the way of life, prevailing in an urban area, while urbanization is the process of evolution of urban units or areas. Jones has defined an urban settlement as "a physical conglomeration of house and streets or it is a centre of exchange and commerce or it is a kind of society or even a frame of mind (Jayasri Raychaudhuri, 2001).

Urbanization means transition from one way of life to another. They become urbanized by going to where the urban way of life is. Urbanization means breakdown of traditional social institutions and values. In the Indian context this means, among other things, that caste system will change into the class system, nuclear families will emerge from joint families, and the religion become highly secularized (Ravinder Singh Sandhu, 2003).

Cause and Consequence of Urbanization

The rural-urban migration is mainly a consequence of the push factor causing the worker to leave the rural areas; and agricultural field. Unemployment, unavailability of socio-economic facilities and services and lower level of income are economic pressure, or push in the countryside which mounts continuously and pushes out the people to the cities in search of employment and livelihood. The demand for labour by developing economic activities in the towns and cities or "pull factor" is also a factor for growth in urban population. Availability of socio-economic services and civic facilities and modern outlook of society also pull the population to migrate to urban areas. Generally the population gained by natural increase or re-classification of urban centre forms a small segment of the total gain to the urban population. Therefore, rural to urban migration is the moving force behind the progress of urbanization (Dr. Sheo Shankar Verma, 1989).

Stages of Urbanization

Urbanization as a process generally follows a sig maid curve it attenuated 'S' shape curve. In the early period of time where initial stage of urbanization prevails, the curve rises gradually. It is characterized by a traditional economic structure and society and relatively small population resides in cities.

The second stage, urbanization accelerate stage when urbanization curve rises steeply indicating a high pace of urbanization. It rises up to 60 per cent or more of the total population. During this period there is not only consecration of population at the cities but also of economic activities. The secondary and tertiary economic sectors gains as increased importance which may employ increasingly large member of people than the primary sector.

The third stage, terminal stage comes after the acceleration stage. Urban population reaches near saturation point (60 to 80%). During this stage, there is a gradually flattering of upper portion of the curve because some segment of population will remain in rural areas to provide food and fiber (Dr. Sheo Shankar Verma, 1989).

Problems of Urbanization

The rapid urbanization had led to serve problems and challenges being confronted by the governments. Besides undertaking day-to-day functions, such problematic zones have not only increased the urban governments, takes but have made their functioning more challenging. The positive rote of urbanization is often over shadowed by the evident deterioration in the physical environment and quality of life in the urban areas caused by widening gap between demand and supply of essential services and infrastructure. With a rapid urbanization and problems arising there from the task of urban governments have become challenging indeed. Urbanization brings demographic, social, economic and physical challenges which generate problems relating to civic urban services, planning, land use, policing and law and order managements (Pradeep Schdeva, 1995).

Urbanization poses several problems such as slums, insanitation, and environmental pollution, scarcity of housing, water, electricity, transport and medical aid. The speed with which the urban population is rising has created difficulties for urban governments.

Slums

Slum basically reflects sub-standard housing insanity living environment and lack of civic amenities. Slum is the result of accelerated urbanization. The slum is the outcome of the inability of the city to provide land and shelter to all its citizens. The poor migrate, who migrate from villages and small urban settlements for livelihood are the worst hit. The slum areas are congested having only narrow lane, open drains with stagnant stinking waste water, heaps of garbage dumps, poor street lighting are the typical symptoms of deteriorating environment of the slums.

Transportation

There are many dimensions to the urban transport problem. Limited physical space and paucity of financial resources is one important aspect.

Historical development and town planning practices of the past is another. To travel in a mass transport system during peak hours is an ordeal for most of the Indian city dwellers. Congestion on roads, crush loads on buses and suburban trains, alarming rise in number of vehicular accidents and high level of traffic generate air and noise pollution (Pradeep Sachdeva, 1995).

Urban Poverty

Urban poverty is a cruel reality which cannot be ignored as it impinges vitally on the designs of urban areas, their living patterns and the supply of civic services. In every growing city there is a huge backlog of urban services and the condition is worsening everyday by the continuous flow of migrants from the villages and small towns. The living environment seems to be deteriorating fast in the face of chronic shortages of all the essential civic amenities like water supply, housing, roads and transportation, education, public health and medical facilities and so on (V.P Dubey, 1990).

Environment

Environmental deterioration is one of the alarming and uncomfortable problems of metropolitan, because it can be seen almost every where in the form of heaps of garbage and other waste material and also in the structure of houses in the slum. Other aspects of environmental deterioration include atmospheric waste from the emission of gases by industries or automobiles etc. It is noteworthy that rush of rapid industrialization and consequents; almost no attention was paid to control the adverse impacts on environment.

Housing

Although movement of population to cities have always created housing problem, the great tidal waves of urbanward migrates that have engulfed many cities in recent years have created housing shortages probably without precedent. The disparity between income and the costs of adequate housing has made it impossible for countless families.

Urbanization poses several problems such as slums, insanitation, and environmental pollution, scarcity of housing, water, electricity, transport and medical aid. The speed with which the urban population is rising has created difficulties for urban governments (Pradeep Schdeva, 1995).

Conclusion

Urbanization is a worldwide process and it has been considered not only as an index of development but also as an important factor of social change. Urbanization helps to contribute to the growth process at large. Urbanization and technological transformation are two key process of economic development. Most of the developed countries of the world have already passed through these processes and derived economic benefits. At the same time urbanization poses several problems of multi-dimensional nature such as slums, housing, pollution, water, poverty, and transport problems etc. But urbanization as such is not an evil rather it is a welcome phenomenon of change and transformation.

References

1. Inderjeet Singh Sodhi (2004), *Challenges and Prospects of Urbanization—Need for Better Approach and Strategy*, Vol. xxxvi, No. 2, April-June, 2004.
2. Pradeep Sachdeva (1995), *Revamping Government in India*, Kitab Mahal, Delhi, 1995.
3. B. Sudhakar Reddy, *India Development Report*, 2002.
4. Shamsher Singh (1992), *Urban Planning and Development: Issues and Imperatives*, Ashis Publishing House, Delhi, 1992.
5. Sheo Shankar Verma (1981), *Urbanization and Regional Development in India*, Chugh Publication, Allahabad, 1981.
6. Jayasri Ray Chandhuri (2001), *An Introduction to Development and Regional Planning*, Orient Longman, Kolkata, 2001.
7. Ravinder Singh Sandhu (2003), *Urbanization in India, Sage* Publications, Delhi, 2003.
8. V.P. Dubey (1990), *Urban Development Administration*, Deep and Deep Publication, New Delhi, 1990.
9. Michael Pacione (1981), *Problems and Planning in Third World Cities*, Vikas Publishing House Pvt Ltd., New Delhi, 1981.

Impact of Urbanization on the Levels of Economic Development

Dr. K. Radhika,
Mr. A. Ramesh

As per the notification of Municipal Authorities and AP Urban Ceiling Act, 2001, the concept of urbanization has comprises of municipal corporation area, cantonment board and notified town areas/nagars/panchayats. An urbanized area included territory encompassing underdeveloped land which indicated transformation of land from rural to urban use as an instrument of social, and economic change and of community's efforts to corresponding urban development. The main characteristic feature is newly created urban area where its population earns its livelihood and also as an independent local government.

According to 1961 census, which militates against the concept of urban area was more responsible for the declassification of towns with a high proportion of workers engaged in agricultural activities. The urban units recognized by the Census Organization are known as Census Town based on the classification of urban areas as it consider the size class. The existing population of the Ist size-class carries a population up to one lakh and above, followed by IInd, IIIrd ranging from 50,000 to 99000 and 20,000 to 49000, but there are other areas in which the 4th, 5th and 6th size classes will be fixed at 10,000 to 19000, 5000 to 9990 and less than 5000.

An important result of urbanization pertains to change in attitudes that accompany it. This process is furthered by the enormous reduction in the costs of organizing disseminating information tend to promote modernization of behavior and motivation along with variety of jobs and existence of cultural activities. The changed attitudes replace the traditional ones. By all means, it is rightly said that urbanization itself becomes a powerful factor in furthering urbanization.

The concept of urbanization has explained by the economics thinkers from their point of view in due course of time. As R.P. MISRA viewed on urbanization as, a process which reveals itself through temporal, spatial, and sectoral changes in the demographic, social-economic, technological and environmental aspects of life in a given society. These changes manifest themselves in the increasing concentration of population in human settlements larger than villages; in the increasing involvement of the people in secondary and tertiary production in the progressive adoption of certain social traits, which are typical of traditional rural societies.

Nevertheless, urbanization can influence rural society depending upon the nature of rural-urban articulation and other factors such as the development of learning process communication skills and economic change. Some how, urban life may transform the migrants. The rural culture may gradually substituted with the urban culture. But it does not mean that he completely abandon the old habits as himself loses perfectly into the multi-dimensional urban culture.

Thus, India is taking part in an earth-wide tide of urban growth, presently creating in developing nations. As a whole, in India, the pace of urban increase but not yet noticeably quickening. The percentage of India's urban population at the time of Independence was 17 per cent, but now it is 24 per cent as per Census of India. India has the slow growth of urban population when compared with G10 countries. Till now, urbanization in India has reflected an increasing magnitude of numbers rather than high urban growth rates, a pattern shared with other developing nations. Urbanisation in India has relatively slow over the past 50 years as compared with many other developing countries. According to 1991 census. its urban population of 217 million, occupies along with China as the countries with the largest urban systems in the world.

History of Urban Growth

The development of urbanization in India has been through a prolonged and slow process of the progress of civilization may be called a 'Cultural Process'. During the past historical background visualized various socio and political change may be called a Political Process, whereas in modern times urbanization has mostly associated with industrialization and economic development and accordingly it may be called an 'Economic Process'.

Not with stand this, the process of urbanization in India was thrashed out in considerable detail at an International Seminar held at Berkeley (California) in 1960. As a result, a major contribution to the study of urbanization in India turns into a new outlook. Gradually the process of urbanization can be divided into four categories namely:

(i) Sub-urbanization,
(ii) Metropolisation,
(iii) Urban-commercialisation,
(iv) Rural-urbanization.

Trends in Decadal Growth of Population

From the general trends of population change and urbanization in the 20th century, it has identified two factors, firstly except during 1911-21 both India and Andhra Pradesh had experienced minus percentage decadal growth and secondly the population growth accelerated in each successive decade with one exception from 1941 to 1951. The reason was mainly due to the deaths caused by the great famine in Bengal and parts of India and Pakistan. The growth of urban population has increased at the rate that exceeds the growth for the whole population and it began to rise in decade of 1911-31, later on it was declined from 1981 to 2001.

Comparative Picture of Urbanization with Selected Countries

From the survey an attempt has been made to examine the levels of urbanization in different countries. The table 10.1 reveals the comparison of the level of the urbanization in India with the developed countries of the world in 1992. Singapore was stood at first position next followed by UK and Argentina, whereas in India and China the percentage of urbanization was too low and it was less than the percentage of the developing nations. Obviously employment strategies should be planned to attract population to urban areas.

Table 10.1: Comparative picture of urbanization with selected countries, 1992

Country	Percentage of Urban Population
Singapore	100
UK	89
Australia	85
Japan	77
USA	76
Russia	74
India	28
China	26
Mexico	73
Argentina	86
Brazil	75
More developed countries	73
Less developed countries	34

Source: Rudder Dutt and Sundaram, KPM, *Indian Economy*, 2003 p. 53. United Nations Estimates Cited in Pradeep Roi S.N. Dass Gupta, Ed, *Urbanizations and Slums*, New Delhi, 1995 p. 31.

Table 10.2: Level of urbanisation in India (in selective states)

State	1961	1971	1981	1991	2001
A.P.	17.4	19.7	23.3	26.8	27.1
Bihar	8.4	10.0	12.5	13.2	10.5
Gujarat	25.8	28.1	31.1	41.0	37.4
Haryana	22.3	24.3	28.9	30.9	34.0
M.P.	14.3	16.3	20.3	23.2	26.7
Maharashtra	28.2	31.2	35.0	38.7	42.4
Orissa	6.3	8.4	11.3	13.4	15.0
Punjab	23.1	23.7	27.7	29.7	34.0
Rajasthan	16.3	17.6	20.9	22.9	23.4
Tamilnadu	26.7	30.3	33.0	34.2	43.9
U.P.	12.9	14.7	18.0	19.9	20.8
West Bengal	24.5	24.7	26.5	27.4	28.0
India	18.3	20.2	23.7	26.1	27.8

Source: 1. Census Reports from 1961-1991.
2. Census on India, paper II of 2001, Andhra Pradesh, Hyderabad.

As the table 10.2 shows that the level of AP urbanization compared per decade i.e., 1991-2001, which recorded as 26.8 per cent and 27.1 per cent as compared to the All India Average. It is almost equivalent to the All India average since 1961 and up to now.

The table 10.2 on the other hand represents a view that there will be fast rate of urban growth confined to the industrially developed states respectively except Gujarat registered a fall from 41 to 37 per cent. As per the Census of 2001 Tamilnadu tops the list with 42.4 per cent followed by Maharashtra, Gujarat, Punjab and Karnataka in respect of the level of urbanization whereas AP was stood at sixth place.

The table 10.3 contains the percentage of urban population in A.P. It shows that the urbanization was slow during 1901 to 1941 and then onwards this has been increasing slowly by one or two per cent. During 1951 the urban population registered an increase of about 3.3 per cent and reached 17.2 per cent. Once again there was rise of urban growth about 3.75 per cent between 1981 and 1991. Later on during the next two decade, the process of urbanization in AP was about 2 per cent. This could be attributed by the various reasons—

1. Construction of huge multi-purpose dams.
2. Creation of additional employment opportunities.

Table 10.3: Urban population in A.P.

Census	Population (000s)		Variation		% of Urban	Population India
	Total	Urban	Total	Urban		
1901	19.1	1.8	—	—	9.42	10.8
1911	21.4	2.2	12.49	17.68	10.26	10.3
1921	21.4	2.2	–0.13	1.03	10.28	11.2
1931	24.0	2.7	12.99	22.17	11.25	12.2
1941	27.3	2.7	12.75	36.07	13.55	13.8
1951	31.1	5.4	14.02	47.86	17.36	17.2
1961	36.0	6.3	15.65	15.76	17.44	18.0
1971	43.5	8.4	20.96	33.92	19.31	19.9
1981	53.5	12.5	23.1	48.62	23.32	23.3
1991	66.5	17.9	24.2	43.24	26.89	25.7
2001	75.7	20.5	13.86	14.63	27.08	27.8

Source: Computed from census reports (1901-2001).

3. Rural migration.
4. Industrialization and significant development in the tertiary sector of road and transportation.
5. Increase in literate rate among the masses.
6. Increased health care facilities and reduction in death rates.
7. Social change and increased mobility.

Table 10.4: Comparative statement of urbanisation of A.P. with other southern states of India (1961-2001)

Sl.No	State	1961	1971	1981	1991	2001
1.	Andhra Pradesh	17.4	19.4	23.3	26.8	27.1
2.	Tamilnadu	26.7	30.2	33.0	34.2	43.9
3.	Karnataka	22.3	24.3	28.9	30.9	34.0
4.	Kerala	15.1	16.3	18.5	26.4	26.0
	India	18.0	20.0	23.7	26.1	27.8

Source: Computed from the census tables (1961-2001).

Table 10.4 reveals the comparative picture of urbanization of A.P. with other southern states during the period 1961 to 2001. The proportion reflects a relatively low levels of urbanization, whereas the credit goes to Tamilnadu stood at first with 43.9 per cent, followed by Karnataka with 34.0, and A.P. at 27.1 per cent and the least was recorded in Kerala with 26.0 per cent. But all the four States have registered a rise nearer to the percentage of India's urbanization on the whole. This pace of urbanization has been faster and

Table 10.5: District wise growth of urban population in Andhra Pradesh, 1981-2001.

S. No.	Name of the District	Urban Population in 1981	% of Urban Population	Urban Population in 1991	% of Urban in Population	Urban Population in 2001	% of Urban Population
1.	Adilabad	316,983	19.34	481,576	23.13	656,343	26.47
2.	Nijamabad	322,653	19.21	412,944	20.27	422,533	18.04
3.	Karimnagar	384,730	15.79	624,319	20.55	678,944	19.53
4.	Medak	216,404	11.97	328,487	14.47	273,131	14.45
5.	Hyderabad	2,260,702	100.00	31,45,939	100.00	3,686,460	100.00
6.	Rangareddy	3,76,997	23.83	12,05,177	47.23	1,878,138	53.27
7.	Mahaboobnagar	267,221	10.93	3,42,192	11.12	3,71,461	10.59
8.	Nalgonda	259,517	11.38	3,31,453	11.87	4,29,458	13.26
9.	Warangal	396,474	17.24	5,46,622	19.39	6,20,791	19.21
10.	Khammam	297,386	16.98	4,48,163	20.23	5,08,048	19.3
11.	Krikakulam	213,404	10.89	2,90,238	12.50	2,78,203	11.00
12.	Vijayanagaram	287,499	15.94	3,63,500	17.22	4,12,093	18.36
13.	Visakhapatnam	805,961	31.28	13,08,583	39.83	15,12,840	39.89
14.	E. Godavari	822,180	22.21	10,80,804	23.80	1,136,714	23.33
15.	W. Godavari	596,874	20.76	7,28,553	20.71	7,47,458	19.69
16.	Krishan	992,062	32.54	13,24,954	35.82	1,365,617	32.37
17.	Guntur	945,702	27.53	12,86,700	28.89	12,31,253	27.95
18.	Prakasam	349,277	14.99	4,53,902	16.45	4,66,709	15.28
19.	Nellore	418,389	20.76	5,69,062	23.79	6,03,634	22.7
20.	Kadapa	374,503	19.37	5,44,973	24.03	6,00,487	23.33
21.	Kurnool	589,599	24.49	7,68,100	25.84	7,92,664	22.57
22.	Anantapur	530,917	20.84	7,48,053	23.5	9,20,079	25.28
23.	Chittoor	462,142	16.88	6,45,832	19.8	8,10,015	21.69
	Andhra Pradesh	8,609,107	23.32	1,78,87,126	26.89	2,05,03,597	27.08

Source: Computed from the census report (1981-2001).

more widespread in the last decade mainly due to the rapid developmental process has been taken place in service sector and overall economic development of the state. Therefore, the study of urbanization trends and strategies for urban growth has great importance to the policy-makers as the economic development is linked with the process of urbanization precisely as one of the key dimensions in the modernization process of society.

It is very interesting to know from table 10.5, the trends of growth of urbanization population to examined the districtwise urban population in AP during 1981-2001. Out of 23 district in AP, Hyderabad had unique development reached for all the three decades. The other district where urban population was higher than the state average in 2001 are Rangareddy (53.27), Visakhapatnam (39.89), Krishna (32.37) and Guntur (27.95) per cent. The lowest percentage of urban population is the Mahabubnagar with 10.59 per cent and all the Rayalaseema districts along with the remaining districts in AP revealed the lowest proportion of urban population as against the percentage of the state.

Concept of Urban Agglomeration

It was first introduced in the 1971 census continued in the 1981 census and further also. Accordingly the urban agglomeration is defined as a continuous urban spread constituting a town and its adjoining urban out-growths or more philosophically contagious town together with continuous and well recognized out-growths if any of such towns. The A.P. state had three such urban agglomerations namely, Hyderabad, Vijayawada and Rajahmundry in 1971. The same were found in the 1981 census also. But the number of urban agglomerations has increased to 15 in the 1991 census.

According to the 2001 census there were 37 urban agglomerations. Out of the 37 urban agglomerations 14 existed at the time of 1991 census and 23 urban agglomerations were newly formed by 2001 census. Jammalamadugu in Kadapa district was deleted from the list of Urban Agglomeration in the 2001 census.

As the economic development is relied upon the development of tertiary sector and its basic indicators linked with urbanization such as:

(i) Literacy,

(ii) Density of population,

(iii) Percentage of sex ratio,

(iv) Percentage of workers in agriculture/non-agricultural activities,

(v) Percentage of means of Transport sector,

(vi) To compute the data related to ranking of District according to Gross Domestic Product.

Urbanisation and Level of Development in A.P.

From the available data of 2001 given in tables 10.6, 107 and 10.8 INE indicators have been selected to identify the levels of development in A.P. as a result of the degree of urbanization. The level of urbanization of a state is a meaningful indicator of economic development. The concept of development can be identified with the increase in employment opportunities, availability of infrastructural facilities, amenities, and services, proper distribution of resources, increased production, investment and consumption and so on. The districts were categorically divided into three types such as:

- High level development refers to those districts exceeding the state average.
- Medium level development can be referred in between high and low development of the state average.
- Low level development is to be identified below the state average.

Therefore, basing on the available State Average data we can measure through the Ranking of the districts levels of economic development in A.P. resultant into urbanization such as:

- *Ranking of districts to the proportion of urban population, 2001:* Among 23 districts in A..P., 5 districts have recorded above the state average and in the first category of development. Among these first three districts i.e., Hyderabad, Rangareddy, and Visakhapatnam are industrially based and the remaining two are agriculture based economies.

  There are 18 districts which are recorded urbanization below the state average among them, the first 14 districts that show above 15 per cent of urban population are counted under medium level development and the other four districts are treated as low level development category i.e., Nalgonda, Medak, Srikakulam and Mahabubnagar.
- *Development on the basis of percentage of literacy:* As the literacy rate would further motivate the mass to reach township in the persuasion of higher education and to improve learning process. The rural migration is one of the cause to consider to take curriculum mainly in English medium to their children. If we examine the state average of literacy rate is 61.1 per cent as per the Census of 2001. The data reveals that eleven districts have recorded a literacy growth above the state averages. Among these, Hyderabad is at the top with a literacy rate of 79.04 per cent, followed by West Godavari with 73.95 per cent, Krishna with 69.91 and Chittoor with 67.46 per cent.
- *According to the sex ratio:* The state average sex ratio is 978/1000 women per men. The data reveals that sex ratio to be favorable to women in Nizamabad, Srikakulam and Vijayanagaram. In Karimnagar the sex ratio is neutral. The lowest sex ratio is registered in Rangareddy, Hyderabad and Anantapur district.

- *Indicator of development measured on the percentage of total workers to total population*: The Vijayanagaram district, the smallest among all districts in the state ranks first in the work participation rate (52.2) per cent, followed by Mahaboobnagar (51.8) per cent and Prakasam (50.03) per cent. There are three districts registered least work participation rates, i.e., Rangareddy (39.9) per cent, East Godavari(39.6) and Hyderabad (29.2) per cent. But in terms of work participation rate, there is upgrading from 27.4 per cent in the Census of 1991to 29.2 per cent in 2001 Census.
- *On the basis of male workers to total male population/female workers to total female population*: The Census of India, 2001 represents that half of the districts have registered a male workers population above the state average i.e., 56.8 per cent. Among the other districts, West Godavari with 60.2 per cent is in the top rank, followed by Vijayanagaram with 60.0 per cent and Guntur with 59.2 per cent. Hyderabad is the only district that had recorded the lowest i.e.,48.2 per cent male work participation rate among the total male population. In spite of it, more than half of the districts registered female workers population above the state average i.e., 35.1 per cent. Districts like Mahaboobnagar Vijayanagaram, and Nijamabad are in the top three ranks with 47.2, 44.6, and 44.2 per cent respectively. East Godavari with 20.4 per cent and Hyderabad with 8.8 per cent stood at the lowest ranks.
- *According to the percentage of agricultural/non-agricultural workers to total workers*: The percentage of workers engaged in agriculture sector of the state average is at 62.3 per cent and in non-agricultural activities, the state average is 37.7 per cent as per the Census of India, 2001 and the Economic Survey, 2003. The survey shows that Mahaboobnagar, Khammam, and West Godavari districts have registered top ranks whereas Hyderabad (0.3), Rangareddy (40.2) and Visakhpatnam (53.5) have registered the lowest ranks in agro-based economy. The other districts showing percentage of agricultural workers are almost highly urbanized and the districts showing high participation rate in agricultural sector are less urbanized district. Apart from, in 23 districts of AP, only 8 districts crossed the state average with regard to non-agricultural labor. The remaining 15 districts recorded an average below the state average. There is a clear indication of slow urbanization process in state. There are two districts namely Khammam and Mahaboobnagar showing very poor performance that is below 30 per cent. The Hyderabad district occupies the first rank as there is no rural area in the district and 99.7 per cent of workers engaged in non-agricultural activity. Predictable Rangareddy district occupies the second rank with 59.8 per cent followed by Visakhapatnam with 46.5 per cent is in the third rank. There is correlation to some extent between urbanization and workers in non-agricultural sector.

- *According to the percentage of Means of Transportation:* Means of Transportation is a positive indicator of urbanization. The most urbanized centers have secured the first 7 ranks i.e. Hyderabad (26.4), Krishna (8.6), Visakhapatnam (7.9), East Godavari (5.4), and Guntur (4.4.) The Economic Survey of 2003 had revealed that five districts recorded a vehicular movement below the state average as Medak 1.4, Mahaboobnagar (1.3), Kadapa (1.3), Vijayanagaram (1.1) and Srikakulam (1.0) per cent.
- *Ranking of the districts according to gross district domestic product at factor cost:* The state GDDP is of Rs. 3,71,834 as per data and also the state average. Eleven districts GDDP have touched above the state average, whereas remaining 12 districts have recorded GDDP below the state average. Among the twelve districts, two districts namely Srikakulam and Vijayanagaram recorded least GDDP at factor cost.

From the above analysis it is found that five districts fall under the category of high level of development from the all ranks of the districts namely, Hyderabad, Krishna, Visakhapatnam, Guntur and Rangareddy. No district from Rayalaseema region fall in this category, rather all the districts have fallen under the category of medium level of development. The reason is that the low level degree of connectivity between industrial development pattern and the agricultural base. The districts which have insignificant development of both agriculture and industrial sector are also responsible for the low level of urbanization in the state reveals under the category of low level of development i.e., Medak, Nalgonda, Srikakulam and Mahaboobnagar.

Findings

The following are some of the findings from the study where we can overcome to solve the problems arises due to the urbanization:

- To check rural migration and to eliminate the idea of posturing about city crazy and false prestige.
- Stop conversion of agricultural lands into real estate zones/centres.
- To arrest deafforestation of forests and to save ozone layers which protect environment at large.
- Unorganized growth of urbanized is accompanied by a sharp deterioration of sanitation and water supply.
- There are many shortcomings due to excess urbanization which reflects in growing urban unrest, crime, prostitution, begging, social tensions, proliferation of slums, congestion, and other essential amenities.
- The housing problems is yet another alarming and unmanageable sanitation with the growing inequalities as it is always inadequate in urban areas as the dwellers have low level of income, lack of education and sub-standard living in slums.

Table 10.6: District wise status of Andhra Pradesh in respect of literacy, density of population, sex ratio and total population ratio.

S.No	Name of the District	% of Population to Total Population	Rank	% of Literacy	Rank	Density of Population Per sq.Kms	Rank	Sex Ratio	Rank
1.	Adilabad	26.5	6	61.1	11	154	23	989	8
2.	Nijamabad	18.0	18	53.3	20	294	11	1016	1
3.	Karimnagar	19.5	15	53.5	19	294	10	1000	4
4.	Medak	14.5	20	53.2	21	274	12	976	12
5.	Hyderabad	100.00	1	79.O	1	16988	1	945	22
6.	Rangareddy	53.3	2	66.3	5	468	4	941	23
7.	Mahaboobnagar	10.6	23	45.5	23	190	18	970	17
8.	Nalgonda	13.3	21	57.8	14	227	15	967	18
9.	Warangal	19.2	16	58.4	13	252	13	973	15
10.	Khammam	19.8	13	57.7	15	160	22	975	13
11.	Krikakulam	11.0	22	55.9	17	233	6	1013	2
12.	Vijayanagaram	18.4	17	51.8	22	343	8	1004	3
13.	Visakhapatnam	39.9	3	59.5	12	340	9	991	7
14.	E. Godavari	23.3	8	65.5	8	351	5	992	5
15.	W. Godavari	19.7	14	73.9	2	490	2	992	6
16.	Krishan	32.4	4	69.9	3	483	3	961	20
17.	Guntur	27.9	5	62.8	10	387	7	984	9
18.	Prakasam	15.3	19	65.9	6	173	20	971	16
19.	Nellore	22.7	10	65.9	7	203	16	983	10
20.	Kadapa	23.3	9	64.0	9	168	21	975	14
21.	Kurnool	22.6	11	54.4	18	199	17	965	19
22.	Anantapur	25.3	7	56.7	16	190	19	957	21
23.	Chittoor	21.7	12	67.5	4	247	14	983	22
	Andhra Pradesh	27.1		61.1		275		978	

Table 10.7: District wise status of Andhra Pradesh in respect of male, female and agricultural workers.

S No	Name of the District	% of Male workers to Total Male Population	Rank	% of Female workers to Total Female Population	Rank	% workers engaged in agricultural works	Rank
1.	Adilabad	52.9	21	37.0	14	61.5	17
2.	Nijamabad	54.3	19	44.2	3	57.2	20
3.	Karimnagar	55.5	16	43.5	4	59.2	18
4.	Medak	55.5	16	41.4	9	67.6	11
5.	Hyderabad	48.2	22	8.8	23	0.3	23
6.	Rangareddy	53.4	20	25.6	21	40.2	22
7.	Mahaboobnagar	56.3	14	47.2	1	73.4	1
8.	Nalgonda	54.9	17	43.1	5	67.9	9
9.	Warangal	54.5	18	41.8	8	68.4	8
10.	Khammam	57.0	10	39.5	11	72.0	2
11.	Krikakulam	56.6	12	38.4	13	68.4	7
12.	Vijayanagaram	60.6	2	44.6	2	68.4	5
13.	Visakhapatnam	55.6	15	27.8	20	53.5	21
14.	E. Godavari	58.7	4	20.4	22	62.2	16
15.	W. Godavari	60.2	1	28.0	19	69.4	3
16	Krishan	29.5	18	40.9	5	8.6	2
17.	Guntur	59.2	3	38.7	12	67.1	12
18.	Prakasam	57.9	9	42.5	6	68.5	4
19.	Nellore	58.6	5	32.2	17	62.6	15
20.	Kadapa	56.8	11	32.6	16	63.5	14
21.	Kurnool	56.4	13	42.2	7	68.4	6
22.	Anantapur	57.9	8	39.5	10	67.7	10
23.	Chittoor	58.3	7	35.3	15	66.4	13
	Andhra Pradesh	56.8		35.1		62.3	

Table 10.8: District wise status of Andhra Pradesh in respect of non-agricultural workers, all type vehicles and GDDP

So. No	Name of the District	% of Wokers engaged in non-Agricultural Works	Rank	% of All Types of Vehicles	Rank	GDDP at Foctor cost at Constant (1993-94) 2000-2001	Rank
1.	Adilabad	38.5	7	1.7	18	2,14,281	21
2.	Nijamabad	42.8	4	2.2	14	2,17,945	20
3.	Karimnagar	40.8	6	3.4	8	4,03,438	10
4.	Medak	32.4	13	1.4	19	4,44,091	8
5.	Hyderabad	99.7	1	26.4	1	5,06,228	5
6.	Rangareddy	59.8	2	6.7	5	4,74,585	7
7.	Mahaboobnagar	26.6	22	1.3	20	2,80,493	18
8.	Nalgonda	32.1	15	1.9	15	3,29,052	13
9.	Warangal	31.6	16	2.9	11	2,98,026	17
10.	Khammam	28.0	21	2.4	12	3,00,292	16
11.	Krikakulam	31.6	17	1.0	23	1,96,696	22
12.	Vijayanagaram	31.6	18	1.1	22	1,72,680	23
13.	Visakhapatnam	46.5	3	7.9	3	5,20,482	4
14.	E. Godavari	37.8	8	7.7	4	5,96,719	1
15.	W. Godavari	30.6	20	5.4	6	4,99,163	6
16.	Krishan	40.9	19	8.6	2	5,22,233	2
17.	Guntur	32.9	12	4.4	7	5,21,665	3
18.	Prakasam	31.5	19	1.6	17	3,18,110	14
19.	Nellore	37.4	9	1.9	16	3,14,488	15
20.	Kadapa	36.5	10	1.3	21	2,72,623	19
21.	Kurnool	31.6	17	2.4	13	3,48,331	12
22.	Anantapur	32.3	14	3.1	4	3,86,730	11
23.	Chittoor	33.6	11	3.1	10	4,13,853	10
	Andhra Pradesh	37.7		100.00		3,71,834	

Source: Census of India, 2001 and Economic Survey, 2003.

- Another findings from the study is to check the menace of pollution and epidemic diseases.
- It is also find a major Herculean task to maintain the law and order to provide security to the people in case of urbanization.
- It creates more regional disparities due to more emphasis has made on the improving of a particular town or city which attracts the people become hue and cry for their settlement.

Suggestions

1. The government should formulate a uniform national urbanization policy in correlation with population policy.
2. To remove regional disparities and priorities shown by the political leaders confine to a particular place/town/district.
3. Irregular urban policies will be checked and controlled.
4. Equal importance should be imparted in promoting both education and health facilities simultaneously.
5. A sound perspective of urban development involving all the specialists, namely architects, town planners, engineers economists, bureaucrats transport authorities, health and medical experts as well as sociologists is need.
6. The rural, urban disparities could be reduced by a balanced approach of development coupled with infrastructure development.
7. Slum improvement and clearance should be undertaken with a determined plan and set targets.
8. The growth of small towns should be encouraged by providing sufficient economic and social infrastructure. It promotes rural industries and also for the improvement of small-scale industries.
9. Massive rural employment programs should be undertaken to prevent the flight from rural to urban areas.
10. To manage urban affairs and their programmes, policies, and strategic plans are taken to appropriate. Political, Techno-Economic Administrative Institutions to be set up for promoting new concepts and leadership in unfamiliar areas.
11. The civil administration has to create awareness among the people, regarding the dubious techniques of real estate businessmen spreading its tentacles and encroaching public assets, and Christian missioners properties.
12. The municipal corporation/district registration office has to strategies to check mal-practices of real estate businessmen. Public places should be notified clearly, so that they cannot be misused by the builders.

The normal phenomenon of accelerating urban growth with industrialization seems to have been muted in the advanced industrial districts in A.P. because of absence of corresponding improvement in agricultural productivity. An over all view reveals that there is an increasing trend in inequalities of the levels development between the districts.

Conclusion

According to the estimates and projections of the United Nations population division. The urban population of the world which doubled between 1950 and 1975 and further it was doubled between 1975 and 2000. The urban explosion in the developing country is mainly responsible for the surging up the world's urban population. As Mr. Tarun Sareen has rightly said that the "Urban Economics is the study of land use, location, decision and the growth of cities and towns. This broad subject encompasses the economic dimension of all activities in urban areas, including industry, housing, crime and poverty". Thus, the rapid urban growth is a problem of both developed and developing countries of the world because there is a wide gap between the rate of growth of urban population and rate of progress of social overhead facilities including employment opportunities for the educated urban population.

References

1. Dr. N.T.K. Naik and Dr. Mansoor Rehman, *Urbanisation of India*, pp. 14.
2. Ashok Mehta, *The Future of Indian Cities: Past and Future; National Issuses and Goals*.
3. Govt. of India, Planning Commission, Third Five Year Plan.
4. Cited in Kundas, Abanti, "Urbanization in India —A Contrast with Western Experience" *In Scientist* April, 1983.
5. Ibid., p. 453.
6. Misra, R.P., '*Million Cities of India,* 'New Delhi, 1978.
7. Ibid., p.9.
8. International Seminar on "Urbanization in India" Sponsored by Kingsley Davis, Richard, L. Park and Catherine Beuer Wurster at Berkeley, California in 1967.
9. Ibid.p.195.
10. K. Siddartha and L. Mukheerji, *Cities, Urbanization and Urban System*, New Delhi, 2001.
11. Nicholas William, H. "Industrialisation Factor Markets and Agricultural Development " in *Journal of Political Economy*, August, 1961.
12. Census of India, 1901-2001, 1961-1991, 2001, Government of India, Publications, New Delhi.
13. *Economic Survey of India*, 2003, New Delhi.
14. United Nations, *Estimates and Projects of Urban, Rural and City Population 1950-2025*, New York, 1981.

15. Tarun Sareen, *Dictionary of Economics*, New Dellhi, p. 713.

16. Rudder Datt and Sunderam, KPM., *Indian Economy*, 2003.

17. "United Nations Estimates" cited in Pradeep Roy, S.D.Gupta (Ed), *Urbanization and Slums*", New Delhi, 1995.

Educational Access in Urban India

Dr. Naraginti Amareswaran

Introduction

Education is a key factor not only for social development, but also for economic development of any nation in the world. Education in general and quality education in particular has a prominent role to change the lives of the students. Today's children are tomorrow's citizens. The future of the nation depends on the roles of the youth. Many researchers say that there is a positive correlation between education and economic development. Urbanization is a symbol for economic development. Some of the rural populace of India is moving to towns and cities for happy and wealthy life and some other to get employment.

According to the latest survey by the National Sample Survey Office (NSSO) in June 2008, the literacy rate among the population with age 7 and above was 72 per cent whereas the adult population (age 15 and above) had a literacy rate of 66 per cent. The level is well below the world average literacy rate of 84 per cent and India currently has the largest illiterate population of any nation on earth. According to 2001 census the urban literacy of India was 79.9 per cent (rural literacy was 58.7 per cent). McKinsey Global Institute estimates that India's population will reach 1.47 billion with around 40 per cent urbanization. That means close to 590 million will be living in cities. There are so many problems for urban people in India. The population of India is increasing day by day. What is the status of provision of primary needs of its citizens including Education?

URBANIZATION

Urbanization is an index of transformation from traditional rural economies to modern industrial one. It is progressive concentration (Davis, 1965) of population in urban unit. Quantification of urbanization is very difficult. It is a long term process. Kingsley Davis (Davis, 1962) has explained urbanization as process of switch from spread out pattern of human settlements to one of concentration in urban centers (Davis, 1962). It is a finite process—a cycle through which a nation pass as they evolve from agrarian to industrial society (Davis and Golden, 1954). He has mentioned three stages in the process of urbanization. *Stage one* is the initial stage characterized by rural traditional society with predominance in agriculture and dispersed pattern of settlements. *Stage two* refers to acceleration stage where basic restructuring of the economy and investments in social overhead capitals including transportation, communication take place. Proportion of urban population gradually increases from 25 per cent to 40 per cent, 50 per cent, 60 per cent and so on. Dependence on primary sector gradually dwindles. *Third stage* is known as terminal stage where urban population exceeds 70 per cent or more. At this stage level of urbanization remains more or less same or constant (Davis, 1965). Rate of growth of urban population and total population becomes same at this terminal stage.

The onset of modern and universal process of urbanization is relatively a recent phenomenon and is closely related with industrial revolution and associated economic development. As industrial revolution started in Western Europe, United Kingdom was the initiator of Industrial Revolution. Historical evidence suggests that urbanization process is inevitable and universal. Currently developed countries are characterized by high level of urbanization and some of them are in final stage of urbanization process and experiencing slowing down of urbanization due to host of factors (Brockerhoff, 1999; Brockerhoff and Brennam, 1998). A majority of the developing countries, on the other hand started experiencing urbanization only since the middle of 20th century.

Indian Census Definition of Urban Area

In Census of India, 2001 two types of town were identified:

- *Statutory towns:* All places with a municipality, corporation, cantonment board or notified town area committee, etc. so declared by state law.
- *Census towns:* Places which satisfy following criteria:-
  - *(i)* A minimum population of 5000.
  - *(ii)* At least 75 per cent of male working population engaged in non-agricultural pursuits.
  - *(iii)* A density of population of at least 400 persons per sq km.

Table 11.1: Urban population

Year/Sector		Population			Decadal Variation
		Male	Female	Persons	Persons
1951					
	Rural	153,444,642	145,199,739	298,644,381	—
	Urban	**32,083,820**	**30,359,889**	**62,443,709**	—
	Total	185,528,462	175,559,628	361,088,090	—
1961					
	Rural	183,504,095	176,794,073	360,298,168	20.64
	Urban	**42,789,106**	**36,147,497**	**78,936,603**	**26.41**
	Total	226,293,201	212,941,570	439,234,771	21.64
1971					
	Rural	225,319,943	213,725,732	439,045,675	21.86
	Urban	**58,729,333**	**50,384,644**	**109,113,977**	**38.23**
	Total	284,049,276	264,110,376	548,159,652	24.80
1981					
	Rural	270,910,547	252,956,003	523,866,550	19.32
	Urban	**82,463,913**	**76,998,634**	**159,462,547**	**46.14**
	Total	353,374,460	329,954,637	683,329,097	24.66
1991					
	Rural	324,321,614	304,370,062	628,691,676	20.01
	Urban	**114,908,844**	**102,702,168**	**217,611,012**	**36.47**
	Total	439,230,458	407,072,230	846,302,688	23.85
2001					
	Rural	381,602,674	360,887,965	742,490,639	18.10
	Urban	**150,554,098**	**135,565,591**	**286,119,689**	**31.48**
	Total	532,156,772	496,453,556	1,028,610,328	21.54

Source: Census of India.

The table 11.1 shows the full information regarding urban population sexwise from 1951 to 2001.

Why Educational Access is Important in India?

In 1950 India made a Constitutional commitment to provide free and compulsory education to all children up to the age of 14. In 2002 constitutional amendment made free and compulsory education a fundamental right for children aged 6-14. Yet, universal access to elementary education remains elusive and quality of provision erratic. Provision of quality education in India is an enormous quantitative challenge. In 2004-2005, data available from the Ministry of Human Resource Development (MHRD) showed that 182 million students were enrolled in 1.04 million elementary schools (grades 1-8) across the country (GoI, 2007a). This accounted for approximately 82 per cent of children in the 5-14 year age group in that year (GoI, 2007b).

Over the past two decades demand for schooling in India has increased, but provision is unequal. The National Policy on Education (NPE) (1986) and its Programme of Action (POA) (1992) state that all children, irrespective of caste, creed, location or gender, should have access to elementary education of a comparable quality. But in reality, schooling provision favours those better off, and disadvantaged groups (including poor children, girls, children from Scheduled Caste (SC), Scheduled Tribe (ST), Other Backward Classes (OBC) groups) have less access and access to poorer quality education. Large variations in access exist across different states, geographical areas, and social categories such as gender, caste and ethnicity. Policy-makers whilst making great strides to improve physical access to schools, have ongoing challenges to provide meaningful access for all children in India.

Indian Policy Context

Education in India is the joint responsibility of the central and state governments, and rights to education are provided for within the Constitution. Further commitments to the universalization of education as well as the legal, administrative and financial frameworks for the government-funded education system are found in two main sources. These are the on-going series of Five Year Plans for National Development and the National Policy on Education (NPE) (1986), with its Programme of Action (1992). Additionally, Sarva Siksha Abhiyan (SSA) is a programme which aims to achieve universal elementary education of satisfactory quality by 2010.

The general pattern of education adopted at the national level, commonly known as the 10 + 2 + 3 pattern, envisages a broad-based general education for all pupils during the first ten years of schooling. The elementary education which has now been made free and compulsory for the children of 6-14 years age group includes primary (I-V) and upper-primary/middle (VI-VIII) stages. Most states conduct examinations after class VIII for entry to secondary school. A policy of automatic promotion has been introduced at the elementary stages to encourage children to continue their education to at least Grade VIII, whilst minimizing repetition and dropout.

As a result of the NPE policy initiatives changes are being made on the ground. A massive infrastructure development and teacher recruitment drive was initiated nationally. NPE (1986) focused on the need for improvements to school environments (including building conditions, availability of tap water and toilet facilities), instructional material and teacher training. The District Primary Education Programme (1994) brought additional resources to the sector through the involvement of bilateral and multilateral donors. Village education committees, parent-teacher and mother-teacher associations have become active across the country. Legislative moves to bring elementary education under Panchayati Raj Institutions (local self-governments) have given further impetus to community mobilization at the grassroots level. Despite these changes, quality of provision continues to be a concern and is highlighted in the Tenth (2002-2007) and Eleventh (2007-2012) Five Year Plans, as well as SSA.

Various government schemes target disadvantaged children. The Alternative, Innovative and Education Guarantee Scheme (EGS/AIE) provides education in smaller, isolated habitations in rural areas and/or urban slums that do not qualify as regular formal schools; and schooling to difficult-to-reach groups such as working and migrating children. The National Programme for Education of Girls at Elementary Level (NPEGEL) and Kasturba Gandhi Balika Vidyalaya (KGBV) target girls often from scheduled castes, scheduled tribes and minorities in difficult areas. Through these programmes scholarships, free uniforms and textbooks are being given to recipients. The Mid-day Meal Scheme offers free lunch to all children attending primary schools and EGS/AS throughout India. Anganwaris provides nutritional support and pre-school education to children aged 0-6 years and early childhood care and education (ECCE) centers are operational in some selected areas. These initiatives have had considerable impact on children's access to education.

Patterns of Educational Access in India

Access to basic education in India is improving, but areas of concern remain:

School Supply: The number of primary schools has grown rapidly from 529,000 in 1986 to 767,000 in 2005 and at upper primary from 134,000 to 275,000.

In 2003 around 87 per cent of habitations had a primary school within a distance of 1 km and 78 per cent of habitations had an upper primary school within 3 km (NCERT, 2005).

In addition, the number of private pre-primary, primary and upper-primary schools has also increased considerably. However, government and local bodies continue to be the main providers managing around 91 per cent of primary and 73 per cent of upper-primary schools. Many new schools particularly those opened under the EGS/AIE scheme are small in size. Most are located in rural areas. Around 28 per cent of children are educated in primary schools with 50 students or fewer (DISE, 2005-6). Questions of quality of provision persist with many schools having weak infrastructure and poor teaching and learning conditions.

Educational Access in Urban India

The essence of human resource development is that education must play a significant and interventionist role in remedying imbalances in the socio-economic fabric of the country. Basic education has also greatly contributed to the quality of human life, particularly with regard to life expectancy, infant mortality, learning levels and nutritional status of children, etc. Several new initiatives have been taken by the government placing emphasis on decentralization with the participation of people at the grassroot level. Consequently, universal basic education has vastly contributed to social justice and equity, and participative economic growth. Education for all programme, makes an effort to universalize elementary education by community ownership of the school system. It is a response to the demand for quality basic education all over the country and seeks to ensure access, retention and quality improvement. It reiterates the need to focus on girls' education to equalize educational opportunities and eliminate gender disparities.

The international movement towards Education for All (EFA) encompasses six goals — early childhood care and education, universal elementary education, adult literacy, adolescent and life skill education, gender equality and all aspects of quality education. These goals are designed to enable children and young adults to realize their right to learn. The Government of India is committed to the Education for All (EFA) goals, which encompass early childhood care and education, primary education, girls' education, as also adult education. Government of India implements a number of programmes for the achievement of the EFA goals, including, *inter alia*, Sarva Shiksha Abhiyan (SSA), Mid-Day Meal Scheme (MDM) and National Literacy Mission (NLM). Sarva Shiksha Abhiyan (SSA), which is a major flagship programme of the government, addresses the national resolve of universalizing elementary education. Under SSA, special focus is on girls, children belonging to SC/ST communities, other weaker sections, minorities and urban deprived children.

Table 11.2: Urban literacy rate

Year	Male	Female	Persons
1991 (7 Years and above)			
Rural	57.87	30.62	44.69
Urban	**81.09**	**64.05**	**73.08**
Total	64.13	39.29	52.21
2001 (7 years and above)			
Rural	70.70	46.13	58.74
Urban	**86.27**	**72.86**	**79.92**
Total	75.26	53.67	64.84

Source: Census of India.

From the table 11.2 we conclude that the literacy rate of urban India is better than rural India. Urban literacy rate of India is low when compared to other developed countries in the world. It is the duty of government and NGOs to take good steps to increase urban literacy rate of India.

Urban Poverty and Education

India Urban Poverty Report-2009 using human development framework provides a good insight on various issues of urban poverty such as basic services to urban poor, migration, urban economy and livelihoods, microfinance for urban poor, education and health, unorganized sector and livelihoods.

- Quality of employment, productivity and returns on education are likely to be better in large cities than small towns.
- Education infrastructure is poorer in cities with larger population base and higher urbanization, thus increasing the possibility of marginalizing children of urban poor from education.
- There is a big difference between the proportion of children accessing education in million plus cities compared to smaller cities. The two critical problems pointed out by the author in this field are access and the quality of education. Quality defines in terms of poor teaching standard and facilities, teacher absenteeism, insensitive curriculum and content, poor motivation of teachers. This is compounded with lack of physical access and infrastructure.
- The analysis also shows that smaller million-plus cities have more schools per capita population when compared to four mega polis. Contrary to health services, education infrastructure is poorer in cities with larger population and there is a huge gap in achieving universal access to education in all cities, impacting the disadvantaged children the most and million-plus cities, which are hub of economic activities, need to improve access of girl children to education. The proportion of children from marginalised communities in mega cities is very low compared to smaller towns.
- There is still a huge gap in achieving universal access to education in all cities, impacting the disadvantaged children the most.
- Effective monitoring and surveillance system for improving the student-to-classroom and student-to-teacher ratio in the cities.
- Vigorous community mobilization campaigns need to be initiated in urban slums urging the poor households to send their children to schools.
- Innovative approaches to increase school enrollment at primary level and retention rate in schools, particularly for girls.
- Convergence of health and education with other basic services for achieving synergy.

Main Features of Right to Education 2010 Act

The salient features of the Right of Children for Free and Compulsory Education Act are—

- Free and compulsory education to all children of India in the six to 14 age group.
- No child shall be held back, expelled, or required to pass a board examination until completion of elementary education.
- A child above six years of age has not been admitted in any school or though admitted, could not complete his or her elementary education, then, he or she shall be admitted in a class appropriate to his or her age;

  Provided that where a child is directly admitted in a class appropriate to his or her age, then, he or she shall, in order to be at par with others, have a right to receive special training, in such manner, and within such time limits, as may be prescribed:

  Provided further that a child so admitted to elementary education shall be entitled to free education till completion of elementary education even after fourteen years.
- *Proof of age for admission*: For the purposes of admission to elementary education. The age of a child shall be determined on the basis of the birth certificate issued in accordance with the provisions of the Births, Deaths and Marriages Registration Act, 1856 or on the basis of such other document, as may be prescribed. No child shall be denied admission in a school for lack of age proof.
- A child who completes elementary education shall be awarded a certificate.
- Calls for a fixed student-teacher ratio.
- Will apply to all of India except Jammu & Kashmir.
- Provides for 25 per cent reservation for economically disadvantaged communities in admission to Class One in all private schools.
- Mandates improvement in quality of education.
- School teachers will need adequate professional degree within five years or else will lose job.
- School infrastructure (where there is problem) to be improved in three years, else recognition cancelled.
- Financial burden will be shared between state and central government.

Conclusion

Educational access in urban India is better than rural India. At the same time it is not so better than neighboring countries like China and Sri Lanka and other developed countries in the world. The poverty rate of urban India is increasing gradually when compared to rural India. Poverty is the main cause for low access of Education. It is the foremost duty of governments (state and central) to take necessary actions towards quality and quantity education. Without education the development of any nation can't take place. Education is the base for all types of development in the world.

References

1. Geetha Gandhi Kingdom, 2007, *The Progress of School Education in India,* Report of Global Poverty Research Group, Oxford.
2. Government of India, 2001, *Census of India-2001,* New Delhi.
3. Government of India, 2007, *Time Series Data,* New Delhi.
4. Government of India, 2009, *Urban Poverty Report-2009,* New Delhi.
5. Report of Crete, 2009, *Educational Access in India.*
6. Reports of Ministry of Human Resource Development, Government of India, New Delhi.
7. Reports of NCERT, New Delhi.

Urbanization: Impact on Education and Health

Dr. T. Mallikarjuna Sharma

Migration from rural to urban areas has reached alarming level compounding problems like congestion and over population and giving rise to numerous socio-economic problems. Lack of health and education facilities, weak economy, recurring droughts, shortage of irrigation and drinking water, poverty, unemployment and quarrels between clans are some of the problems, forcing people to leave their homes for urban areas. Migration is a natural process and it has been taking place since centuries but this migration has on the one hand defaced the beauty of villages and on the other increased burden on limited resources of urban areas. In urban areas the colonies lacked infrastructure for education and health facilities, supply of clean drinking water and sanitation and other social services. Most of the children living in these colonies were found begging in the streets. The migrants discovered that their needs were neglected and in towns where income inequality was more evident, some of them had resorted to petty crimes, beggary and sex work to make both ends meet. This increasing gap between demand and supply of public services gives rise to many problems such as the emergence of slums, shortage of resources, inadequacy of public transport, education, health and increasing crime rate along with social costs such as inte-rethnic conflicts and imbalances.

Population explosion is the prime concern of today. India is no more an under-developing country particularly with the reference to its growing population. As the population increases so is the urbanization which is resulting in many adversaries. Unless we think, plan and implement some modifications sincerely the rapid urbanization may result in total devastation. And children education and health are on the first line to be affected with.

Education is an internationally recognized basic human right. UNESCO and UNICEF report addressed the need for a human rights-based approach to education that goes beyond goals of universal access and quality education. The report highlights three interrelated rights that, when implemented, help ensure all children have the opportunity to attend school and receive a quality education in a safe, respectful environment:

(i) *Right of Access to Education*—Education must be available for, accessible to and inclusive of all children.

(ii) *Right to Quality Education*—Education needs to be child-centered, relevant and embrace a broad curriculum, and be appropriately resourced and monitored.

(iii) *Right to Respect within the Learning Environment*—Education must be provided in a way that is consistent with human rights, equal respect for culture, religion and language and free from all forms of violence.

Migration of highly skilled individuals or brain drain is an integral part of the globalization. Education is a crucial determinant of human capital accumulation in the country and therefore, a source of economic growth. The interaction between education and migration remains unexplored in the literature.

In an educational environment students should be the first priority. Globalization and innovation are revolutionizing the higher education forcing to create new market trends. Educational institutions are also seeking different organizational and behavioral changes for their better future. As with every other part of human development we have continued down the path of innovation and change to what some today call the "creative society". It might be early to say that we are entering a new age but it is clear that changes happen faster and with greater impact across the globe and that is creating a society that is different from earlier. Poverty remains the largest barrier to access. Paying school fees in urban area private schools is an impossibility for many families struggling to make ends meet, especially in light of the ongoing food crisis and when faced with the burden in their families and communities. The next step was to address the fact that the schools in urban areas were under-staffed and under-equipped to accommodate the influx of new students.

Cultural, socio-economic and gender barriers also stand in the way of a quality education for all children in an environment where they feel safe and where their rights are protected. According to UNESCO, "Children from poor, indigenous and disabled populations are at a systematic disadvantage, as are those living in slums in urban areas."

Girls are less Likely to have access to education. It is noted that due to sexual violence, insecure school environments and inadequate sanitation that adversely affect girls' self-esteem, participation and retention. Textbooks, curricula and teacher attitudes have sometimes enforced negative stereotypes and have kept girls from receiving the education they need and deserve.

Beyond the basic need for education to support one's self and family in later years, many social ills accompany the lack of free and accessible education. 70 per cent of all child laborers work in agriculture in rural areas where access to schools, availability of trained teachers and educational supplies is severely limited. In urban areas, poor and marginalized children are unable to benefit from greater access to school facilities because of cost, caste and culture and without educational opportunities; these children are forced to work.

Urban environments have been linked to a range of human health issues, and as the pace of urbanization accelerates, new challenges arise to understand their positive and negative implications for health. Data that are available indicate a range of urban health hazards and associated health risks: substandard housing, crowding, air pollution, insufficient or contaminated drinking water, inadequate sanitation and solid waste disposal services, vector-borne diseases, industrial waste, increased motor vehicle traffic, stress associated with poverty and unemployment, among others. Urban health risks and concerns involve many different sectors, including health, environment, housing, energy, transportation, urban planning, and others.

Environmental hazards and sanitation

An effective environmental sanitation programme are necessary for a primary health care (PHC) programme such as availability, accessibility, affordability, acceptability, and practicability. Poor housing conditions give rise to stress, delinquency, and crime, as well as to helminthic and other parasitic infestations. Environmental hazards in urban areas mainly affect low-income people, especially women, children, and migrants—the people who are least able to avoid the hazards and/or least able to deal with the illness or injury they cause. Poor people are priced out of safe, well-located, well-serviced housing and land sites. Hazards include biological pathogens; chemical pollutants; scarce, over-priced, or poor quality natural resources; physical hazards; natural resource degradation; and national/global environmental degradation. These preventable health burdens cause disease, accidents, and premature death. Biological pathogens have the most serious impact on human health. Crowded conditions, poor sanitation, and inadequate water supplies, poor facilities for preparing and storing food, and inadequate hygiene contribute to biological pathogen induced ill-health. Common chemical pollutants in urban areas are lead, indoor air pollutants from fuel combustion, toxic/hazardous wastes, and ambient air pollution. A shortage of fresh drinking water is also one of the prime concerns as some urban households do not have safe and adequate water supply. Limited land in cities prevents the urban poor from growing their own crops or maintaining livestock. Common physical hazards in cities are traffic accidents and accidental fires. Overcrowding, poor building material, and settlements on dangerous sites (e.g., flood plains, steep hillsides, and dumps) are example of physical hazards. Noise, overcrowding, inappropriate design, and stresses contribute to the growing psycho-social health problems of many urban dwellers in developing countries, especially of adolescents and young adults.

Access to health care

Equity in access to health care is now accepted as a basic ethical principle for health development. The glaring inequalities in health suffered by poor people living in slums are a strong justification for urgent action. The problem is rapidly increasing the study of urban health considers how characteristics of the urban environment may affect population health. The key factors affecting health in cities can be considered within three broad themes:

(i) Physical environment

(ii) Social environment

(iii) Access to health and social services.

Unauthorized squatter settlements and health implications

Urbanization gives rise to creation of unauthorized squatter settlements on the peripheries of large cities and these settlers share a low standard of housing resulting from lack of employment and low income. Very often large households are crowded into poor quality structures with no running water or sewage disposal. Health consequences are serious. Residents of squatter settlements generally fall below the rest of the urban population in health indicators. Settlers in these makeshift communities all tend to be disadvantaged, but there are significant differences in the health and living conditions of different low income zones on the urban periphery. It must also be remembered that conditions of the physical and social habitat are mediated by social practices such as hygienic habits, diet, use of medications, and reproductive patterns.

Contamination of drinking water

Pathogenic contamination of drinking water poses the most significant health risk to humans, and there have been countless numbers of disease outbreaks and poisonings throughout history resulting from exposure to untreated or poorly treated drinking water. However, significant risks to human health may also result from exposure to non-pathogenic, toxic contaminants that are often globally ubiquitous in waters from which drinking water is derived. In assessing the relative risk of toxic contaminants in drinking water to humans, the major sources of contaminants from anthropogenic activities to aquatic surface and groundwater and the pathways along which these contaminants move to become incorporated into drinking water supplies should be considered as priorities. The point source and non-point-source pollution should be identified and corrected with urgency. Point-source pollution originates from discrete sources whose inputs into aquatic systems can often be defined in a spatially explicit manner. Examples of point-source pollution include industrial effluents (pulp and paper mills, steel plants, food processing plants), municipal sewage treatment plants and combined sewage-storm-water overflows, resource extraction (mining), and land disposal sites (landfill sites, industrial impoundments). Non-point-source pollution, in contrast, originates from poorly defined, diffuse sources that typically occur over broad geographical scales. Examples of non-point-source pollution include agricultural runoff (pesticides, pathogens, and fertilizers), storm-water and urban runoff. Environmentalists proposed a basic framework that is probably suitable for development of indicators of exposure to environmental health risks that would facilitate the; assessment of the health effects of risk factors, design and evaluation of interventions and programs to deliver the interventions, appraisal and quantification of inequalities in health effects of risk factors, and benefits of intervention programs and policies. Specific emphasis is put on the features of environmental risks that should guide the choice of indicators, in particular the interactions of technology, the environment, and human behavior in determining exposure.

Conclusion

One of the main characteristics of urbanization is the very rapid increase in population movement from rural to urban centers leading to changing population structure, composition and lifestyles in the cities and its fringes. As consequently, the urban concentrates are faced with several social and socio-economic problems. Rural poverty has pushed villagers to the cities resulting in public health, education and social problems that lower the quality of life.

A lack of free education encourages sexual exploitation of children. The link between education and public health is strong. Access to education affects HIV/AIDS infection rates, child survival figures and maternal health. According to a survey if all children received a complete primary education, as many as 700,000 cases of HIV could be prevented each year.

Educating girls and concern for their health in urban areas is the key to smart international development. Women with some formal education are more likely to seek medical care, ensure their children are immunized, be better informed about their child's nutritional requirements, and adopt improved sanitation practices. As a result, their infants and children have higher survival rates and tend to be healthier and better nourished.

According to a research on women, the education that a girl receives is the strongest predictor of the age she will marry and is a critical factor in reducing the prevalence of child marriage. Educating girls in urban areas is a big step in stopping the poverty cycle for future generations. Increased funding and better use of funding for the development of school and children, trained teachers recruitment in appropriate time where teachers must be properly trained and paid in order to provide quality education and flexible programs (school programs must take into account social, economic and cultural barriers) and flexible school schedules would certainly helps to overcome the problems of children education under the Urbanization. It is also concluded that the local, state and central governments should establish and enforce socio-economic, educational and the health policies for redistribution of population, policies for revitalization of urban centers, and policies for decentralization of development, and measures to stabilize the population within cities. Health providers working with inner-city populations must consider an array of social, health, and environmental factors in their assessments of health problems. Many of the societal issues, which negatively impact health, such as poverty, lack of a universal health program, unemployment, violence, drugs, and other factors, can be corrected in our society only if the political will to do so is present. Health workers have a responsibility to advocate for programs and environments in which all citizens can maximize their full potential. Populations in urban areas who are at risk for disease, disability, and premature death make cities special places for focusing on the promotion of health and the prevention of diseases.

Access to Health and Education Services

Mr. P. Raju

Introduction

India's vision stays in the development of education and health which utterly needs the absolute development of it. To attain its inclusive development our country needs to fortify the improvement of health and education. Here urban areas need the complete development. Health and education are the critical sectors for achieving overall equitable human development in the country. Several constraints exist in the health and education sectors in India. The major challenges for the health sector include accessibility and coverage in rural areas, ineffective management of existing infrastructure, inadequate number and quality of health care professionals. In the education sector, the primary and upper-primary schools are constrained by several factors, including inadequate basic physical infrastructure (toilets, electricity, and drinking water), absenteeism of teachers and poor quality of training, and lack of leadership and ineffective management at school level.

Poverty is often given as an important reason for why learners drop-out of school. Inability to pay school fees, the costs of uniform, shoes, transport, stationary, added to the opportunity costs of what children might be contributing to household labour, eat away at meagre resources and push children from school. School fees have been singled out for blame as a particularly burdensome cost and organizations such as the Education Rights Project have been campaigning for their complete abolition (Roithmayr, 2002). Fleisch and Woolman (2004), arguing that fees do not feature as a primary reason for dropout, contend that absolute or "abject" poverty inhibits educational access where the full range of costs associated with attendance, particularly of uniforms and transport, are taken into account.

Status in Urban

We can say that India's development of backbone lies in rural areas but that rural development is based on urban. Only 66 per cent of the Indian people are literate (76% of men and 54% of women). While close to 90 per cent children in the 6-11 age group are formally enrolled in primary schools, nearly 40 per cent dropout at the primary stage. The enrolment ratios of slum residents, especially girls, still remain far lower than the national average. Malnutrition, hunger and poor health remain core problems, which comprehensively affect attendance and performance in classes. The added burden of home chores and child labour influence a large number of children, especially girls, to drop out of school. While India has successfully developed physical infrastructure and adequate coverage of primary health services, significant shortfalls remain.

The top three challenges for the health sector are accessibility and coverage in rural areas, ineffective management of existing infrastructure, inadequate number and quality of services. A rapid assessment of the health and education sectors in India is to understand how might usefully be applied for delivering sustainable and enhanced health care and education services was considered a crucial task. Our country hopes for a better future depend in large part on improving the health and education of the people. India is experiencing a period of extraordinary change. Here, policy reforms are contributing to dynamic economic growth. Greater political openness has strengthened the commitment of Indian government to meet the basic needs of their people. Much of our country's population remains desperately poor. Our nation struggles to provide health and education services to populations expanding at a gradual per cent a year. In many countries, rapid population growth is contributing to degradation of the environment and undermining prospects for prosperity. Our country's hope for a better future depends in large part on improving the health of its people. Better access to good quality health and education services improves the area with tremendous planned growth.

Agricultural performance average per capita food production has declined in many countries, per capita calorie consumption had stagnated at very low levels, and roughly 100 million people in rural parts of India are food insecure. The average Indian consumes only about 87 per cent of the calories needed for a healthy and productive life.

Challenges that Urban Areas Meet

The fundamental problem is low demand for fewer children. Environmental degradation, agricultural problems, food insecurity and poverty, and the heavy work burdens of woman all play a part in this respect in remote educational efforts, directed at both men and women, are needed to raise awareness of the benefits of fewer children. Women's work loads need to be eased to reduce the need for child labour. Dynamic agricultural development and improved food security will also reduce the demand for children. Promoting environmentally Sustainable Agriculture Farm productivity per unit area must be raised significantly to generate more output with little increase in the area farmed. To minimize negative impacts on the environment, much more emphasis is required on "environmentally benign and sustainable" technologies. Increased use of fertilizers will be especially important to raise yields and maintain soil fertility. Intensive and resource-conserving agriculture must be made less risky and more profitable. This requires appropriate marketing, price, tax and exchange rate policies as well as investments in rural infrastructure, health and education facilities. Creating parks, reserves and community-owned range land and protecting these against conversion into crop land will be important to conserve natural resources and bio-diversity. The high rate of population growth intensifies existing social, political, economic, and environmental pressures. Taking account of the quality of health services is a major challenge. To meet this, there needs to be debate about what health care is for, how to measure the dimensions of quality, how to isolate the specific contribution of the health sector from other influences on the quality domain, and how to attach weights to each domain the education sector, consideration of output measurement yielded the following insights.

- There is a lack of consensus about the primary purpose of education, with suggestions including equipping recipients with qualifications, making them rounded citizens, or enhancing their earning potential. This lack of consensus makes it difficult to define education 'outcomes'.
- Output measurement in education is more straightforward than in health, because students are reasonably homogenous within each educational level and because they can be tracked over time. It is said that the output of higher education institutions is not confined to teaching activities, and their research and other undertakings need to be incorporated into their measure of output.
- Quality adjustment in education is challenging, and countries are adopting different methods.
- Some make adjustment for class size, recognising that countries with smaller classes appear 'less productive' unless the enhanced student experience is accounted for. However, it is not a simple matter to put a value on this experience.
- The key to this will be continued commitment by government to community consultation along with dynamic leadership. It is probable only when it gains in social capital and responsiveness of the services be realised.
- Can make education and health investment more effective and equitable by extending the impact and reach of services and through better nutrition.

- Act as incentives to increase poor people's demand for services and improve their education and health outcomes, even if they are given unconditionally are most effective when complementing health and education services.

Health in India—Key Indicators

- India accounts for more than 20 per cent of global maternal and child deaths, and the highest maternal death toll in the world estimated at 138,000.
- United Nations calculations show that India's spending on public health provision, as a share of GDP is the 18th lowest in the world.
- Per cent Nearly 67 per cent of the population in India do not have access to essential medicines.
- Infant Mortality Rate (IMR) in India was 67.6 in 1998-99 and has come down to 57 in 2005-06. Kerala heads the progress made so far with an IMR of 15/1000 births. Uttar Pradesh has the worst IMR in the country of 73/1000 births.
- Maternal Mortality Rate (MMR) is currently 4 deaths per 1000 births. India accounts for the largest number of maternal deaths in the world.
- 79 per cent of the children between the age of 6-35 months, and more than 50 per cent of women, are anemic, and 40 per cent of the maternal deaths during pregnancy and child-birth relate to anemia and under-nutrition.
- There are 585 rural hospitals compared to 985 urban hospitals in the country. Out of the 6,39,729 doctors registered in India, only 67,576 are in the public sector.

The ratio of hospital beds to population in rural areas is almost fifteen times lower than that for urban areas.

The key conclusions that emerge from this Research are:

1. *It is a Right, not Charity*

Both health and education are rights under the Constitution of India, the latter being a Fundamental right. It is therefore the duty of the Indian government to deliver these services to the citizens. Health, education and water and sanitation are neither commercial service to be delivered nor charity to be given to citizens; citizens are neither customers nor alms seekers when it comes to basic human rights.

2. *Public not Private*

The responsibility to ensure that each citizen receives good education and health care lies squarely with the government. Given the scope and scale of delivery that is required, the state cannot abandon its role as the primary deliverer of services. For instance, in order to achieve the coverage of services visualized through the National Rural Health Mission, about 21,983 new sub-centers and 200,000 ANMs (Auxiliary Nurse Midwives) are required in keeping with the population norm of the 2001 census. No private or voluntary agency can meet this requirement. Utilize the private and non-government sectors for innovation and monitoring, not as a substitute provider.

3. *Education and Health Are Social Investments, Not Just Public Expenditure*

The NCMP aims to increase public expenditure on education to 6 per cent of the GDP, and public expenditure on health to 2-3 per cent of the GDP as one of the strategies to meet this promise. However, to date, the total investment on Health and Education in India remains dismally low. Less than one per cent of India's GDP is spent on public health, which is even lower than the public health expenditures of countries like Sri Lanka and Sierra Leone. Public expenditure on education in India is a little over three per cent of the GDP.

Even poorest families spend as much as Rs. 350 per child per year (which amounts to more than 10 per cent of the monthly income of a family that is able to earn Rs. 100 per day) for uniforms, stationery, transport, and more if tuition is added. The introduction of User Fees further adds to the burden of the 'invisible' costs that are borne by families who struggle to access health and education, and also deny the 'costs' that are already paid by the poor by way of their recognized economic contribution to the overall GDP of the country.

4. *Planning Around the Poorest*

The government must prioritize the needs of traditionally marginalized groups in planning its investments and outreach. The poorest districts of the country and most vulnerable groups–including women, children, people with disabilities, and communities like the dalits, adivasis, denotified tribes and muslim minorities must be the focus while planning for infrastructure and allocating resources.

5. *Uniform Quality of Service*

The quality of health and education is a crucial factor in ensuring the achievement of the human development outcomes intended through these services. In states that have more teachers (where teacher-pupil ratio is low), where funds are received and utilised, and where there are more classrooms and fewer single-teacher schools—the overall educational achievements have been recorded to be much better. The quality of services even in the poorest areas of the country should be commensurate with the standards and norms envisaged by the National Development Goals at the very least, and encourage further improvisation and enhancement through active local participation, information sharing and accountability.

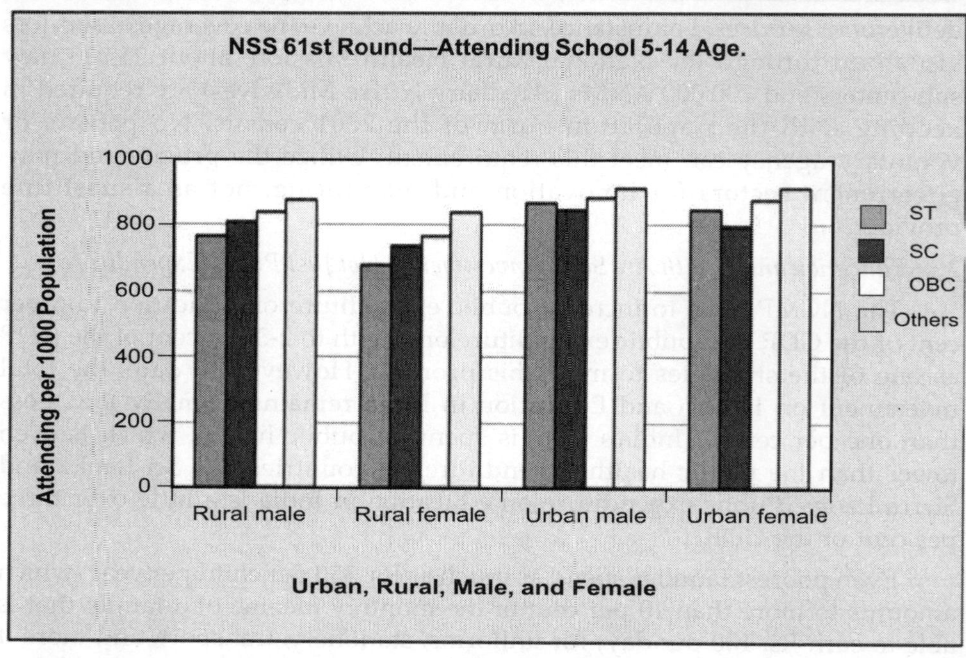

Health Indicators: Unable to Reach Out to the Poor

When we compare the morbidity and mortality profiles in India against the infrastructure and investments in health, the picture is not very impressive. Marginal declines in morbidity and mortality or stagnation seem to be the only achievement. In fact, it seems to be an achievement fraught with poor recording and misreporting. If we take the data on leprosy published by the government, it shows that the estimate of life of number of people suffering from leprosy were much lower as compared to the actual detections all through. The reason is simple: the programme puts a stop to the treatment of individuals after two years of medication. In official records that person is cured. So the estimated treatment simply reduces the severity of the disease; it does not necessarily lower its prevalence. The incorrect targets were based on the assumption that India has succeeded in eliminating the disease when the truth lies somewhere else. Similarly, vaccine preventable infections of childhood flourish. Dengue, pneumonia, enteric fever, viral hepatitis and other infections are large in number.

Dismal Performance

This brief overview shows that achievements in health indicators have been far less promising than expected, both in terms of the present status of health and reaching out to the poor as well as in terms of building health infrastructure. Also, whatever has been achieved is due to the overall socio-economic development overtime that has no doubt touched the lives of the people. To understand the inability of the health services to effectively deal with health problems, we need to implement the Primary health education awareness from schooling children. A review after 10 years pointed out the problems of financing programmes in the health sector. It is suggested the access of health and education into a system of in-depth planning.

National Rural Health Mission: Keynotes to Health Sector

The state too has been conscious of these trends. In 2005 it launched the National Rural Health Mission (NRHM) to target the poor and provide relief. The main components of NRHM are:

- Train accredited social health activists (ASHA) to provide essential health-care at the village level and work under the ANM and anganwadi worker (a functionary of the ICDS).
- Provide a fund of Rs.10,000 to the ANM to use as and when necessary.
- Strengthen the subcenters.
- Strengthen all CHCs and convert them into first referral hospitals.
- Post additional public health and health management personnel to bring about efficiency in work.
- Develop national public health standards for each level of services.

Access to Services: Priced out by Privatisation

Three rounds of National Sample Survey (NSS) data from 1986-87 onwards show that the utilisation of private sector services has been increasing over time. According to the 2004 NSS, 20 for ailments not needing hospitalisation, 22 persons per 1,000 use government facilities against 78 per 1,000 who frequent the private sector. In the urban areas the corresponding figures are 19 and 81 per cent.

The instant conclusion one draws from this is that:

- People prefer the private sector.
- The Private Sector is more efficient.
- Making the available quantity of essential drugs should be another priority.
- Implementation by the group states in improving health indicators and social sector development.
- Human Poverty Index Measure (HPIM) seems to be a good tool to assess differential needs of the states.
- All the essential drugs should be brought under price control.

The National Policy of Education (NPE) 1996, as revised in 2010 indicated the following thrust areas in elementary education:

(i) Universal access enrolment.

(ii) Universal retention of children up to 14 years of age.

(iii) A substantial improvement in the quality of education to enable all children to achieve essential levels of learning.

(iv) To upgrade the nutrition level, implementation of mid-day meal programme is to be strengthened.

(v) Financial allocation of fund for the adult education and strength.

There is also the challenge of quality in Indian education, which has many dimensions, such as providing adequate physical facilities and infrastructure, making available adequate teachers of requisite quality, effectiveness of teaching-learning processes, Attainment levels of students, etc.

Conclusion

Enhancing the quality of the services delivered and tailoring them to the needs of specific groups to protect the health of communities and the right of everyone to the highest attainable standard of physical and mental health. Sponsoring a comprehensive approach to health maintenance and the treatment of disease by fostering, for instance, a range of care is needed.

Teacher training alone cannot improve teaching and learning processes. Addressing administrative, personnel and other issues alongside accountability systems could help us turn the corner. A systemic approach is needed even though we may start from one point. Expanding access to health care services to ensure universal and equitable coverage, including through social protection and cash transfer programmes, and through reforms to extend health coverage to all.

The economic welfare perspective on educational access does not account for meaningful access. Physical access alone is not sufficient as a robust definition of access, which must include a notion of learners making cognitive progress and attaining curricula outcomes. Most importantly, interventions to increase access beyond the basic school phase of grade nine need to be based on a recognition of the inextricable link between access and quality.

References

1. www.hsrc.ac.za/Document-1838.phtml
2. www.unicef- irc.org/datasets/access_public_services.pdf
3. www.educationforhealth.net

Role of Migration in Growing Urbanization and the Impact of Urbanization on the Development Process

Dr. K. Gaanesh Babu

Introduction

Migration is the chief mechanism by which all the world's great urbanization trends have been accomplished. Urbanization has come to be viewed as a reflection of overall socio-economic development, and its attainment is considered crucial to the overall strategy of progress. The urban economy which provides opportunities for raising productivity by generating employment in the high productivity industrial sector, and contributes towards eradicating poverty in the developing countries.

Economic development plays a very significant role in producing rapid urban growth. The low rate of growth of industrial employment and the high rate of rural-to-urban migration make for excessive and even explosive urbanization involving a transition from rural under employment to excessive urban unemployment and underemployment, a visible proliferation of poverty of slums in cities.[1]

Urbanization is a process whereby increasing proportions of the population of a region or a country live in urban areas. Urbanization is an index of transformation from traditional rural economies to modern industrial one. It is a long term process. Urbanization has become a major demographic issue in the 21st century not only in India but also all over the world.

Objectives of the study

The present study chiefly aims at the following objectives:

1. To study the concept of migration and urbanization.

2. To analyze the causes/factors for the migration of the people.
3. To focus the role of migration for growing urbanization.

Concept of Migration, Urbanization

A great deal of analysis of urbanization process crucially hinges on how an urban area is defined. According to census definition, all settlements which have corporation, municipality, and cantonment board or notified area committee are eligible to be classified as urban. Settlements which satisfy three demographic criteria:

1. A minimum population of 5,000.
2. A density of at least 400 persons per sq. km.
3. At least 75 per cent of male workers in non-agricultural activities can also be treated as urban.[2]

In India, migrants are not required to be registered either at the place of origin or at the place of destination. However, the Indian census counts the migrants and provides data on migration based on place of birth (POB) and place of last residence (POLR). If the POB or POLR is different from the place of enumeration, a person is defined as a migrant.

The commutation from the rural areas to the nearby urban centre is an important phenomenon, but this form of spatial mobility along with seasonal and circular migration shows more the magnitude of rural-urban linkages rather than significantly influencing urban growth.

It is important for the number of internal migrants to be disaggregated into the different migration streams in order to assess the role of migration in urban growth. The streams of migration include rural to rural, rural to urban, urban to rural, and urban to urban areas. Rural to urban migration adds to urban population, whereas urban to rural depletes the urban population; the net balance of the two streams is the actual contribution to the process of urbanization.

There are four main components of urban growth, namely:

(i) natural increase;

(ii) net migration to urban areas;

(iii) reclassification of settlements as towns or its declassification as a result of changes in the nature of economic activities and acquisition of urban characteristics; and

(iv) the extension of boundaries of cities and towns.

The natural increase in urban areas of the initial population as well as migrants continues to be the largest contributor to the urban growth.[3]

Migration is an integral part of rural and national development, and societal change. It allows individuals to respond to economic opportunity and helps to manage risks and accumulate assets. Mobility is frequently viewed as a critical livelihood strategy for many individuals. Migration and increasing urban poverty raises issues in health care, education, food provision etc.[4]

The three great socio-economic revolutions—the industrial revolutions, the agrarian revolution and transport revolution—sparked off another revolution: urban revolution. In fact, higher urbanization is regarded as one of the indicators of development because it is an integral part of the process of industrialization and development. The process of development entails a massive shift of labour and other inputs from sectors that are predominantly rural to sectors that are predominantly urban.

Thomson has viewed urbanization in the form of migration and described it as "the movement of people from communities concerned chiefly with agriculture to other communities, generally larger, whose activities are primarily centered in government, trade, manufacture and allied interests".[5]

Migration is the barometer of changing socio-economic and political conditions at the national and international levels. It is also a sign of wide disparities in economic and social conditions between the origin and destination. Migration and development is a growing area of interest. There has been much debate on the negative impact of migration on development and vice versa. On the one hand, it is argued that under development is a cause of migration, and on the other hand, prosperity also leads to migration.

Migration is a natural outcome of inequality in the distribution of resources. Studies and evidence reflect that it is positively related to modernization, industrialization and development. Migration is essential for development. It is a desirable phenomenon. But what is not desirable is the distressed migration, found in most of the developing countries resulting in overcrowding of cities and mushrooming of slums.[6]

Urbanization is the growth in population residing in urban areas, due to both growth in population of current residents and net migration into urban areas. They get easier access to primary and advanced health care, at close distance, and with much better service quality than in rural areas. In terms of all the basic human development parameters, urban areas stand out as significantly different from rural belts, both in the provisioning of services essential for human development, and in the basic capabilities that citizens can, and do, acquire while living and growing in an urban area as compared to that in a rural area. The urban dwellers get to access schools more easily and in greater quantity.[7]

Migration and urbanization are direct manifestations of the process of economic development in space, particularly in the contemporary phase of globalization. The capacity of the cities and towns to assimilate the migrants by providing employment, access to land, basic amenities etc. are limited. Rural urban migration has often been considered the major factor for growth of slums in urban areas.

It would be interesting to look at the migration pattern in relation to that of urbanization. The pattern of urban growth (or urban-rural growth differential) across states during the first four decades since Independence exhibit negative relationship with their level of economic development articulated through income or consumption expenditure in per capita terms, share of industries in state income, agricultural productivity etc. The poor states like Orissa, Bihar, Rajasthan and Madhya Pradesh that experienced rapid demographic growth in urban areas were also those that reported low productivity and high unemployment in agrarian sectors and heavy pressure on urban infrastructural facilities, suggesting presence of push factors behind rural-urban migration.[8]

Causes/Factors of Migration

Actually, migration flows are determined by a complex interaction of economic, environmental and demographic factors. These causes/factors have differential impact on the rate and direction of migration.

1. Migration is caused by the income disparity between rural and urban sectors.
2. Economic factors such as transportation costs, income and job opportunities significantly affect individual's decision to migrate to a city in a developing country like India.
3. The expansion of labour-force, unemployment and underemployment in rural areas, for seeking employment, better employment for better life standards, better prospective opportunities in progressive business and industries forced people to migrate to urban areas.
4. Increasing educational facilities, wider expansion of transportation and effective communication system, improved, sophisticated and comfortable living conditions are the factors responsible for the rapid rate and huge magnitude of migration.
5. 'Push' and 'pull' forces affecting the trend of rural-urban migration in the form of two hypotheses viz., *(i)* unusually rapid rates of population growth pressing limited farm acreage, pushing landless labour into cities and *(ii)* economic forces pulling migrants into the cities as an explanation of urban growth.
6. Social and cultural factors such as quest for independence, the desire to break away from traditional constraints of social organization, conflict among family members also play their role in migration.
7. Geographical and physical factors like distance, natural barriers, size of the country, weather and climate conditions also make an effect on the movement of people.

Thus migration blows are determined by a complex interaction of economic, environmental and demographic factors.

In case of our country, economic factors exercise a dominant influence on the rural-urban migration process. Because of population pressure, the agriculture sector is now overcrowded and the problem of disguised unemployment has become very acute in this sector. Frequent occurrences of droughts and lack of proper irrigation facilities are the factors responsible for the reduction of employment opportunities in this dominant sector. Again in this era of globalization, agriculture itself is not proving a reliable source of income. High cost of cultivation, scarcity of irrigation water, stagnation of productivity in this sector and fluctuations in prices of agricultural products are the main factors responsible for converting agriculture into non-profitable sector of employment. In such 'distress' conditions, rural labourers and farmers are compelled to move from villages to urban areas and cities in search of employment and better livelihood.[9]

Urbanization in other Countries

A comparison of the level of urbanization in India with the developed countries of the world reveals that India is far behind the high income countries. The proportion of urban population to total population in 2001 was 73 per cent in Russia, 77 per cent in USA, 79 per cent in Japan, 91 per cent in Australia and 89 per cent in UK compared to them, the Indian percentage of 27.8 in 2001 was too low.

Industrialization and modern technologies have played an important role in modifying settlement and population pattern over the countries. Nearly three-quarters of the population of more developed countries now live in urban areas, with many more living near major metropolitan areas.

Urbanization in India

More than one-fourth of the total population of India is urban. The total urban population has increased eleven fold from 25.85 million in 1901 to 285.35 million in 2001. Such a rapid growth has been possible by migration of population to urban places. India has a long tradition of urbanization which has continued since the days of the Indus valley civilization. The development of cottage industries and tertiary activities has helped in the process of urbanization.[10]

According to the 2001 census, out of the total population of 1027 million (or 102.7 crore) in India, about 742 million, or 72.2 per cent live in rural areas and 285 million or 27.8 per cent, live in urban areas. Rural India thus accounts for an overwhelming majority of the country's population. However, in recent years, the population growth rate in rural India has come down to one per cent per annum, while urban population is growing at two per cent per annum. This is a sign of increasing urbanization in India.[11]

Urbanization in Different States of India

Goa is the most urbanized state in India with 49.77 per cent urban population followed by Mizoram, Tamilnadu and Maharashtra. All union territories are highly urbanized except Dadra Nagar Haveli and Andaman & Nicobar Islands. The degree of urbanization is high in southern, western and north-eastern states whereas low urbanization level is found in northern, central states. Maximum concentration of the country's urban population is found in Maharashtra, Uttar Pradesh, Tamilnadu, West Bengal and Andhra Pradesh.

Features of Indian Urbanization

1. The Indian urbanization is of subsistence type whereby rural illiterate and semi-literate workers swarm into the cities to seek employment. This badly affects the quality of the urban life creating slums and squatter settlements.
2. The Indian urbanization has poly-metropolitan effect in which four premier cities—Mumbai, Kolkata, Delhi and Chennai play dominant role.
3. The big cities of India are experiencing explosive population growth while the small towns are stagnating.
4. The Indian urban system is not integrated both functionally and spatially. Hence, there are breaks and imbalances in urban hierarchy and rural-urban profile.
5. The Indian urban centers are growing more on the basis of tertiary sector rather than on the basis of secondary sector. It is only in recent years that some efforts are being made to create proper industrial base at the district level.
6. The western and southern parts of the country are more urbanized than their eastern and northern counterparts due to differential resource potential and history of urban development.[12]

Consequences of Migration

Migration or movements of population may result in both positive consequences and negative consequences. Mobility of population at large-scale and the consequent redistribution of population have a number of economic, ecological, social, political and demographic implications.

Mobility of people may have essentially economic effects on both the place of origin and destination. Shift of labour force from the region where it is surplus or in disguised unemployment usually provides increase in the average and marginal productivity of labour in that region. According to this view, the migration disfavours the emigrating region and favours the immigrating region and the consequent result effect is disparity in development between the place of origin and the place of destination due to the shift of resourceful persons.

Most of the migrants have moved in search of better economic opportunities. The availability of good agricultural land continues to be a most powerful economic factor determining magnitude and direction of population migration. The increasing pressure of population has led to division and fragmentation of land resulting in small and uneconomic holdings giving low yields. In the absence of other non-agricultural activities available in the area, a high majority of population tends to migrate to the urban areas. So the technological improvements are particularly relevant to analysis of mobility of rural manpower.

Migration is not a labour problem but it is closely associated with the problems of urbanization, slums, pollution, poverty, unemployment, and many other institutional, social, cultural, and educational problems. The labour migration has brought many more positive changes than negative ones. The majority of migrant workers and their households have definitely made economic and non-economic gains. The remittances they sent home improved the household economy substantially and through the overseas work experience they accumulated skills and became more productive than before. In addition, many of them improved their families both socially and economically in the community. The new elements like the role of women, inter-generational relations, expectations relating to children and wider international awareness were introduced into villages. Thus, it would appear that migration has brought economic well-being and human development to a large proportion of migrants and their households.

The urban areas attract a large number of labourers of different skills, since there has been a significant expansion of employment opportunities. Thus, the mobility of people from rural to urban areas accelerates economic growth both in the place of origin and in the place of destination. However, it should be seriously thought that overcrowded urbanization gives negative problems and evils in many dimensions.

Role of Migration in the Process of Growing Urbanization

Ever since the origin of human race, migration has been one of the inevitable activities of man. The primitive man used to move/migrate from one place to another in search of food. It is quite evident in human history that man moves from one place to another where he is afforded with sufficient livelihood. Hence, it is a demographic/geographic phenomenon.

The primitive men used to move from one forest to another in search of forest products to feed themselves and for water to quench their thirst. As days passed people tamed animals, they learnt to utilize the natural resources to till the ground and developed harvesting crops, where natural water resources were available and to get adapted to civilized life. As a result, mobility of mankind increased considerably and man started to establish settlements, at the place where he would be afforded comfortable life.

When the industries were established in the developing countries the need for human resources had increased and when facilities for movement got developed, the rulers of the some of the developed countries started establishing colonies in various parts of the world. It was followed by the process of rural-urban migration and it caused the growth of urbanization and industrialization. As a result explosion of population to urban areas had grown uncontrolled and the green pastures in the rural areas were left barren.

India, being one of the developing countries has been experiencing population explosion and large-scale rural urban migration as well. Having the Indian rural economy been characterized by spontaneous and overwhelming explosion of population, the consequent result is rural to urban migration.[13]

Impact of Urbanization in the Development Process

Rural poor workers migrate to the urban areas. Many of them live in the urban slums. This process of migration actually exports poverty from rural areas to urban areas and thus reduces the average per capita income of urban areas and consequently becomes instrumental in under-estimation of the rural-urban economic disparity.[14]

If well managed, migration can ensure a better living for the rural poor. In terms of the impacts of migration, it generally seems to have a positive impact on the households involved and migration has the potential to contribute to poverty reduction, with widespread and generally beneficial impacts. Migration between urban and rural areas has fundamentally changed interactions between rural and urban settlements and the way in which we perceive the countryside.

Many rural urban migrants retain strong links with their home villages to the benefit of household members in both locations (for example, through remittances, food supplies, childcare, work at harvest time etc.). Long distance migration, usually to cities and sometimes international, contributes an increasing share of household income. It helps individuals and their families to increase their income, learn new skills, improve their social status, build up assets and improve their quality of life. Migration can influence social and political development, with internal labour mobility being seen as essential to economic growth.[15]

No doubt, these big cities are engines of growth as they are not only creating opportunities for learning skills and earning wealth but also generating employment opportunities for rural migrants. But the problem is that these cities, growing uncontrollably, have generated unmanageable problems whose symptoms include slums, congestion, pollution and unhygienic living conditions.

According to Indian Union Urban Development Ministry, 20 per cent of the country's urban households are denied access to safe drinking water, 58 per cent do not have access to sanitation facilities. Our 'metropolitan cities' are overcrowded, urban land has become extremely scarce, services are breaking down and human misery has increased beyond belief. Thus, the main cause of concern is the concentration of urban population in large 'primate cities'. With the increase in city size, the per capita investment requirements in the infrastructure and overheads are also increasing at a rapid pace.[16]

The uncontrolled growth of the population of urban areas, i.e. urbanization there is a negative impact on the people, environment, income etc. They are pointed out below:

- Due to migration open spaces were shrinking and were encroached upon for building houses. Vanishing open spaces have serious health and environmental implications for the city.
- The vehicles and factories spew out hydro-carbons and other toxic substances affecting the quality of cities.[17]
- Due to uncontrolled urbanization in India, environmental degradation has been occurring very rapidly and causing shortages of housing, worsening water quality, excessive air pollution, noise, dust and heat, and the problems of disposal of solid wastes and hazardous wastes.
- The large and metropolitan cities present a particularly depressing picture today. The situations in metropolises like Mumbai, Kolkata, Chennai, Delhi, Bangalore, Kanpur, Hyderabad etc., is becoming worse year by year.
- The problems of finding space and housing for all have been intensified. Slums have become an inevitable part of the major Indian metropolises.
- Environmental pollution in India can broadly be attributed to rapid industrialization, energy production, urbanization, commercialization, and an increase in the number of motorized vehicles.[18]

Streamlining of metropolitan transport, provision of housing, increase in protected water supply, improvements in drainage sanitation and solid waste disposal system are all necessary to make our cities and towns more able to live.

Ban on the location of industries in congested cities, fiscal incentives for setting up of industries in backward areas, promotion of small and cottage industries, use of labour-intensive technologies, more investment in infrastructural facilities in small towns and identifying and nurturing the growth centers and growth poles, all must form part of a package for industrial and urban dispersal.

Above all, urban development, to be effective, must maintain a certain harmony with rural development. Making rural life better would help keep the villagers stay put in their villages. It could be a more effective way of solving the problems of unsanitary conditions, overcrowding and slum living—the bane of developing world's urbanization.[19]

Measures to Minimize the Migration to Decrease the Growing Urbanization

1. The "gloomy" picture of cities forces us to root-out the factors which have forced the rural labourers to migrate to big cities so that the tide of migration to these big cities can be effectively controlled.
2. Effective policy measures should be taken to check the flow of migration from these rural areas to the big cities.
3. An impetus should be given to the development of small and medium towns so that the flow of migration to large cities can be checked. Their infrastructure should be developed so that their economic bases are consolidated strengthened and expanded.
4. Population control measures must be made effective in both urban and rural areas in order to sustain urban situation.
5. Rural and urban settlements should not be considered as competitive but they should be treated as complementary to each other. Urban and rural areas constitute parts of an organic whole. Balanced development of urban and rural areas is the only possible long term solution.
6. The problems of metropolitan cities must be looked in a comprehensive manner and on a regional basis. The civic services in big urban centers must be augmented to make the fit for a reasonable level of living.[20]

Suggestions

The following are some suggestions to minimize the migration of rural people to the urban areas:

1. Providing primary health, transport, communication and education facilities to the rural people.
2. Providing technical assistance to the rural farmers as well as people to improve agriculture, horticulture, dairying, animal husbandry, fishery, poultry, etc.
3. Increasing the income of the rural people through income generating activities, giving financial assistance and providing better employment opportunities in rural areas.
4. Introducing high yield varieties of seeds in the farming land to increase their production.
5. Giving awareness about the problems of migration like security, food, shelter, education etc.

Conclusion

The expansion of trade and commercial activities, industrial development, better facilities of education and other sources of employment in big cities are the factors responsible for the rapid flow of migration to the big cities.

The rapid growth of urbanization in India has resulted in the emergence of many towns, cities and metropolises. They have attracted people, but have failed to absorb and assimilate them. A major reason is their incapacity to proportionately expand employment opportunities for this expanded labour force in the organized sector.

Migration and urbanization should be managed in such a way that they can play a positive role in the process of economic development and can provide a sound basis for national prosperity.

References

1. Edwin S. Mills, Arup Mitra, *Urban Development and Urban Ills,* Common Wealth Publishers, New Delhi, 1997, pp. 1-3.
2. Johnson Samuel, "Urbanization and Urban Development", in Shenol P.V. (ed.,), *Contours of Social and Economic Development Policy Issues,* Institute for Social and Economic Change, Bangalore, Concept Publishing Company, New Delhi, 1997, pp. 191-192.
3. http://www.informaworld.com/smpp/section? content = a909780783&fulltext=71324 0928.
4. Sankaran, P.N., "Rural and Urban Development—A Partnership Perspective", *Kurukshetra,* December–2004, p. 18.
5. Anita Modi, "Role of Migration in Urban Growth", *Kurukshetra,* December 2010, p. 7.
6. Anupam Hazra, "Migration: Still a Survival Strategy for Rural India", *Kurukshetra,* December 2010, pp. 3-5.
7. http://www.mp.gov.in/difmp/mphdr%5CChap5_E_2007.pdf
8. http://www.networkideas.org/ideasact/jun07/Beijing_Conference_07/Amitabh_ Kundu.pdf
9. Anita Modi, op. cit., pp. 8-9.
10. Barkha Tondon and Singh, D.K., "Rural-Urban Migration in India: Status and Direction", *Kurukshetra,* June 2007, pp. 23, 27.
11. Rajagopalan, S., "The Rural–Urban Divide in India", in Rajagopalan, S., (ed.), *Rural-Urban Dynamics: Perspectives and Experiences,* the ICFAI University Press, Hyderabad, 2010, p. 47.
12. Barkha Tondon and Singh, D.K., op. cit., pp. 26-27.
13. Raghavendar, B.V., Swarna, M.N., and Sambasiva Rao, B., "Migration and Economic Development: Causes and Consequences (A Study of Mahaboobnagar District in Andhra Pradesh)", *ANU Journal of Social Sciences,* Vol.1, No.2, December 2009, pp. 58-60.

14. Singh, S.P., "Growing Rural-Urban Disparities in India", *Kurukshetra*, November 2007, p. 8.
15. Anupam Hazra, op. cit., p. 5.
16. Anita Modi, op. cit., pp. 9-10.
17. Johnson Samuel, op. cit., pp. 204-205.
18. http://www.krepublishers.com/02-Journals/JHE/JHE-17-0-000-000-2005-Web/JHE-17-4-237-317-2005-Abst-PDF/JHE-17-4-277-287-2005-1233-Maiti-S/JHE-17-4-277-287-2005-1233-Maiti-S.pdf
19. Johnson Samuel, op. cit., pp. 206-207.
20. Anita Modi, op. cit., p. 10.

Urbanization in India

Dr. C. Sujathamma

Introduction

Urbanization is the process of population concentration in towns and cities. It is a gradual but dynamic phenomenon which changes through time and space. A country is said to become more urbanized when its cities grow in number, its urban population increase in size and the proportion of its population living in urban areas rises.

The process of urbanization involves a rapid growth of urban population at a higher rate than that of the increase in the total or rural population. "Urbanization is the process of increase in the number and size of centers of concentration" (Ranganatham,1984). Thus, the urban centers grow in population size as well as multiply in number resulting in the increase of the degree of urbanization in any region. "Urbanization, being a complex socio-economic process closely connected with scientific-technological revolution, exercises a growing influence on all aspects of society's life affecting the nature of economic development, the demographic, ethnic and many social processes" (Kanstebovskaya, 1976). This further explains an increased human interaction and linkage of human activities, besides concentration of productive forces, especially concentration of the more dynamic part of the population.

Historical evidences suggest that urbanization process is inevitable and universal. Currently developed countries are characterized by high level of urbanization and some of them are in final stage of urbanization process and experiencing slowing down of urbanization due to host of factors (Brockerhoff, 1999; Brockerhoff and Brennam 1998). On the other hand a majority of the developing countries started experiencing urbanization only since the middle of the 20th century.

Objectives

The main aim of studying urbanization in this context is to examine the trends and patterns of urbanization in India during the period 1901-2001 using Indian Census data. It will try to focus the causes and problems of urbanization, and related policy issues.

Criteria to define urban area

Most of the countries use a combination of common criteria as: population size, population density and extent of the built-up area. In U.S.A the place with population of 2500 and in UK 1000 is treated as urban. In India, the criteria to define urban area:

1. All the places with municipality, corporation etc.
2. All other places with
   a Minimum population of 5000;
   b At least 75 per cent male working population in non-agricultural pursuits;
   c Density of population of at least 400 persons/sq.km.
3. Some other places with distinct urban characteristic are also considered as urban, even though they don't satisfy the above criteria.

Definition of urban agglomeration

An urban agglomeration is a continuous urban spread constituting a town and its adjoining urban outgrowths (OGs) or two or more physical contiguous town together and any adjoining urban outgrowths of such towns. Examples of outgrowths are railway colonies, university campus, port area, military campus etc. that may come up near a statutory town or city. For Census of India, 2001 it was decided that the core town or at least one of the constituent towns of an urban agglomeration should necessarily be a statutory town and the total population of all the constituents should not be less than 20,000 (as per 1991 Census). With these two basic criteria (R.G., 2001) having been met the following are the possible different situations in which urban agglomerations could be constituted.

1. A city or town with one or more contiguous outgrowths.
2. Two or more adjoining towns with or without their outgrowths.
3. A city or one or more adjoining towns with their outgrowths all of which form a continuous spread.

History of urbanization

The urbanization process in India is very ancient one, started during Indus civilization continued up to the fall of the Gupta period, revived through Turks and Sultanate period, and again continued during the Moghul period.

Table 15.1: Trends of urbanization

Census years	Total population in Million	Urban population in Million	Rural population in Million	Annual exponential growth rate	% of decadal variation of urpop
1901	238.39	25.85	212.54	—	—
1911	252.09	25.94	226.15	0.03	0.35
1921	251.32	28.08	223.23	0.79	8.27
1931	278.97	33.45	245.52	1.75	19.12
1941	318.66	44.15	274.5	2.77	31.97
1951	361.08	62.44	298.64	3.47	41.42
1961	439.23	78.93	360.29	2.34	26.41
1971	598.15	109.11	489.04	3.21	38.23
1981	683.32	159.46	523.86	3.83	46.14
1991	844.32	217.17	627.14	3.09	36.19
2001	1027.01	285.35	741.66	2.73	31.39
2011*	1192.5	357.94	834.56	2.07	25.56
2021*	1339.74	432.61	907.13	2.5	20.86

Source: Census of India (1981, 1991 & 2001).

*Population Projections for India, 2001-26, Registrar General of India, 2006.

During this period many cities were great commercial centers connecting India with the Central and Western Asia. Calcutta, Bombay and Madras grew and prospered during British period with the establishment of railways, industries and irrigation canals. After the independence it is at accelerating stage with emergence of a large number of new towns.

Trends in Urbanization

India's urban population has gained from 25.85 million in 1901 to 285.4 million in 2001, and projected to 357.94 million and 432.6 million in 2011 and 2021, Whereas total population has increased from 238.39 million in 1901 to 1027.01 million in 2001, estimated to 1192.5 and 1339.74 million in 2011 and 2021 respectively. Although the urban population attained more than 11 fold increase but the total population by four times only over a century (1901-2001). It shows a gradual increasing trend of urbanization (Table 15.1 and Fig.15.1).

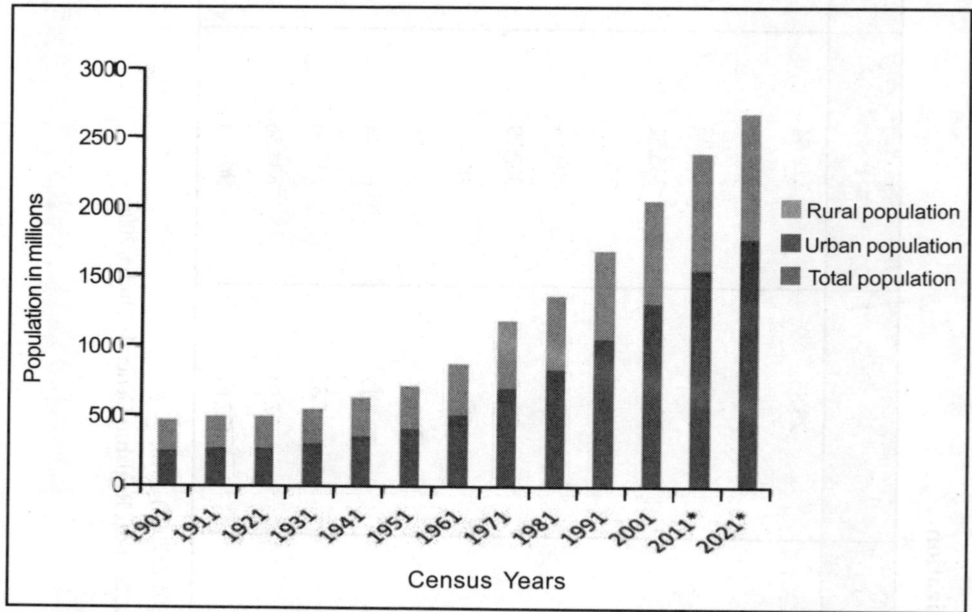

Source: Census of India (1981, 1991 & 2001).

*Population Projections for India, 2001-26, Registrar General of India, 2006.

Fig. 15.1: Trend of Urbanization —1901-2021

The urban growth in India remained stable for a period of four decades that is from 1901 to 1941. Even the total urban population remained more or less the same for this period. The decadal growth rates of urban population in India from 1901 to 2001 show slight fluctuations. During the last six decades, that is from 1941-2001 growth rates of urban population have been significant.

The decade 1941-51 is more significant (41.4%), which led to very faster growth period till 1961-81, slowing down during 1981-91 (36.2%) and from 1991-2001 (31.39%). The highest percentage of increase of urban population of 46.14 per cent was recorded in the decade 1971-81 and the lowest of 0.35 per cent was recorded in the decade 1901-11 (Table 15.1). But the rate of urbanization has gone down significantly from 1901-2001. The annual exponential growth rate of urban population grew with faster pace from 1921-51 and a sharp decline during 1951-61 was due to formalization of criteria to define urban centres in 1961. The decades 1961-71 and 1971-81 claimed a significant growth, and came down to 3.1 and 2.7 per cent. During the last ten decades, i.e. 1901-2001 it reveals that urbanization has progressed markedly.

Level of Urbanization

The level or degree of urbanization is related to number of people living in urban areas. The percentage of urban, rural and urban-rural ratio are generally used to measure the degree of urbanization. The level of urbanization picked up a gradual increasing trend starting from 11 per cent in 1901 to14 per cent in 1941, 23.3 per cent in 1981and 28 per cent in 2001(Table 15.2 and Fig. 15.2)

Table: 15.2: Level of urbanization

Census years	%Urban to total population	%Rural to total population	%Urban-rural ratio
1901	10.84	89.15	12.16
1911	10.29	89.71	11.47
1921	11.18	88.82	12.58
1931	11.99	88.01	13.63
1941	13.86	86.14	16.08
1951	17.29	82.71	20.91
1961	17.97	82.03	21.91
1971	19.91	81.76	22.31
1981	23.34	76.66	30.44
1991	25.72	74.28	34.63
2001	27.78	72.22	38.47

Source: Census of India (1981, 1991 & 2001).

From the table 15.2 and figure 15.2 it is evident that the percentage of urban population and urban-rural ratio experiences an increasing trend whereas the percentage of rural has shown gradual decreasing trend over a period of century.

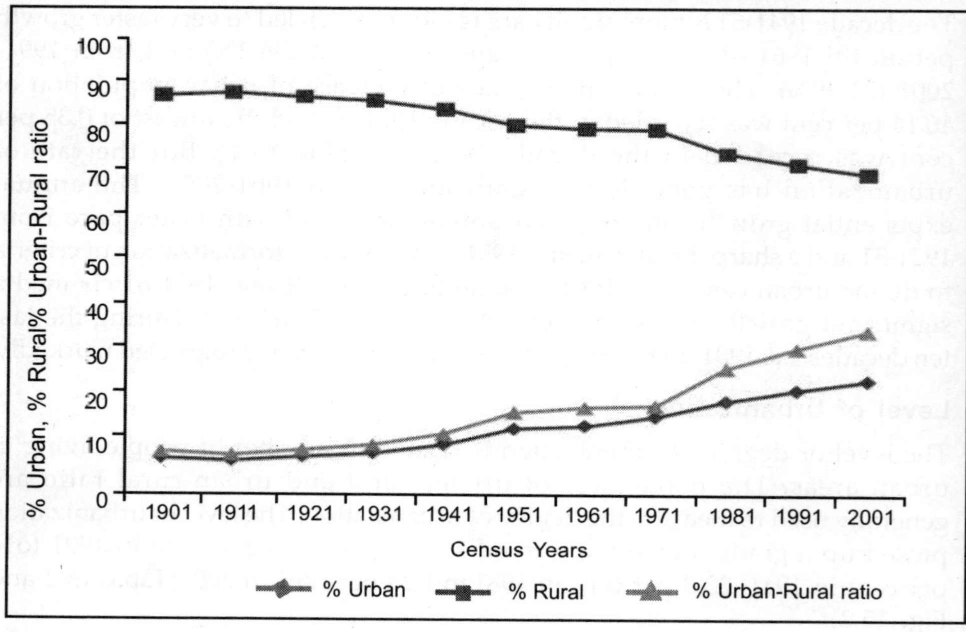

Source: Census of India (1981, 1991 & 2001).

Fig. 15.2: Level of Urbanization

Urbanization Pattern Across Size Class of Urban Settlements

The state of urbanization of a region can be studied not only with degree of urbanization, but also with size and distribution of the urban settlements. The cities and towns in different size categories have been growing at different rates altering the size composition of urban population. India had 1827 urban settlements in 1901, of which 24 class I, 43 Class II, 130 class III, 391 class IV, 744 class V and 479 class VI towns. The total no of urban settlements had increased from 1811 in 1901 to 5161 in 2001 showing an increase of 3334 towns. It is visible from the figure 15.3 that there has been a decadal increase in total number of urban settlements in all categories from 1901 to 2001 except class VI towns. But the rate of change showed considerable fluctuations. This is due to the development of new urban centres and some centres have lost their urban status in view of the change in the definition of the concept of urban from census to census.

Population Share of Towns

Table 15.3 presents the number of towns and percentage of urban population by size class urban settlements for the periods from 1901-2001.

Table 15.3: Number of Towns and Percentage of Urban Population by Size Class

Census Years	No of Towns by size class						Percentage of urban population by size class					
	I	II	III	IV	V	VI	I	II	III	IV	V	VI
1901	24	43	130	391	744	479	26.0	11.2	15.6	20.8	20.1	6.1
1911	23	40	135	364	707	485	27.4	10.5	16.4	19.7	19.3	6.5
1921	29	45	145	370	734	571	29.7	10.3	15.9	18.2	18.6	7.0
1931	35	56	183	434	800	509	31.2	11.6	16.8	18.0	17.1	5.2
1941	49	74	242	498	920	407	38.2	11.4	16.3	15.7	15.0	3.1
1951	76	91	327	608	1124	569	44.6	9.9	15.7	13.6	12.9	3.1
1961	102	129	437	719	711	172	51.4	11.2	16.9	12.7	6.8	0.7
1971	148	173	558	827	623	147	57.2	10.9	16.0	10.9	4.4	0.4
1981	218	270	743	1059	758	253	60.3	11.6	14.3	9.5	3.5	0.5
1991	300	345	947	1167	740	197	65.2	10.9	13.1	7.7	2.6	0.3
2001	393	401	1151	1344	888	191	68.6	9.67	12.2	6.8	2.3	0.2

Source: Census of India (1981, 1991 & 2001).

Population Size	Category
100,000 and more	Class I
50,000 to 100,000	Class II
20,000 to 50,000	Class III
10,000 to 20,000	Class IV
5,000 to 10,000	Class V
Less than 5,000	Class VI

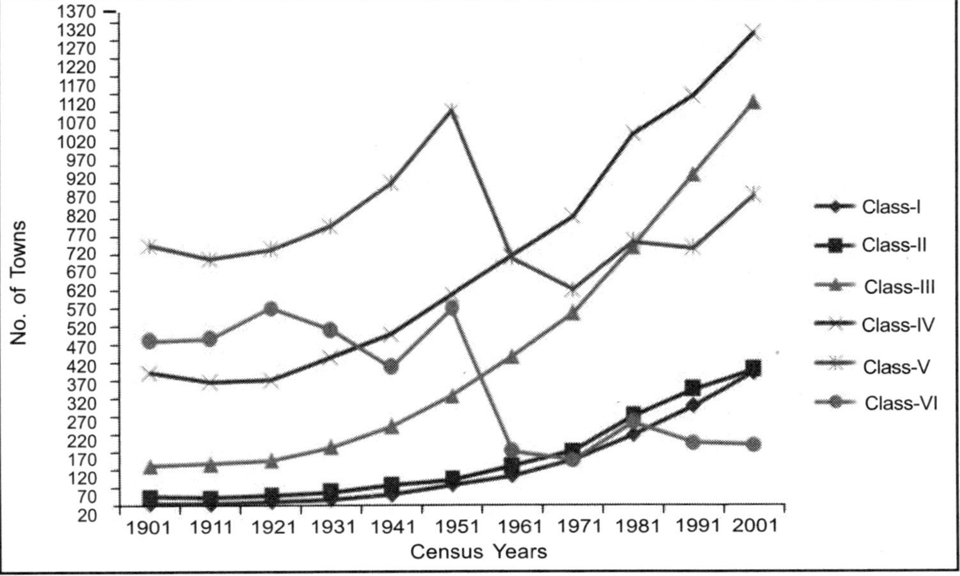

Source: Census of India (1981, 1991 & 2001)

Fig 15.3: No. of Towns by Size Class

Table 15.4:

	1961-71	1971-81	1981-91	1991-2001
Urban population increase (million) out of which	30.18	49.45	56.45	67.81
Natural increase (million)	19.68 (65.2)	25.56 (51.3)	35.37 (61.3)	40.17 (59.4)
Net R-U Migration (million)	5.91 (18.7)	9.83 (19.6)	12.76 (20.7)	14.32 (20.9)
Residual Component (million)	4.59 (16.1)	14.06 (29.1)	8.32 (18.0)	13.32 (19.7)

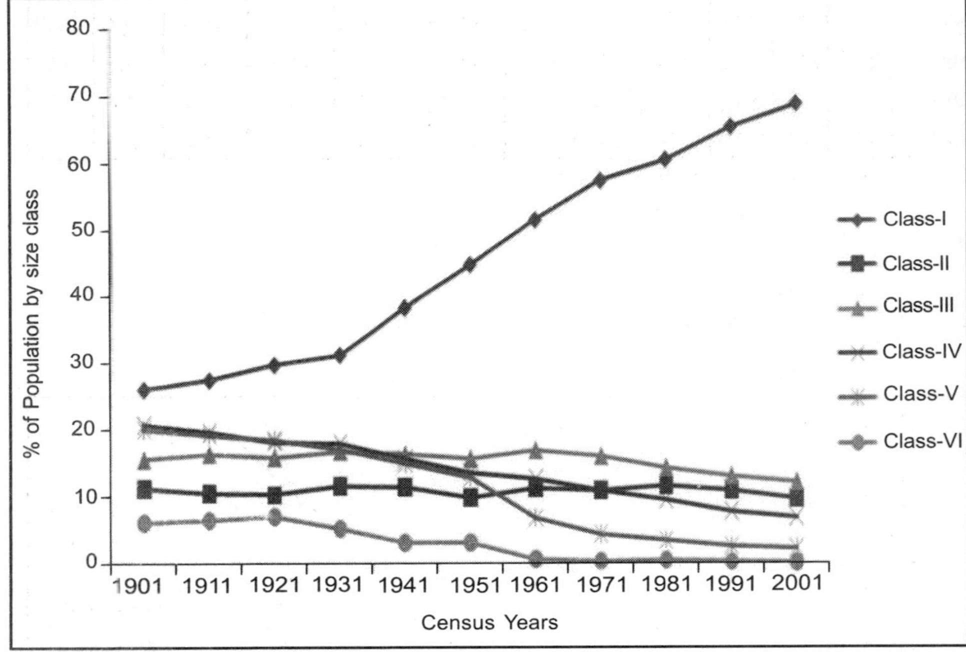

Source: Census of India (1981, 1991 & 2001).

Fig. 15.4: Growth of City by Size Class

From the point of view of population of the different classes of towns, it may be observed that class I towns over the decades accounted for a high percentage. According to 1901 census percentage of population in class I, IV and V were 26, 21 and 20 per cent respectively. In 1991 and 2001census 65 per cent and 67 per cent of people are living in class I towns. In case of class II and III towns the parentage is more or less the same (Fig. 15.3). The distribution of population in different size class of settlements is likely to become more and more skewed. The share of class I towns or cities, with population size of 100,000 or more, has gone up significantly from 26 per cent in 1901 to 68.6 per cent in 2001 that is more than three times. The percentage share of class IV, V and VI towns, having less than 20,000 people, on the other hand, has gone down drastically from 47 to 10 only. This is largely due to the fact that the towns in lower categories have grown in size and entered the next higher category. However, there has not been a corresponding increase in the number of urban centers, especially at the lower levels, through transformation of rural settlements during the period from 1901 to 2001 (Kundu, 1994). An analysis of the distribution of urban population across size categories of urban centers reveals that the process of urbanization in India has been top heavy or large city oriented. This is because of higher demographic growth in larger cities, in addition to the factor of upward movement of towns.

Causes of Urbanization

In developing countries like India, natural population increase and rural to urban migration are significant factors in the growth of towns/cities. Component of urban growth (Bhagat, 1992) has attributed to mainly three components and the largest contributor is natural growth (Table 15.4). The natural increase is caused by improved medical facilities, better sanitation and improved food supplies, and cause populations to grow, whereas migration caused by poverty drives people from the rural to urban areas in search of employment, food, shelter and education. In rural areas, people become victims of unpredictable weather conditions like drought and floods, which can affect their livelihood. Due to this many farmers from villages move to cities in search of jobs and other facilities. In contrast, cities offer job opportunities and other services and are known to be areas where wealth and money are centralized. Educational institutions and more industries are located in cities. This leads to migration to cities.

Problems and Policy Implications of Urbanization

Urbanization is an indicator of socio-economic development and modernization; can also become the cause of several problems. The urban problems are not all of recent making. In India the urban situation had become serious because of the large increase in population since 1921. The growth of cities in India has been haphazard and largely unplanned. These cities have their characteristic problems such as explosive increases in population, gross inadequacy of infrastructural facilities and services, overcrowding and traffic jams, crumbling old city centers, neighborhood degradation, expansion of slums etc. Our cities are a mixture of splendor and squalor. They provide better employment opportunities, higher income levels, better education, health and social services. At the same time, they are also congested, chaotic and squalid. Various types of problems like shortage of housing and sanitation, growth of slums, environmental pollution, urban poverty, lack of pure drinking water, unemployment, traffic congestion, poor public transport, improper treatment of sewage, uncollected solid waste, etc. are at present we are facing in India due to urbanization. Inequality in access to services, housing, land, education, health and employment opportunities within cities have socio-economic, environmental and political repercussions, including rising violence, urban unrest, environmental degradation, and under employment, which threaten to diminish any gains in income and poverty reduction. These problems cannot be tackled without the joint endeavor of the local elected bodies and a conscious group of city people acting through the NGOs and other institutions at the local level. Urban policy formulation and implementation have never received the attention they deserve from the highest policy-making levels in India.

India is the world's fifth-largest producer of global warming gas and emissions (USA first). Lopsided and unchecked urbanization lead to environmental degradation and deterioration of urban quality of living. The problem of pollution is more severe in big cities. The contamination of water and rising level of toxins in almost all major rivers of India due to heavy disposal of sewage wastes, excreta and chemical wastes. Fairly high rate of urbanization coupled with a low rate of investment in urban development, in the public as well as the private sector, are responsible for a serious deficiency in the availability of infrastructure and basic amenities. According to World Bank report on urbanization only 58 per cent of urban population of India has access to improved sanitation facilities. If job opportunities are productive and lead to gainful employment, urbanization becomes a means of economic development otherwise it is merely a process of transfer of rural poverty to an urban environment resulting in concentration of misery.

Counter urbanization is essential. Policy should relate to proper urban planning/master planning where city planning will consist of operational, developmental and restorative planning. Proper implementation of such plans is crucial in the regulated development of urban areas, which in turn have resulted in mushrooming of slums and squatters, unauthorized and haphazard development and above all environmental degradation and transportation problems within and around the urban areas. Further, the development plans/master plans are mostly documents prepared with limited forecasting capabilities without capturing the entire dynamics and are generally not responsive to dynamic problems and policy changes. It is therefore necessary to enable the administrators and planners to graduate and equip with better understanding, methods and tools to tackle the problem of urbanization.

Conclusion

Urban population in India experienced 11- fold increase from1901-2001, while the total population increased by four times. The size class distribution of urban population over the decades highlights that the recent trend is a sharp departure from the past. The total number of towns/urban areas increased in case of all size classes, except class VI. Small cities/towns are experiencing low demographic and economic growth. It can be suggested that a case can be made for providing special capital support to the less-developed urban centers for development, particularly, small and medium towns. Need research to understand trends and patterns of different migration streams and assess their contribution for growth of different town size class. Urban planning in medium and small towns needs emphasis as they are likely to grow in the coming days. Studies are also needed to understand growth of slums and slum population and their quality of life.

References

1. Bhagat, R. B. (1992), "Components of Urban Growth in India with Reference to Haryana: Findings from Recent Censuses", *Nagarlok,* Vol. 25, No. 3, pp. 10-14.
2. Brinkerhoff, M. (1999), "Urban Growth in Developing Countries: A Review of Projections and Predictions", *Population and Development Review,* Vol. 25. No. 4, pp. 757-778.
3. Brinkerhoff, M. and Brenna, E (1998), "The Poverty of Cities in Developing Regions", *Populations and Development Review,* Vol. 24, No 1, pp. 75-114.
4. Census of India, (1981), *Paper 2 of 1981: Rural–Urban Distribution of Population,* Government of India Publications, New Delhi.
5. Census of India (1991), "Emerging Trends of Urbanizations in India", *Occasional* pp. No. 1 of 1993, Registrar General, New Delhi.
6. Census of India (1991), *Paper 2 of 1991: Rural–Urban Distribution of Population,* Government of India Publications, New Delhi.
7. Census of India (2001), *Paper 2 of 2001: Rural–Urban Distribution of Population,* Provisional Population Totals, Government of India Publications, New Delhi.
8. Kanstebovskaya, I.V. (1976), *Some Definitions in Geographical Literature and the Relevant Idea,* Osmania University, Hyderabad.
9. Krishan, G. (1993), "The Slowing Down of Indian Urbanization", *Geography,* 78 (1): 80-84.
10. Kundu, A (1983), "Theories of City Size Distribution and Indian Urban Structure—A Reappraisal", *Economic and Political Weekly,* 18(3).
11. Kundu, A. and N. Sarangi (2005), "Employment Guarantee in India: The Issue of Urban Exclusion", *Economic and Political Weekly,* 40(33), pp. 3642–46.
12. Kundu, A. (1997), "Trends and Structure of Employment in the 1990s: Implications for Urban Growth", *Economic and Political Weekly,* 32(24): 1399–1405.
13. Ministry of Urban Development and Poverty Alleviation (1988), The National Commission of Urbanization, Government of India, New Delhi.
14. Mohan, Rakesh and C. Pant (1982), "Morphology of Urbanization in India: Some Results from 1981 Census", *Economic and Political Weekly,* 18 September–25 September.

15. National Commission on Urbanisation (1988), *Report of the National Commission on Urbanization,* Vol. II, August, Ministry of Urban Affairs, Government of India.

16. Pathak, P. and Mehta, D. (1995), "Recent Trends in Urbanization and Rural-Urban Migration in India: Some Explanations and Projections", *Urban India,* Vol. 15, No. 1, pp. 1-17.

17. Ranganadham, N. (1984), "Metropolitan Transport System Planning", *Journal of the Institute of Town Planners,* Vol. 3, No.1.

18. Ramakrishna, N. (2005), "Regulatory Impacts on Land and Housing Markets in Mumbai", Paper Presented in the Tenth International Conference on Asian Real Estate Society, Sydney, Australia.

19. Singh, R.L. (2003), *Fundamentals of Human Geography,* Sharada Pustak Bhawan, Allahabad.

20. Sivaramkrishnan, K. C., A. Kundu, and B. N. Singh (2005), *A Handbook of Urbanization,* Oxford University Press, New Delhi.

21. United Nations (2005), *World Urbanization Prospects, the 2003 Revision,* Population Division, New York.

22. World Bank (1998), *Reducing Poverty in India: Options for More Effective Public Services,* World Bank, Washington, D.C.

Trends of Migration

Mrs. B. Anupama Devi

Introduction

Urbanization occurs naturally from individual and corporate efforts to reduce time and expense in commuting and transportation while improving opportunities for jobs, education, housing, and transportation. Living in cities permits individuals and families to take advantage of the opportunities of proximity, diversity, and marketplace competition.

People move into cities to seek economic opportunities. A major contributing factor is known as "Rural Flight". In rural areas, often on small family farms, it is difficult to improve one's standard of living beyond basic sustenance. Farm living is dependent on unpredictable environmental conditions, and in times of drought, flood or pestilence, survival becomes extremely problematic. In modern times, industrialization of agriculture has negatively affected the economy of small and middle-sized farms and strongly reduced the size of the rural labour market.

There are better basic services as well as other specialist services that aren't found in rural areas. There are more job opportunities and a greater variety of jobs. Health is another major factor. People, especially the elderly are often forced to move to cities where there are doctors and hospitals that can cater to their health needs. Other factors include a greater variety of entertainment (restaurants, movie theaters, theme parks etc.) and a better quality of education, namely universities. Due to their high populations, urban areas can also have much more diverse social communities allowing others to find people like them when they might not be able to in rural areas.

These conditions are heightened during times of change from a pre-industrial society to an industrial one. It is at this time that many new commercial enterprises are made possible, thus creating new jobs in cities. It is also a result of industrialization that farms become more mechanized, putting many labourers out of work. This is currently occurring fastest in India. In recent years, urbanization of rural areas has increased.

Village profile

Ramanuja Palle village is located in Tirupati (rural) mandal at a distance of four km to the south-east of Tirupati town. As per our field survey Ramanuja Palle village consist total of 4028 population of which 3012 people are engaged in various works. The village has 762 households and total of 2578 hectares of geographic land. The village gets drinking water through Swarnamukhi river canal, tanks, wells and hand pumps. The Ramanuja Palle village has various facilities like schools, electricity, transport, post and telegraph. Medical facility is also available at a distance of four kms from this village.

Hypothesis

Ramanuja Palle village of Tirupati (rural) mandal is selected for case study to know the urban impact on this village as it is closer to the town of Tirupati. It is also selected because of frequent interaction of villagers of Ramanuja Palle with Tirupati town for day-to-day activities. It is hypothesized that the village my exhibit more development features of demography such as literacy, percentage of working population, sex-ratio, out-migration and in-migration.

Land use

Table 16.1 illustrates the land use. The total geographical area of Ramanuja Palle village was 2578 hectares during 1991, which is remained same during our field survey. During 1991 the cultivable waste land was 166.70 hectares (6.47%) which is decreased to 40.25 hectares (1.56%) in 2011. During 1991 the area not available for cultivation was 1121.05 hectares (43.49%), which is decreased to 1012.35 hectares (39.27%) in 2011. The arable land was 1205.25 hectares (46.75%) during 1991, which is increased to 1429.40 hectares (55.45%). This change indicates that the people are taking more land for agriculture. This village was covered by 85 hectares (3.30%) of forest area during 1991, which is increased to 96 hectares (3.72%) during 2011.

Irrigation

Table 16.2 shows area under irrigation, during 1991 there was 43.48 per cent of net sown area under irrigation, while 56.52 per cent area was un-irrigated, while during 2011, the irrigation is increased to 56.53 per cent, while un-irrigated land is decreased to 43.47 per cent. This change indicates the agricultural development in the village.

Table 16.1: Land use

Category	1991	2001	2011
Cultivable waste land (in hectares)	166.70 (6.47)	39.02 (1.51)	40.25 (1.56)
Area not available for cultivation (in hectares)	1121.05 (43.49)	1032.61 (40.05)	1012.35 (39.27)
Arable land (in hectares)	1205.25 (46.75)	1410.25 (54.70)	1429.40 (55.45)
Forest	85.00 (3.30)	96.05 (3.73)	96.00 (3.72)
Total	2578.00 (100.00)	2578.00 (100.00)	2578.00 (100.00)

Table 16.2: Area under irrigation

Category	1991	2001	2011
Irrigated	524.00 (43.48)	636.00 (45.10)	808.00 (56.53)
Un-irrigated	681.25 (56.52)	774.25 (54.90)	621.40 (43.47)
Total	1205.25 (100.00)	1410.25 (100.00)	1429.40 (100.00)

Population aspects

The details of population aspects in Ramanuja Palle village are shown in Table 16.3. During 1991 the total population of Ramanuja Palle village was 1900, which is increased to 3062 during 2001, showing 1162 absolute increase with 61.15 per cent decadal growth and 6.11 per cent yearly growth. During 2011, the population of this village was increased to 4208, showing an absolute increase of 1146 persons with 37.42 per cent decadal growth and 3.74 per cent yearly growth.

Table 16.3: Decadal growth

Decades	Populations	Absolute Variation	Percent Variation	Yearly Percentage of Growth
1991	1900	—	—	—
2001	3062	1162	61.15	6.11
2011	4208	1146	37.42	3.74

Density of population

General density: Table 16.4 explains decadal growth of general density, agricultural density, psychological density in Ramanuja Palle village. During 1991, the general density of Ramanuja Palle village was 109 persons per sq km., which was increased to 184 persons per sq km. during 2001. During 2011 the general density was increased to **298** persons per sq km.

Agriculture density: During 1991, the agriculture density of Ramanuja Palle village was 78 persons per sq. km. During 2001, it was increased to 127 persons per sq. km. During 2011, the agriculture density of this village was 236 persons per sq. km. This study reveals that there is an increasing pressure of agricultural population on net sown area.

Physiological density: During 1991, the physiological density of Ramanuja Palle village was 198 persons per sq. km. During 2001, it was increased to 316 persons per sq. km. The physiological density of this village was increased to 412 persons per sq. km. in 2011. This study reveals that there is an increasing pressure of total population on net sown area of Ramanuja Palle village.

Table 16.4: Decadal growth

Density	1991	2001	2011
General density per sq. km.	109	184	298
Agricultural density per sq. km.	78	127	236
Psychological density per sq. km.	198	316	412

Male-Female Composition

Table 16.5 gives the clear picture of sex composition of Ramanuja Palle village. During 1991, out of total population of 1900 Ramanuja Palle village 1020 (53.68%) were males, while 880 (46.32%) were females. During 2001, out of 3062 total population 1668 (54.47%) were males and 1394 (45.53%) were females. During 2011, out of 4208 population 2534 (60.22%) were males and 1674 (39.78%) were females. The sex ratio of Ramanuja Palle village shows 862 females per 1000 males during 1991. During 2001, females per 1000 males were 835. During 2011 females per 1000 males were 660, which shows decreasing trend of female sex ratio.

Table 16.5: Sex composition

Sex	1991	2001	2011
Males	1020 (53.68)	1668 (54.47)	2534 (60.22)
Females	880 (46.32)	1394 (45.53)	1674 (39.78)
Total	1900 (100.00)	3062 (100.00)	4208 (100.00)

Age Structure of Population

Age structure of population in Ramanuja Palle village can be ascertained with the help of Table 16.6. The age structure of Ramanuja Palle village shows dominance of child population with 10.42 per cent males and 5.10 per cent females in the age group of below 6 years. Similarly there is about 13.22 per cent males and 7.75 per cent females in the age group of 6 to 14 years. Thus the age structure of Ramanuja Palle village is dominantly based on child and working population, being dependent population. This kind of age structure will effect the growth of economy of the village. In the age group of 15 to 30 years we noticed about 32.25 per cent males and 35.56 per cent females, which is very much prone to reproduction of population. Similarly in the age group of 31 to 40 years we noticed about 18.47 per cent males and 18.67 per cent females, which is also engaged in reproduction of population. In the age group of 15 to 50 years about 66.83 per cent males and 76.28 per cent females being accounted as working population in this village. We noticed about 6.83 per cent males and 6.76 per cent females in the age group of 51 to 60 years. There is only 2.01 per cent males and 2.55 per cent females noticed in the age group of 61 to 70 years, which is dependent population of the Ramanuja Palle village.

Table 16.6: Age structure

Age Groups	Total	Male	Female
Below 6 years	336 (7.98)	238 (10.42)	98 (5.10)
6 to 14 years	451 (10.72)	302 (13.22)	149 (7.75)
15 to 21 years	632 (15.02)	365 (15.97)	267 (13.88)
22 to 30 years	789 (18.75)	372 (16.28)	417 (21.68)
31 to 40 years	781 (18.56)	422 (18.47)	359 (18.67)
41to 50 years	792 (18.82)	368 (16.11)	424 (22.05)
51 to 60 years	286 (6.80)	156 (6.83)	130 (6.76)
61 to 70 years	95 (2.26)	46 (2.01)	49 (2.55)
Above 70 years	46 (1.09)	16 (0.70)	30 (1.56)

Literates

Table 16.7 shows the literates of Ramanuja Palle village. During 1991, out of 1900 total population 701 (36.89%) were literates, while 1199 (63.11%) were illiterates. During 2001, the literates were increased to 1528 (49.90%), while 1534 (50.10%) were illiterates. During 2008, out of 4208 population, 2092 (49.71%) were literates, while 2116 (50.29%) were illiterates. The percentage of literates have increased to 12.82 per cent and percentage of illiterates is decreased to 12.82 per cent from 1991 to 2008, which indicates increasing trend of literates.

Table 16.7: Decadal growth

Category	1991	2001	2008
Literates	701 (36.89)	1528 (49.90)	2092 (49.71)
Illiterates	1199 (63.11)	1534 (50.10)	2116 (50.29)
Total	1900 (100.00)	3062 (100.00)	4208 (100.00)

Level of education

The educational level of Ramanuja Palle village shown in Tabl 16.8. 637 (30.58%) persons having primary level of education, out of which 361 were males and 276 were females. There were 609 (29.24%) persons having secondlly level of education, of them 334 were males and 275 were females. About 754 (36.20%) persons having higher secondary level of education, of them 478 were males and 276 were females. There were 71 (3.41%) persons having gone to graduate level of education, of them 40 were males and 31 were females. There were 5 postgraduates and 7 technical/diploma holders are noticed in Ramanuja Palle village.

Table 16.8: Educational level

Category	Primary	Secondary	Higher Secondary	Graduation	Post-Graduation	Technical
Males	361 (29.59)	334 (27.38)	478 (39.18)	40 (3.28)	3 (0.25)	4 (0.33)
Females	276 (31.98)	275 (31.87)	276 (31.98)	31 (3.59)	2 (0.23)	3 (0.35)
Total	637 (30.58)	609 (29.24)	754 (36.20)	71 (3.41)	5 (0.24)	7 (0.34)

Composition of working population

Table 16.9 shows the composition of working population in Ramanuja Palle village. During 1991, out of 1900 total population of the Ramanuja Palle village had 58.32 per cent (1108) workers and 41.68 per cent (792) non-workers. During 2001 the percentage of workers were increased to 55.55 per cent, while the percentage of non-workers were decreased to 44.45 per cent. During 2011, the working population of Ramanuja Palle village was increased to 71.58 per cent, while non-working population was decreased to 28.42 per cent as per our field survey. Here we noticed the 13.26 per cent increase of working population from 1991 to 2011.

Nature of occupation

A detailed analysis of the native occupation presented in Table 16.10. There were 928 (22.05%) persons engaged in household works out, of them 18 (1.94%) were males and 910 (98.06%) were females. About 56 (1.33%) persons

Table 16.9: Composition of workers

Category	1991	2001	2011
Workers	1108 (58.32)	1701 (55.55)	3012 (71.58)
Non-workers	792 (41.68)	1361 (44.45)	1196 (28.42)
Total	1900 (100.00)	3062 (100.00)	4208 (100.00)

engaged in government services, of which 44 (78.57%) were males and 12 (21.43%) were females. About 98 persons (2.33%) persons were engaged in private employment, of them 54 (55.10%) were males and 44 (44.90%) were females. There were 1402 (33.32%) persons who were engaged in agriculture works, of them 710 (50.64%) were males and 692 (49.36%) were females. In Ramanuja Palle village about 1328 (31.56%) were persons engaged in coolie and labour works, of them 670 (50.45%) were males and 658 (49.55%) were females. There were (396 9.41%) persons engaged in self employment, of them 122 30.81%) were males and 274 (69.19%) were females.

Table 16.10: Nature of occupation

Nature of Occupation	Total	Male	Female
Household work	928 (22.05)	18 (1.94)	910 (98,06)
Government service	56 (1.33)	44 (78.57)	12 (21.43)
Private employment	98 (2.33)	54 (55.10)	44 (44.90)
Agriculture works	1402 (33.32)	710 (50.64)	692 (49.36)
Self employment	396 (9.41)	122 (30.81)	274 (69.19)
Coolie and labourers	1328 (31.56)	670 (50.45)	658 (49.55)

Marital status

From Table 16.11 it is observed that, out of 4208 total population 2319 (55.11%) were married, of them 1504 (52.13%) were males and 815 (61.14%) were females, 1841 (43.75%) persons were unmarried, of them 1351 (46.99%) were males and 490 (36.76%) were females. There were 48 (1.14%) persons, belonging to other status like widows, widowers, of them 20 (0.70%) were males and 28 (2.10%) were females.

Economic status

Table 16.12 shows nature of occupation. There were 18 households, consisting of 86 persons (2.25%), of them 44 (51.16%) were males and 42

Table 16.11: Marital status

Status	Persons	Males	Females
Married	2319 (55.11)	1504 (52.13)	815 (61.14)
Unmarried	1841 (43.75)	1351 (46.99)	490 (36.76)
Other Status	48 (1.14)	20 (0.70)	28 (2.10)

(48.84%) were females, belonging to rich class, whose annual income was more than Rs.1,00,000. There were 35 households consisting of 232 persons (6.06%), of them 118 (50.86%) were males and 114 (49.14%) were females, belonging to upper-middle class, whose annual income was Rs. 50,000 to 1,00,000. There were 64 households consisting of 422 persons, of them 217 (51.42%) were males and 205 (48.58%) were females, belonging to middle class, whose annual income was Rs. 25,000 to Rs. 50,000. There were 208 households consisting of 1318 persons, of them 661 (5015%) were males and 657 (49.85%) were females, belonging to lower-middle class, whose annual income was Rs.15,000 to Rs. 25,000. There were about 402 households consisting of 1900 persons (45.15%), of them 964 (50.74%) were males and 936 (49.26%) were females belonging to poor class, whose annual income is less than Rs.15,000. We noticed about 35 households (250 persons) in Ramanuja Palle village, who have not responded about their annual income.

Table 16.12: Nature of occupation

Groups	No. of Houses	Persons	Males	Females
Rich Class Rs. Lakh More than	18	86 (2.25)	44 (51.16)	42 (48.84)
Upper Middle Class Rs.50,000 to 1 Lakh	35	232 (6.06)	118 (50.86)	114 (49.14)
Middle Class Rs.25,00 to 50,000	64	422 (10.03)	217 (51.42)	205 (48.58)
Lower-Middle Class Rs.15,000 to 25,000	208	1318 (31.32)	661 (50.15)	657 (49.85)
Poor Class Below Rs.15,000	402	1900 (45.15)	964 (50.74)	936 (49.26)
Not Reported	35	250 (5.94)	133 (53.20)	117 (46.80)

Migration

As per our field survey shown in table 16.3, about 132 persons (24.18%) have in-migrated to Ramanuja Palle village from some urban areas of Chittoor district, while 106 persons (23.98%) have out-migrated to some urban areas of Chittoor district. There were about 278 persons (50.92%) have in-migrated from some rural areas of Chittoor district, while 302 persons (68.33%) have out-migrated to some rural areas of Chittoor district. There were about 136 persons (24.91%) have in-migrated from outside the Chittoor district, while 34 persons (7.69%) have out-migrated from Ramanuja Palle village to outside the Chittoor district.

Table 16.13: Migration

Places	In-migrants in Percentages	Out-migrants in Percentages
Urban areas of Chittoor District	132 (24.18)	106 (23.98)
Rural areas of Chittoor District	278 (50.92)	302 (68.33)
Outside the District	136 (24.91)	34 (7.69)

Causes of Migration

Table 16.14 shows that there were about 194 females who have out-migrated from Ramanuja Palle village due to marriage, while 318 females have in-migrated for same purpose. In connection with occupation 114 females and 66 males have in-migrated, while 55 females and 79 males have out-migrated for same purpose. Only 6 males out-migrated for some other purposes, while 19 males have in-migrated to Ramanuja Palle village from other places for other purposes. The tested hypothesis is disproved.

Table 16.14: Causes of migration

Causes	In-migrants in Percentage		Out-migrants in percentage	
	Females	Males	Females	Males
Marriage as primary	318 (58.24)	—	194 (43.89)	—
Education as primary	13 (2.38)	11 (2.01)	12 (2.71)	96 (21.72)
Occupation as primary	114 (20.88)	66 (12.09)	55 (12.44)	79 (17.87)
Others	5 (0.92)	19 (3.48)	—	6 (1.36)

Conclusion

Out of total migrants 23.98 per cent of people have out-migrated to urban areas of Chittoor district, while 24.18 per cent of people have in-migrated to some other rural areas of Chittoor district, while 50.92 per cent of people have in-migrated from rural areas of Chittoor district, whose purposes of migration are associated with occupation and marriages. The village Ramanuja Palle has shown constant increase in population. Similarly agricultural density of population and physiological density are also on rise. Sex ratio is 660 females per 1000 males. About 45.15 per cent of villagers belong to very poor economic class. Therefore, the population resource in Ramanuja Palle village need qualitative development in literacy, health, family planning and agriculture development so as to foresee wholesome development.

References

1. Bhattacharya, P., (1998), "The Informal Sector and Rural to Urban Migration: Some Indian Evidence", *Economic and Political Weekly*, 33 (21), pp. 1255-1262.

2. Shah, F. (1998), *Rural-Urban Migration Jaipur India,* Print Well Publishers, Distributors, p. 200.

3. Misra, S.N., (1998), *Dynamics of Rural-Urban Migration in India,* Anmol Publishers, New Delhi, India, p. 211.

4. http://web.unfpa.org/swp/2007/english/chapter-1/urbanization.html

5. http://www.un.org/esa/population/publications/WUP2005/2005wup.htm

6. http://esa.un.org/unup

Urbanization and the Aged
A Sociological Perspective

Dr. K. Dhanalakshmi,
Mr. B. Ramesh

Prologue

We naturally see the beauty of youth, but must learn to see the beauty of age.

—Chinese proverb

India is a country where traditions, values, systems were highly respected. In the olden days the social bonds were very strong, relationships among the human beings and in the society as well in the family were strong, emotional feelings were highly cherished and the moral ideals and the ethics were greatly valued. As time rolls out the situation gradually started mortifying and the joint families were replaced by the nuclear families. The social structure became diluted, moral values have been degraded. It is because of the adventure of modernization and industrialization. There the significant all changes have taken place in the family system. Joint family's disintegrated, the small and nuclear families have emerged where the young couple find no time to look after their old parents. In such families the position of the old became crucial factor. The old themselves find it difficult to adjust with the modern ways of living of their young children. In such situation how the old in urban set-up are being looked after by the family is worth enquiring. In the cities where there is a growth of individualism and with it the desire to be self-reliant. The clashes between generations distress the old in the cities. Hence, many of the problems are facing the urban elderly do not exist in the villages. In contrast to the rural population the city elderly population is quite different. Majority of this group have taken recourse to old age homes. Along with the lonelyness and helplessness they have difference with their kin and kith, perhaps the next generation, which force them to leave their own home and enter the premises of old age homes. They enjoy relatively contended life in these homes, though they often remember earlier life as golden past. Their new life in the public environment is no doubt problems free as far as interrelation with family members is concerned, but after all it is an institutional life certainly artificial being uprooted from ones familiar surroundings and implanted in a strange atmosphere which one has to accept and remain contended with.

Recently in India, technological developments have caused tremendous changes in the lifestyles and values of the younger generation. Their respect for and dependence on the old is reduced. New standards of behavior, new ways of spending time and the like provide specific grounds for conflicts between the two generations. The disagreement which would have remained suppressed in the past are now openly expressed. Unless the old generations remain silent, suppressing its feelings of disapproval before the young, there are risks to verbal argument and contradictions, within their cultural frame work, this constitutes the antithesis of appropriate modes of inter-generational communication. In all the above ways, families include the older people are affected by the social transition taking place in an urban set-up. The impact of changes on the socio-economic structure, geographical mobility, education, cultural values, is felt at all economic and social level.

Urbanization

India is the fastest developing where rapid economic growth is underway. Urbanization is an index of transformation from traditional rural economy to modern industrial one. It is a sign of progressive concentration of population in urban unit. India occupy second place after china in urban population. Barring China, America and Russia; in numerical terms India's urban population is higher than the total urban population of all countries of the world. The U.N. has stated that we are living in the urban century. By 2030 more than 70 per cent of the world will be urbanized. Analyst Paragh Khan wrote in "Foreign Policy" paper that in future the cities are becoming the islands of governance on which the world will be built. This, in fact has become a threat to India. 30 per cent of the India's population is living in urban areas and this 400 million people are generating two-thirds of the Gross Domestic Product (GDP) of our country and 90 per cent of the government's revenue. Five of the most densely populated cities in the world are in India. This rapid growth of urban areas is the result of two factors—natural increase in population (excess of births over deaths), and migration to urban areas. Today the movement of people from rural to urban areas (internal migration) is the most significant. It has been estimated by 2020, 140 million people will be migrating to the urban areas and it will reach to 700 million by 2050. (Sai Sujatha, 2011). The process of urbanization affects the rural community particularly the rural elderly because their younger generations migrates to urban places for their livelihood behind leaving their elderly parents.

Methodology

The present study is intended to know the problems, feeling and other relevant issues of the elderly. Based on the review of the secondary data this article has been prepared. Various books and reports, journal and monographs are referred.

Objectives

1. To look at the status of the aged in the past.
2. To understand the differences between urban and rural.
3. To investigate the problems of the aged in the context of urbanization.

Status Enjoyed in the Olden Days/Status of the Aged in Joint Families

Indian traditions, social values and norms enjoin an exalted position for the elderly, proper care and a say by them is the most matters connected with the family. In early society, the role and authority of the elders was both supportive and upheld. All ancient and sacred literature including the Veda and the epics portray parents almost god. As a consequence, young people would be differential and respectful towards the elderly. They would abide by the wishes and authority of older persons. Seldom would they think of deviating and protesting against them. According to the Veda, man's life is divided in to four *ashramas* or stages:

(i) *Brahmacharya* (student life).

(ii) *Grihasta ashrama* (married life).

(iii) *Vanaprasta* (retired life).

(iv) *Sanyasa* (life of renunciation).

The movement from one stage to another was gradual with prescribed duties and observances associated with each stage. This minimized the inter-stage conflict. When a son would enter in to *Grihasta ashrama,* father would usually proceed to *vanaprastha,* passing on the responsibilities to the son. Another Indian society's characteristic is joint family system. Social systems, traditions sustained and reinforced joint family system as primary groupings. The joint families were headed by "*Karta*" who would invariably be the eldest male who would oversee assets and liabilities together wtih joint family traditions, preserving the positions of the elderly in the family and society as well. Under this system three generations would live together beneath the same roof and all social economical affairs were controlled and managed within the domain of the household. Hence, the joint family prescribed the way of life and deviating from it was not easy. All these reduce the chances of strain caused by differences within the family. In early part of the century the status of the elderly in the family and in the kin group and the community was reinforced by the impact of tradition in society. The elders in India in ancient time enjoyed the power, authority, respect and security. Denise (1991) reports that family is one of the institution that has survived the challenges presented over many centuries and will have to survive the senior challenge. However, in contemporary society the social status is degraded and for which several factors facilitated.

Type of Aged

In 1962, Susan Reichard identified five categories of older persons based on the response to the ageing process.

1. Mature type—Free from conflicts, accepting themselves, no regrets for the past.
2. Rocking chair type—Passive welcoming a change to rest and be free of responsibility.
3. Armored type—Having a highly developed set of defenses to protect themselves against the anxieties of aging.
4. Angry type—Balancing others, unable to accept their aging status.
5. Self-haters—Blaming themselves, seeing life as disappointing.

Urban and Rural Differences

India is a country of villages, and nearly three quarters of its population is rural. Urban and rural areas provide striking contrasts in terms of living conditions, availability of resources and facilities. There are regional variations in the condition of villages but in general, most villages have poor sanitary conditions and less access to education and health facilities. Most rural folk work on their own land or as agricultural labourers. There is no income security or any systematic provision for old age. In most surveys, the urban old people are found to have better health and better economic security than those in rural areas. Urban areas in India have benefited disproportionately from improvements in housing, sanitation, education and health care. Urban males are in the most advantageous position compared to urban females, rural males and rural females. Urban men are better educated, likely to work in the organized sector, to retire with a pension and to be insured. They are also more likely to use health facilities often and have better health status (Prakash, 1997). Senior citizen clubs are becoming popular in cities. In metropolitan areas, older people organize themselves to fight for better facilities and to pressurize the government for tax benefits and user-friendly public services.

In general the rural aged, compared with urban older people, have substantially smaller incomes, are restricted in mobility because of inadequate transportation facilities, report poorer physical health, and reveal a more negative outlook on life. Evidence suggests that the industrialization of rural communities may have a negative impact upon the rural elderly. Periodic longitudinal studies of rural older persons in strategic locations of the nation are needed to provide guidance for programs and services.

For most persons, old age brings limitations of one kind or another. The cumulative effect of these decrements tends to have a negative impact upon the subjective life of many older persons. Each person has within his lifespan a potential for developing a positive outlook, depending on a variety of biological, psychological, and sociological forces influencing his behavior. It is believed that the rural environments have less potential than urban settings for producing a favorable mental outlook among older people.

Vijay Kumar (1999) in his study best expressed that declining joint family system and the increased nuclear families and the declining moral support from family and society, increasing migration rate from rural to urban and the money order economy and intimacy at distance become the major factors contributing to the aged became helpless and economically poor and impoverished. Aparajita Chattopadhyay (2004) in his study explores the needs and demands of the elderly, based on a survey in Mumbai, highlights the importance of intervention of developmental and social security policies for the welfare of the aged. Besides, keeping in mind the heterogeneous nature of India's elderly, it is more practical to develop a plan of action for a specified group of people, instead of having a single policy directed at the entire population. Moneer Alam (2004) emphasizes in his articles that much of the recent growth of India's elderly population is expected to comprise persons with adverse life course experiences, clouded by excessive socio-economic backwardness. Such an ageing process suggests the need for a multi-pillared income security system. The analysis of his paper that focuses on three major income security plans for the aged reveals that the government is instead working to dilute much of its responsibilities. This study strongly argues for—

(i) strengthening of the social assistance programme for older persons and modification of the ceiling formula used for capping the size of its beneficiaries;

(ii) providing a guarantee against diminution of investments in the reformed pension policy; and

(iii) devising long-term old age savings instruments with higher terminal yield.

Meena Gopal (2006) argues in the context of the state's withdrawal from the social sectors. This paper makes a case for the increasing need to ensure social security for older people, especially women. It touches upon some problems in implementing social security legislation, locating elderly women including widows, the deserted and the destitute women as a vulnerable group. The gender implications of the various policies and schemes of assistance for older people, including the National Policy for Older Persons, are also discussed. The manner of implementation of the schemes is situated in the overall context of the vulnerability of older women in India. Tapan Benerjee (2002) in his research work emphasie how the social and situational factors showed its impact on the biological and psychological conditions on the elderly and further he gives more importance to these factors— how they are reducing the role of elderly in family decision-making and in society and political and further discuss about the social stratification and problems of adjustment and the behavioral attitude of children and the society towards the elderly people to improve the moral support among them for healthy life. Ashish Bose and Malakapur Shankardass (2004) in their book evidently illustrate about the problems of elderly with live examples through case studies.

Impact of the Urbanization

Rapid urban growth is responsible for many environmental and societal changes in the urban areas and its effects are strongly related to global change issues. The rapid growth of cities strains their capacity to provide services such as energy, education, health care, transportation, sanitation and physical security. One of the major effects of rapid urban growth is "Urban sprawl"— scattered development that increases traffic, saps local resources and destroys open space. The high density cities are often highly polluted owing to the lack of urban services, including running water, trash pickup, electricity or paved roads. It has been presumed that global warming (and consequent climate change) is one of the problem resulting from increased urbanization. There has also been a poorer air qualities noted in the buildings and households in the urban areas. The population density resulting from urbanization has further been attributed to rising crime rates in urban areas. In big cities there is also the serious problem of housing. The authorities are always failing in their efforts to meet the housing demands of the people. It has been estimated that there will be a shortage of 30 million houses by 2020. The shortage of houses leads to overcrowding, in sanitary conditions and it result in slums. As per 2001 census the slum population of India was 42.6 million which constitute 15.0 per cent of the total urban population of the country. The Planning Commission of India estimated that the slum population will be increased to 93 million by 2011. Around 12.7 per cent of total Indian towns have reported slums.

The huge population of cities also leads to many transport problems like traffic jams, accidents, heavy pollution etc. The trains in the Mumbai are designed to carry 1700 passengers, however carry 5000 commuters during the rush hours. In Delhi, 60 per cent of increase has been observed in the registration of cars in five years. Land is in short supply, which is leading to homelessness, encroachment and crimes. In Mumbai the streets account for only 11 per cent of the Mumbai land, compared to 22 per cent in New York. The number of vehicles on roads will grow five folds by 2020. Over 160 GW of generation capacity has to be added in 10 years in urban India alone. Over population and overcrowding in cities always create many problems such as water shortage, electricity breakdown and so on. India although has enormous resources of water, but it still suffers from shortage of water supply in urban areas. The growing demand of water, along with poor water resource management and mounting pollution levels contributes shortage of to water supply in and around cities. Poor water management practices exacerbate local water shortages. Inefficient water distribution system is another major source of water loss in cities.

There is a tremendous pressure on civic infrastructure like water supply, sewerage and drainage, solid waste management etc. Recent data suggests that water supply is available for 2.9 hours per day across cities and towns. Urban India also needs 200 million additional water connections. About 30 to 50 per cent households do not have sewerage connections. 250 million more people will be in need of sanitation facilities. More than half the residents of Indian slums do not have access to toilets. While this is a question of basic human dignity, it also relates to issues of public health and safety. With growing poverty and slums, Indian cities have been grappling with the challenges of making the cities sustainable, i.e., inclusive, productive, efficient and manageable. According to CII study "Intelligent urbanization: Road map for India" the government alone will have to invest $1 trillion in urban services by 2020 to cater to basic demands.

The sustainability of urban development in India has to be seen in the context of shelter and slums, basic urban services, financing urban development and governance and planning. India has to improve its urban areas to achieve objectives of economic development. However, urban governance and management of the services is far from satisfactory. Some of the ways to save our cities are to plan them small, rethink public transport, reinventing slums, reimagining public spaces, recycle buildings, conserve water resources, and restore forests, save the sewerage system and so on.

In the past villages were endeavored as a self prospered and agriculture was in a position to provide work to all the people who enjoy the rural atmosphere and they were very happy. In the recent past there are several changes in the social system, it is because of high population growth and due to agricultural low yield, decreasing the joint families and changes or shifts in the occupations. Previously people adhere to their occupations but as time progress there is a change in occupations. Parents eagerness to give good education to their children, and for better earnings etc. they migrat from rural to urban areas. In the recent time migration from villages to cities has become a common phenomenon. There are several factors which contribute in the migration of people from rural areas to urban, i.e. low yielding in the agriculture, lack of employment opportunities etc.

The investigations shows that the elderly are suffering from the following problems

Economical

A growing and difficult problem of the elderly is their financial problems. The economic status of elderly is linked with the overall economic status of its general population. Melvin W. Reder see R.R Singh (1995) highlight the economic problems of the aged his study. Economic security during the working years provides an opportunity for its continuation in to later year's through appropriate investments. An older person experience difficulties in regard to raising material resources for day-to-day existence. Inversely debts, absence of regular steady income, absence of primary necessity of life are some of the frequently experienced problems by the older people. Elderly people in the rural areas are the worst sufferers. As in the era of urbanization the economic security has greatly increased. The absence of saving and social security compels most of the elders to continue their work status as long as they can. The situation is truism for those whose main income is either agriculture-oriented or employed in the unorganized sector. The elders who have no savings, pension benefits have to depend on their sons, daughters or near relatives for their livelihood. The situation is worse for women whose primary role is within the household. The NSSO survey (1985-87) has said that this economic problem more acute when the prices of essential commodities rise and the public distribution system does not function effectively. In general the rural areas having less economical viability if compared with the urban areas. Low income leads to several problems.

Health

As a person gets older along with his age some ninor health problems follow due to negligence and lack of care such as defensive eye sight, general weakness, pain in joints, cough and cold, defective hearing, blood pressure, digestive complaints, breathing trouble, trembling of limbs etc., chronic diseases, accidents, non-adoption of preventive measures and lack of health insurance scheme for the aged. The urban elderly for some extent are better than the rural because in rural areas there is no proper medical facility and they cannot go a long distance for treatment.

Psychological and emotional aspects

Personality changes appear when a person gets older. With the advancement of age, apart from the likely impairment in the physical aspects of human body, there are also many adverse effect on the psychological and emotional status of the person. It does not always correspond to physical changes. The problem may become worse, if the aged are physically, economically dependent. These affect adversely their psychological make-up and attitude towards life. The psychological age is characterized generally by a decline in the mental ability of an elderly. Individual worthy attitudes and behavior plays significant roles in the process of psychological ageing. There is no age at which one loses his ability. This situation has to be observed by the children and try to give proper care to the elder parents.

The feeling of isolation and withdrawal

Another major problem which is being faced by the rural elderly is isolation and withdrawl. Very often elderly persons create isolation for themselves by distracting people time and again with tales of their achievements in the past. Sometimes younger people avoid the elders because of this boredom. Although replaying their past gives comfort and consolation to the aged. He may think he knows all, but in reality the younger generation far more knowledgeable and able to contribute much more to the society than expected of them. Because of his personal inadequacy, mannerism, hearing defects, style of living, generation gap, paucity of accommodation with this children and absence of wife, family or peer group, an aged may feel isolated which is social in itself, a great social and emotional handicap for an elderly person. On the other hand, an elderly may feel withdrawn. This may also be interpreted as a non-interfering typed and hence of acceptable behavior.

Diminish the social status and erosion of role

Respect for the aged is the basic characteristic of the Indian family system *honor thy father and thy mother* express the veneration of the elders in our scriptures and literature. The system of ancestor's worship that dominated Indian social life for centuries and even now, continues to dominate and gives Indians a philosophy to care and honor their old parents. (Nasreen, 2009). Social scientists report about the social status of older Indians, that there is a general lowering of social status of elderly in India. Increasingly, older people may be perceived as burdens due to their disability or dependence. Rapid changes in the family system, even in rural areas, are reducing the availability of kin support. With modernization of the country, older values are being replaced by 'individualism'. The family's capacity to provide quality care to older people is decreasing. The government had been complacent that the joint family system and traditional values would provide the social security cover in old age. This view is being drastically revised. In non-agrarian societies older persons who are 'economically unproductive' do not have the same authority and prestige that they used to enjoy in extended families where they had greater control over family resources. The unconditional respect, power and authority that older people used to enjoy in rural extended. The traditional families being gradually eroded in India in recent years. The erosion of the authority of the aged in the family decision making, isolation from children or coupled with abundance of leisure time without much work creates problems for the elderly. Thus retirement may be seen as period of emptiness, in activity loneliness and despair. The retirement period decrease the confidence because of the cut off from the participation of the most important interests and activities of the society. Children also do not involve the elderly in the decision-making process, this make the elderly to feel more despair and unhappy.

Dependency and loneliness

Many of the studies on the elderly highlights that majority of the elderly have been suffering from loneliness and are depending on others to serve their needs. He may not be able to undertake the task which he had easily done during his younger days. This creates a feeling of inadequacy which he may try to meet through a variety of mechanism. Some times when he is ill he has to depend upon others and he may have the feeling of unwanted not being consulted by his sons or daughters. When the children are staying away, their dependency will be more on others. For each and every need they have to depend on others. This leads them to insecurity feeling and makes them suffer as they have no body to serve them. This pushes them in to psychological problems. Psychologically elders feel very unhappy and despair. Another crucial factor which being faced by the elderly is loneliness. Loneliness is lack of social contacts or interaction with the outside world. One of the problems from which the aged is suffers is isolation and loneliness. They give up their job and retire. Accordingly their communications are gradually cut-off from their colleagues. For want of energy, money and means of transport, visits to their friends and relations may become infrequent. If the aged are quarrelsome or off the interfering type, they have constraints in dealing with their son's family. The isolation become worst if the aged loses his/her spouse.

Conclusion

India, with its predominantly agrarian based economy, joint family system has given adequate care, affection, and love for its elder people. They were treated as asset and got all sort of services and they were peaceful at their end of the life. In the modern times, the social matrix has however not remained what it used to be. Moreover several notable changes are observed in joint family system. The joint family system is replaced by the nuclear family; women accepting paid work outside the household, urbanization, commercialization, modernization, industrialization have influenced, modified or even altered many social values and traditions particularly relating to older person. Even technological changes have adversely affected the elder persons. To illustrate, they were earlier the storehouse of anecdote and stories for grand children before TV, video games and comics usurped this role from them. Sodan (1975) points outs that in old-age people in particular have role less role. From the individual part Providing necessary care and support to elder people within the family and the community setting is recommended, instead of putting them in the old-age home or leaving them as a destitute at outside. A small amount of affection gives them great boost and enable them to lead a peaceful life at their last days. The urbanization has much impact on the rural elderly as they are deserted by their young generations and there is no proper care. Often the children must visit their parents and give proper affection and there is a need to intervene the family members for taking care of the elderly.

References

1. Anu Priya Mallik (2009), "The Twist Light Years", *Asian News*, August 28, September 3.
2. Aparajita Chattopadhyay (2004), "Population Policy for the Aged in India", *Economic and Political Weekly*, October 23.
3. Bali Arun P. (1999), *Understanding the Graying People of India* (Ed.), Inter India Publication, New Delhi.
4. Benarjee Tapan (2002), *Senior Citizens of India–Issues and Challenges*, Rajat Publications, New Delhi.
5. Bose Ashish, Malakapoor Shankardass (2004), *Growing Old in India; Voices Reveal, Statistics Speak*, B.R. Publishing Corporation, New Delhi.
6. Chakraborti Rajagopala Dhar (2004), *The Greying of India: Population Ageing in the Context of Asia*, Sage Publications, New Delhi.
7. Debbie Plath (2009), "International Policy Perspectives on Independence in Old Age", *Journal of Aging & Social Policy*, Vol. 21, No. 2, April, pp. 209-223.
8. Denise, Eldemire-Shearer (1999), "Challenge Family Life, Coping Strategies and Seniors", In Randel, Judith and Germa, Tony (ed.) *The Aging and Development Report*, Help Age international, Earthscan.
9. Dewi Rees, W. (1974), Senior Citizens and Their Problems, *The British Medical Journal*, Vol. 2, No. 5916, May 25, p. 452.
10. Dharmalingam A. (1994), "Old Age Support: Expectations and Experiences in a South Indian Village" *Population Studies*, Vol. 48, No. 1, March, pp. 5-19.
11. Ellen Winston (1947), "Social Problems of the Aged," *Source: Social Forces*, Vol. 26, No. 1, October, pp. 57-61.
12. Gary Nelson (1980), "Contrasting Services to the Aged", *The Social Service Review*, Vol. 54, No. 3, September, pp. 376-389.
13. Guhan S. (1993), "Ageing in Kerala", *Economic and Political Weekly*, Vol. 28, No. 35, August 28, p. 1802.
14. Hussain M.G. (1997), "Changing Indian Society and Status of Aged" (ed), Manak Publications Pvt Ltd., New Delhi.
15. Jayakumar B., (2004), "Ageism in Kerala: Protecting Old Age", *Kerala Calling*, August 2004.

16. Jayant V. Deshpande, Subhash C. Kochar, Harshinder Singh (1986), *Aspects of Positive Ageing, Applied Probability,* Vol. 23, No. 3, September, pp. 748-758.

17. Joseph James (1991), *Aged in India: Problems and Personalities,* Chugh Publications, New Delhi.

18. Ken Tout (1989), *Ageing in Developing Countries,* Oxford University Press for Help Age International, p. 334.

19. Kumudini Dandekar (1993), "The Aged: their Problems and Social Intervention in Maharashtra, *Economic and Political Weekly,* Vol. 28, No. 23, June 5, pp. 1188-1194.

20. Leela Gulati and S. Irudaya Rajan (1999), "The Added Years", *Elderly in India and Kerala,* Economic and Political Weekly, October 30.

21. Maithreyi Krishna Raj (1999), "Ageing Women in a Welfare State, Cracks in the Utopia, *Economic and Political Weekly,* October 30.

22. Mark Gorman (1995), *Older People and Development: Development in Practice,* Vol. 5, No. 2, May, pp. 117-127.

23. Mead T. Cain (1991), "The Activities of the Elderly in Rural Bangladesh", *Population Studies,* Vol. 45, No. 2, July, pp. 189-202.

24. Meena Gopal (2006), "Gender, Ageing and Social Security", *Economic and Political Weekly,* October 21.

25. Moneer Alam (2004), "Ageing, Old Age Income Security and Reforms: An Exploration of Indian Situation", *Economic and Political Weekly,* August 14.

26. Nasreen Asiya (2009), *Urban Elderly Coping Strategies and Societal Responses,* Concept Publishing Company, New Delhi.

27. Penny Vera-Sanso (2006), "Experiences in Old Age: A South Indian Example of How Functional Age is Socially Structured", *Oxford Development Studies,* Vol. 34, No. 4, December, pp. 457-472.

28. Phoon, W.O.; S. B. Tan; C. Y. Tye (1983), "A Study of Residents of Five Old People's Homes in Singapore, *Journal of Public Health,* Vol. 5, No. 1, February, pp. 38-49.

29. Pravin Visari (2001), "Demographics of Ageing in India", *Economic and Political Weekly,* June 2.

30. Saxena. D.P. (2006), *Sociology of Changing,* Concept Publishing Company, New Delhi.

31. Shah A.M. (1999), "Changes in the Family and the Elderly", *Economic and Political Weekly,* Vol. 34, No. 20, May 15-21, pp. 1179-1182.

32. Sharon R. Kaufman (1994), "Old Age, Disease, and the Discourse on Risk: Geriatric Assessment in U.S. Health Care", *Medical Anthropology Quarterly,* New Series, Vol. 8, No. 4 (Dec., 1994), pp. 430-447.

33. Shewanti N. Kashyap, P. (2008), "Health Status of Inmates of Old Age Homes of Uttarakhand, India", *Journal of Ddirying Foods & Home Sciences,* Vol. 27, No. 1, March.

34. Srinivas M. N. (1993), Changing Values in India, *Economic and Political Weekly,* Vol. 28, No. 19 (May 8, pp. 933-938.

35. Steven M. Albert; Moneer Alam; Mohammed Nizamuddin (2005), "Comparative Study of Functional Limitation and Disability in Old Age: Delhi and New York City", *Journal of Cross-Cultural Gerontology,* Vol. 20, No: 3, September, pp. 231-241.

36. United Nations Symposium (1988), "Economic and Social Implications of Population of Ageing", Proceedings of the International Symposium on Population and Development, United Nations, New York.

37. Vijay Kumar S. (1991), *Family Life and Socio-Economic Problems of the Aged,* Ashish Publishing House, New Delhi.

38. Vijay Kumar S. (1995), *Challenges before the Elderly an Indian Scenario* (ed.) MD Publications, New Delhi.

39. Vijay Kumar S. (1999), *Aging in India: A Report,* of Council for Social Development, Hyderabad.

40. Visweswara Rao K. (2007), *Aging in Rural India,* Associated Publishers, Ambala Cantt.

41. Warren A. Peterson and Jill Quadagno (1985), *Social Bonds in Later Life,* Sage Publications, London, New Delhi

42. Wm. Neal Phelps (1957), Our Senior Citizens, *Journal of Educational Sociology,* Vol. 31, No. 2, Guidance in Operation: The Southern Illinois University Program, November, p. 117.

Millennium Development Goals

Strategy to Handle Urbanization

Ms. A. Mary Princess Lavanya

Introduction

Urbanization can be handled by using different strategies, specially implementing the Millennium Development Goals. MDGs are eight international development goals that all 192 United Nations member states and at least 23 international organizations have agreed to achieve by the year 2015. They include eradicating extreme poverty, reducing child mortality rates, fighting disease epidemics such as AIDS, and developing a global partnership for development. The aim of the Millennium Development Goals is to encourage development by improving social and economic conditions in the world's poorest countries.

Causes of Urbanization

- Urbanization is not always attributed to high density. In Chennai, the cost of living has forced residents to live in low quality slums.
- Urbanization occurs naturally from individual and corporate efforts to reduce time and expense in commuting and transportation while improving opportunities for jobs, education, housing, and transportation. Living in cities permits individuals and families to take advantage of the opportunities of proximity, diversity, and marketplace competition.
- People move into cities to seek economic opportunities. A major contributing factor is known as "rural flight". In rural areas, often on small family farms, it is difficult to improve one's standard of living beyond basic sustenance. Farm living is dependent on unpredictable environmental conditions, and in times of drought, flood or pestilence,

survival becomes extremely problematic. In modern times, industrialization of agriculture has negatively affected the economy of small and middle-sized farms and strongly reduced the size of the rural labour market.

- Cities, in contrast, are known to be places where money, services and wealth are centralized. Cities are where fortunes are made and where social mobility is possible. Businesses, which generate jobs and capital, are usually located in urban areas.
- There are better basic services as well as other specialist services that aren't found in rural areas. There are more job opportunities and a greater variety of jobs. Health is another major factor. People, especially the elderly are often forced to move to cities where there are doctors and hospitals that can cater to their health needs.
- Other factors include a greater variety of entertainment (restaurants, movie theaters, theme parks, etc) and a better quality of education, namely universities. Due to their high populations, urban areas can also have much more diverse social communities allowing others to find people like them when they might not be able to in rural areas.

Effects on Economic Aspect

In recent years, urbanization of rural areas has increased. As agriculture, more traditional local services, and small-scale industry give way to modern industry the urban and related commerce with the city drawing on the resources of an ever-widening area for its own sustenance and goods to be traded or processed into manufactures. Larger cities provide more specialized goods and services to the local market and surrounding areas, function as a transportation and wholesale hub for smaller places, and accumulate more capital, financial service provision, and an educated labor force, as well as often concentrating administrative functions for the area in which they lie. This relation among places of different sizes is called the "urban hierarchy". Urbanization is often viewed as a negative trend, but can in fact, be perceived simply as a natural occurrence from individual and corporate efforts to reduce expense in commuting and transportation while improving opportunities for jobs, education, housing, and transportation.

Changing Forms

- Different forms of urbanization can be classified depending on the style of architecture and planning methods as well as historic growth of areas.
- In cities of the developed world urbanization traditionally exhibited a concentration of human activities and settlements around the downtown area, the so-called in-migration. In-migration refers to migration from former colonies and similar places. The fact that many immigrants settle in impoverished city centers led to the notion of the "peripheralization

of the core", which simply describes that people who used to be at the periphery of the former empires now live right in the centre.

- Recent developments, such as inner-city redevelopment schemes, mean that new arrivals in cities no longer necessarily settle in the centre.
- When the residential area shifts outward, this is called suburbanization. A number of researchers and writers suggest that suburbanization has gone so far to form new points of concentration outside the downtown both in developed and developing countries such as India.
- Rural migrants are attracted by the possibilities that cities can offer, but often settle in shanty towns and experience extreme poverty.

Challenges of Urbanization

Meeting the needs of India's soaring urban populations is and will therefore continue to be a strategic policy matter. Critical issues that need to be addressed are: poor local governance, weak finances, inappropriate planning that leads to high costs of housing and office space; in some Indian cities these costs are among the highest in the world, critical infrastructure shortages and major service deficiencies that include erratic water and power supply, and woefully inadequate transportation systems, rapidly deteriorating environment, Extreme poverty, child mortality rates and the prevalence of HIV, TB, malaria, poor sanitation. These challenges in a broad spectrum are due to poor, planning, housing, service delivery, infrastructure and environment neglect.

Planning

- Many urban governments lack a modern planning framework.
- The multiplicity of local bodies obstructs efficient planning and land use.
- Rigid master plans and restrictive zoning regulations limit the land available for building, constricting cities' abilities to grow in accordance with changing needs.

Housing

- Building regulations that limit urban density, such as floor space indexes, reduce the number of houses available, thereby pushing up property prices.
- Outdated rent control regulations reduce the number of houses available on rent—a critical option for the poor.
- Poor access to microfinance and mortgage finance limit the ability of low income groups to buy or improve their homes.
- Policy, planning, and regulation deficiencies lead to a proliferation of slums.

- Weak finances of urban local bodies and service providers leave them unable to expand the trunk infrastructure that housing developers need to develop new sites.

Service delivery

- Most services are delivered by city governments with unclear lines of accountability.
- There is a strong bias towards adding physical infrastructure rather than providing financially and environmentally sustainable services.
- Service providers are unable to recover operations and maintenance costs and depend on the government for finance.
- Independent regulatory authorities that set tariffs, decide on subsidies, and enforce service quality are generally absent.

Infrastructure

- Most urban bodies do not generate revenues needed to renew infrastructure, nor do they have the creditworthiness to access capital markets for funds.
- Urban transport planning needs to be more holistic. There is a focus on moving vehicles rather than meeting the needs of the large numbers of people who walk or ride bicycles in India's towns and cities.

Environment

- The deteriorating urban environment is taking a toll on people's health and productivity and diminishing their quality of life.

MDGs as a Strategy

The MDGs focus on three major areas of human development (humanity)— bolstering human capital, improving infrastructure, and increasing social, economic and political rights, with the majority of the focus going towards increasing basic standards of living. The objectives chosen within the human capital focus include improving nutrition, health care (including reducing levels of child mortality, HIV/AIDS, tuberculosis and malaria, and increasing reproductive health), and education. For the infrastructure focus, the objectives include improving infrastructure through increasing access to safe drinking water, energy and modern information/ communication technology; amplifying farm outputs through sustainable practices; improving transportation infrastructure; and preserving the environment. Lastly, for the social, economic and political rights focus, the objectives include empowering women, reducing violence, increasing political voice, ensuring equal access to public services, and increasing security of property rights. The goals chosen were intended to increase an individual's human capabilities and "advance the means to a productive life".

The MDGs emphasize that individual policies needed to achieve these goals should be tailored to individual country's needs; therefore most policy suggestions are general. The MDGs also emphasize the role of developed countries in aiding developing countries, as outlined in Goal Eight. Goal Eight sets objectives and targets for developed countries to achieve a "global partnership for development" by supporting fair trade, debt relief for developing nations, increasing aid and access to affordable essential medicines, and encouraging technology transfer. Thus developing nations are not seen as left to achieve the MDGs on their own, but as a partner in the developing-developed compact to reduce world poverty.

The Millennium Development Goals (MDGs) were developed out of the eight chapters of the United Nations Millennium Declaration, signed in September 2000. There are eight goals with 21 targets, and a series of measurable indicators for each target. They are— eradicating extreme poverty and hunge; achieving decent employment for women, men, and young people; increasing the proportion of family-based workers in employed population, reducing the proportion of people who suffer from hunger; achieve universal primary education. By 2015, all children should complete a full course of primary schooling both girls and boys. Promoting gender equality and empowering women, eliminating gender disparity in primary and secondary education preferably by 2005, and at all levels by 2015, also reducing child mortality rate, improving maternal health, by 2015 achieving universal access to reproductive health. Most important aim is to combat HIV/AIDS, malaria, and other diseases. Ensuring environmental sustainability and also reducing the proportion of the population without sustainable access to safe drinking water and basic sanitation by 2015. By 2020, to improve the lives of at least 100 million slum-dwellers, and finally developing a global partnership for development. Thus, if these drastic steps of MDGs are followed the challenges of urbanization can be handled carefully and sustainable development can be sought.

Conclusion

The Millennium Development Goals can enhance the standard of living of the people despite of growing urbanization. The aim of the MDG is to encourage development by improving social and economic conditions in the world's developing countries. In the recent past there has been a tremendous development in the urban areas, which paved way for urbanization. The MDG Declaration asserts that every individual has the right to dignity, freedom, equality, a basic standard of living that includes freedom from hunger and violence, and encourages tolerance and solidarity. But it is disheartening to know that the growing urbanization and the MDGs don't always go hand-in-hand. The above mentioned MDGs are, in fact, fighting the problems caused by urbanization. The problem is that the MDGs has not reached people as a package but a segment of it now and then, which has poor impact on people. Only when people begin to concentrate on MDGs the growing urbanization can be managed effectively. The professionals must find ways to create awareness and impart the right information on different aspects of MDGs so that we can manage the growing urbanization. It's never too late to revamp our educational curriculum to include lessons and training sessions on MDGs a compulsory paper for both the arts and science students at both school and college level. Young people who are the future of our society will be better equipped to make right choice to live a happy life even in the rural areas. Thus, MDGs can be used as a strategy to handle urbanization effectively. Together these challenges can be addressed and thus the fruits of urbanization can be enjoyed by all.

References

1. Bhagat, R.B. (1992), "Components of Urban Growth in India with Reference to Haryana: Findings from Recent Censuses", *Nagarlok*, Vol. 25, No. 3, pp. 10-14.
2. Brockerhoff, M. (1999), "Urban Growth in Developing Countries: A Review of Projections and Predictions", *Population and Development Review*, Vol. 25. No. 4, pp. 757-778.
3. Grant, Ursula (2008), *Opportunity and Exploitation in Urban Labour Markets*, London: Overseas Development Institute.
4. Glaeser, Edward (1998), "Are Cities Dying?" *Journal of Economic Perspectives.*
5. Lovelace, E.H. (1965), "Control of Urban Expansion: The Lincoln, Nebraska Experience", *Journal of the American Institute of Planners.*
6. Mukherji, Shekhar (2001), "Linkage between Migration, Urbanization and Regional Disparities in India: Required Planning Strategies", *IIPS Research Monograph*, Bombay.
7. Nayak, P. R. (1962), "The Challenge of Urban Growth to Indian Local Government" in Turner (ed.) *India's Urban Future*, University of California Press, Berkley.
8. Pathak, P. and Mehta, D. (1995), "Recent Trend in Urbanization and Rural-Urban Migration in India: Some Explanations and Projections", *Urban India*, Vol. 15, No.1.
9. Premi, M. K. (1991), "India's Urban Scene and Its Future Implications", *Demography India.*
10. Sridhar, K. (2007), "Density Gradients and their Determinants: Evidence from India", *Regional Science and Urban Economics.*
11. http://www.un.org/millenniumgoals/poverty.shtml

Challenges of Urban Development

Mr. N. Sagar,
Mr. V. Parameswar

Introduction

Poverty is the main challenge in urban development. The definition of poverty is according to the World Development Report 2000/01 states that poverty is a pronounced deprivation in well-being. The voices of poor people bear eloquent testimony to its meaning. To be poor is to be hungry, to lack shelter and clothing, to be sick and not to be cared for, to be illiterate and not schooled. The report accepts the now traditional view of poverty as encompassing not only material deprivation (measured by an appropriate concept of income or consumption) but also low achievements in education and health. The report also broadens the notion of poverty to include vulnerability and exposure to risk-and-voicelessness and powerlessness. All these forms of deprivation severely restrict what Amartya Sen calls the capabilities that a person has, that is, the substantive freedom he or she enjoys to lead the kind of life he or she values. This broader approach to deprivation, by giving a better characterization of the experience of poverty, increases understanding of its causes. This deeper understanding brings to the fore more areas of action and policy on the poverty reduction agenda in urban development.

Poverty in India

India is still among the poorest nations in the world in per capita terms. Almost 30 per cent of the population still lives below the poverty line of less than US $100 per capita annually. The poverty alleviation in India leaves a lot to be desired. As Kothari (1993, p.p. 147) aptly puts across, "Laws have been enacted but rarely implanted. Policies have remained on paper, as collection of pious intentions without workable action plans. Few programs that have been implemented have rarely reached the intended beneficiaries, especially in the manner required. Reservations, representations and various fiscal benefits have either been fraudulently diverted to ineligible individuals or have been restricted to very narrow elites of the economically weaker and minority communities."

Model of Poverty—Causes and Manifestation

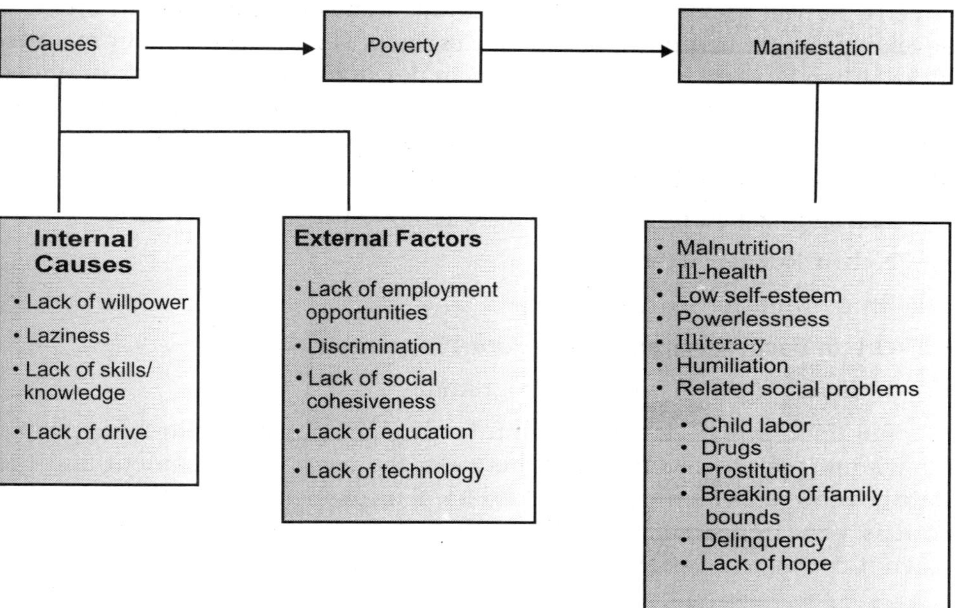

Overview of Poverty

It is interesting to note that the ratio of urban poverty in some of the larger states is higher than that of rural poverty leading to the phenomenon of 'Urbanisation of Poverty'. Urban poverty poses the problems of housing and shelter, water, sanitation, health, education, social security and livelihoods along with special needs of vulnerable groups like women, children and aged people. Poor people live in slums which are overcrowded, often polluted and lack basic civic amenities like clean drinking water, sanitation and health facilities. Most of them are involved in informal sector activities where there is constant threat of eviction, removal, confiscation of goods and almost non-existent social security cover. With growing poverty and slums, Indian cities have been grappling with the challenges of making the cities sustainable, i.e., inclusive, productive, efficient and manageable. The sustainability of urban development in India is seen in the context of shelter and slums, basic urban services, financing urban development and governance and planning.

India has entered the Eleventh Plan period with an impressive record of economic growth. However, the incidence of decline of urban poverty has not accelerated with GDP growth. In fact, urban poverty will become a major challenge for policy-makers in our country as the urban population in the country is growing, so is urban poverty. Therefore, a need has arisen to develop new poverty reduction tools and approaches to attack the multi-dimensional issues of urban poverty. For this, policy-makers at the national and local levels should have a good understanding of the nature of urban poverty as well as accurate data on various issues relating to it, in order to develop programme/policies to manage urban poverty in a systematic manner. India Urban Poverty Report using human development framework provides a good insight on various issues of urban poverty such as basic services to urban poor, migration, urban economy and livelihoods, microfinance for urban poor, education and health, unorganized sector and livelihoods.

The steps taken by government to remove urban poverty are:

- Nehru Rozgar Yojana.
- Prime Minister Rozgar Yojana.
- Urban Basic Services for the Poor Programme.
- National Social Assistance Programme.

But these processes can be helpful only if the policies go to those people for whom it is meant. The clash between the central government and the state governments often results in the lack of implementation of these policies. So it is very important that the governments do not play power politics when it comes to a serious issue such as poverty.

Conclusions

We want to prevent poverty in urban areas by elevation programs in urban areas by following systematic development by stopping political interference in developing programs and following systematic town development by following building byelaws of local governments.

Provide basic requirements like drinking water supply, sanitation, solid waste management, road networks, electricity and banking facility, etc. in slum areas.

By giving nutritious food to poor children to reduce health problems.

Providing employment to the people in urban areas also help to prevent poverty.

References

1. E.J. Anzorena, (1994), *Housing the Poor: The Asian Experience*, Philippines: The Asian Coalition of Housing Rights.
2. *Economist* (1999), August 14 "Helping the World's Poorest", pp. 17-20.
3. Galhardi, Regina, M.A.A. (1995), *Biotechnology for Poverty Alleviation in Third World.*
4. J.Bhagwati, (2001), "Growth, Poverty and Reforms", *Economic and Political Weekly*, March 10.
5. J.C. Glenn, and T.J. Gordon (2000), *State of the Future at the Millennium*, American Council for the United Nations University, Washington.

Urban Development and Urban Ills

Mr. T. M. Prasad

Introduction

"This whole collection of cattle-sheds for human beings was surround on two sides by houses and a factory, an on third by the river, and besides the narrow stair up the bank, a narrow doorway alone led out into almost equally ill-built, ill-kept labyrinth of dwellings.... on re-reading my description, Iam forced to admit that instead of being exaggerated, it is far from black enough to convey a true impression of the filth, ruin, and uninhabitableness, the defiance of all considerations of cleanliness, ventilation, and health which characterize the construction of this single district, containing at least twenty to thirty thousand inhabitants. And such a district exists in the heart of the second city of England, the first manufacturing city of the world" **Engels**, 1845.

"Homeless people are living in cardboard boxes next to gleaming skyscrapers occupied by corporations whose budgets exceed those of many developing countries" **UNCHS**, 2001.

Urbanization has come to be viewed as a reflection of overall socio-economic development, and its attainment is considered crucial to the overall strategy of progress. Upward income mobility involving lavational, occupational and industrial shifts of individuals and their incomes, along with progressively better economic opportunities, is one of the most important features of economic growth (Kuznets, 1966). And it is the urban economy which provides opportunities for raising productivity by generating employment in the high productivity industrial sector, and contributes towards eradicating abject poverty in the developing countries. To put it slightly differently, with increasing incomes demand and production shift in favour of commodities which have declining ratios of land use to that of other inputs, in particular labour. This leads to an increase in population density, and hence urbanisation. Urbanisation, therefore, like industrialization is a concomitan of economic development. A country's overall development strategy or policies connected with the implementation of sectoral objectives are almost certain to have an impact on urbanisation. As Krugman (1994) argues... "whatever changes are made in economic policies, their implementations for urban and regional development within countries are an important, neglected issue."

The urbanisation process in the Third World has been approached through four major alternative perspectives (McGee, 1982). The *first* one is the 'world political economy approach' in which urbanisation and urban centres of the Third World countries are taken as an important manifestation of the role that the national systems play in the international economic system. The contributions from the perspectives of demographers, geographers and anthropologists constitute the *second* major approach to this issue. Of the remaining two one is derived from the body of development theory with its growing concern about the persistent poverty in general and urban poverty in particular and the other is related to the concept of the 'informal sector'. Our analysis in the present volume corresponds mainly to the latter two approaches.

Urban theory is useful in looking at the differences in culture and values between the Middleeast and the United States because cities develop according to those factors (Drennan). Cities have been built-up over many hundreds of years, and each successive wave of invaders or settlers has added its own character to the city. The urban is composed of successive layers of new features superimposed on what has survived from previous cycles of development. The urban landscape expresses the social and economic development of society, and by constraining what alterations can be made, shapes future social and economic organization. The evolving global economy has an impact on urban areas. Their economies are restructuring, and some evolve successfully while others do not.

Urban rioting was highly publicized and fundamentally unsettling to the nation's social fabric (Olzak, Shanahan, and McEneaney,,1996). Examination of the content of media accounts during this period brings this to bear. The dominant media frame was with respect to the notion of "urban crisis", which captures both expansive and debilitating social ills, as well as physical deterioration. During the 1960s, crisis coverage etched the spatial relationship of urban problems—such as poverty, crime, failing buildings, and racial troubles—into the public consciousness. The *New York Times* Index doubled its coverage over the five-year period between 1964 and 1968. Evolving mass opinion reflected these concerns, undergoing a six-fold increase over the same period and capturing just under one-quarter of the public agenda space in 1968. Public interest in urban affairs peaked in 1968 then continued its descent through to the late 1980s. Systemic interest plummeted from the mid-1970s through early 1990s.

The conflicts between the objectives of growth and employment in the organised industry have been reinforced in the Third World countries in general, and India in particular (Edgren, 1989). The reasons usually cited include— the emphasis on the heavy industry and the adoption of capital intensive techniques of production—the presumed superiority of capital intensive methods being based on the idea that they would generate bigger investible surpluses than labour intensive methods. The unionisation of labour that the organised industry faces and the subsidisation of capital are other features which have influenced the choice of capital intensive techniques. Subsequently the growth in value added of the organised manufacturing has not been accompanied by concomitant growth in labour absorption. Despite slowing down of the growth rates of labour force in a number of Asian countries including the Indian subcontinent, growth in demand for labour is too sluggish to eliminate unemployment (ILO-ARTEP, 1990). The surplus labour has, therefore, spilled over into the sector which has been loosely termed as the urban 'informal sector' (Todaro, 1969).

In the face of limited demand for labour in the high productivity sector rapid population movement, as the 'over-urbanisation thesis' would suggest, from rural areas due mainly to 'push' factors aggravates the 'employment problem' in the urban areas. Deficiency of reproducible tangible capital (relative to labour) in the face of a low land-man ratio is taken to. Cause a sizeable volume of unemployment and under-employment ultimately being manifested in the form of immigration to cities. Rural-to-urban movement of labour without concomitant growth of demand for labour originating from the organised segment of the industrial sector increases the urban labour supplies. The result is a residual absorption of labour in low productivity activities, unemployment and growing poverty in the urban areas. In this process of labour transfer the urbanisation rate gets inflated while the proportion of labour engaged in high productivity secondary sector stagnates or dwindles and even when it increases, it continues to remain at a low level relative to the historical experience of the present day developed countries. Thus, urban poverty and rural poverty co-exist and in such a situation city growth ceases to be dynamic, that is conducive to economic development. The low rate of growth of industrial employment and the high rate of rural-to-urban migration make for excessive and even explosive urbanisation involving a transition from rural under-employment to excessive urban unemployment and under-employment, a visible proliferation of poverty and vast stretches of slums in cities. The major concern of the planners has, therefore, been to evolve policy mechanisms that help control city sizes and restrict immigration to cities.

Other recurrent concerns of town and country planning policies in many developing countries are the decentralisation of industrial development and attainment of a balanced pattern of urban settlements. Given high levels of under-employment and unemployment in large parts of India and regional inequality employment generation through industrial dispersal is considered to be essential. Industrial location policies in India which aim at spreading industrial activities across space can be summarised under the following heads:

(a) Policies encouraging small-scale enterprises.

(b) Industrial estates programme.

(c) Rural industries project programme.

(d) Metropolitan planning in the major states.

(f) Incentives to promote industrial development in backward areas.

Mohan (1993) provides a comprehensive review of the studies which attempted an evaluation of location policies and their effectiveness particularly in South Korea (Lee, 1985; Lee et al., 1987; and Murray, 1988). In order to make location policy effective these studies suggest that:

(i) the input which is used extensively by the firm and is a poor substitute for other inputs is to be subsidised by the government.

(ii) if government has to make infrastructure investment then the public input for which the firm is otherwise more willing to pay high prices and which is a good substitute for other inputs needs to be subsidized.

However, the impact of specific industrial location or regional policies on the actual location of industry has been quite limited not only in India but in various countries in the world (Mohan, 1993).

An important fact which is often forgotten is that urbanization may also influence aggregate growth. Although computable general equilibrium models tried in the context of urbanization address themselves to quite a few complex problems, and aim at harnessing the empirical associations between economic development, structural change and urban dynamics, the impact of urbanization on economic growth is not discussed very extensively therein. However, the literature on city scale economies considered this aspect. Some industries are said to induce concentration of economic activity as they exhibit high economies of scale in operation, and some others benefit from concentration because of the operation of agglomeration economies. From concentration of activities a new firm not only benefits in terms of forward and backward linkages, but the existence of the complementary services also reduces his cost of operation. The effective price of infrastructure services like power, water supply, roads etc. is reduced if there is concentration of users of these services. Government action, however, has mostly failed to recognise the merits of concentration, and this has often led to suboptimal utilisation of resources. As Mills and Becker (1986) argued, "...misguided attempts to reduce the sizes or growth rates of large cities can do great harm. The greatest danger is that desperately needed industrial production will be made unviable or will be unable to grow to its full potential because it is forced or induced to locate in the wrong place by misguided government decisions. Government programmes to alter city sizes should be studied with the greatest care as to their desirability, various means of achieving their goal, and the benefits and costs of doing so."

Reconceiving National Urban Policy

Since the late 1960s, public policy theory has developed tremendously. Yet, if one was to take a look at the bookshelf of any given policy scholar, he or she might find just a smattering of works on the process of federal urban policymaking. In Harold Wolman's (1999) quick and dirty survey of the contents of nearly a dozen public policy textbooks, he found many a chapter devoted to national urban policy processes. Calling attention to this informal survey is not to suggest that political scientists have ignored federal urban policy outright. It is to suggest that the majority of scholarship on the subject relies too heavily on electoral and partisan explanations to the detriment of a more nuanced understanding of changes to the urban policy process. I briefly outline this prevailing narrative of the rapid rise and decline of urban affairs on the federal policy agenda. I then make the case for a more encompassing conceptualization of urban policies to help explain historical ebbs and flows in federal policymaking that targets urban problems.

The present study makes an attempt in this direction, in addressing itself to some of the issues concerning urban development in developing countries in general and India in particular. (*Urban Development and Urban Ills*–Edwin S. Mills, Arup Mitra).

Objectives of the Study

- To improve the growing urban development programmes.
- To examine the socio-economic background of urban people.
- To understand the factors lead to the making of the urban ills.
- To know the background characteristics with which urban development professionals have centered urban ills.
- To understand the migration in the process of growing urbanization.
- To develop the sanitation, drainage systems, solid wasteges, living conditions in slums and urban poverty.
- To improve the access to health and education services.

Cause and Effect

- Slums symbolise urban poverty. For the families living in them, they create hazardous and unsafe conditions that compound the poverty which forced them to set up home there in the first place.

- With lack of freely available safe clean water in the cities, families living in slums have often no choice but to buy it at high cost from vendors.
- With inadequate sanitation, waste disposal or drainage facilities, open sewers are created by rubbish and human defecation.
- Alongside walkways between the densely packed shelters–disease thrives and people, especially children become ill.
- In these conditions simply being ill can have severe implications. It can mean loss of livelihood, leaving families struggling to buy food or water let alone medicines.
- With weak ownership rights to the land, residents are vulnerable and cannot build safe, sturdy homes, so they become easy victims of weather conditions, fire and crime.
- With no voice to change policy decisions or demand essential services, slum dwellers face an enormous challenge in such uncertain and unfair circumstances.
- In this environment, with no land, traditional coping mechanisms like relying on extended family or small-holder farming falter. The result is that people's homes and neighborhoods become both a cause and an effect of poverty and something that can be extremely difficult to break out of recognition of this growing problem culminated in 2000 when the world's richest governments pledged through the Millennium Development Goals to improve the lives of 100 million slum dwellers by 2020.

Urban Poverty Facts

- Cities in the developing world will absorb 95 per cent of the world's expected population growth between 2000 and 2030.
- According to recent estimates there are now over 900 million people who can be classified as slum dwellers.
- Based on 2001 estimates, 43 per cent of the urban population in the developing world lives in slums. In the least developed countries, this percentage rises to more than 78 per cent.
- If present trends continue, 1.5 billion people out of 3.3 billion urban residents will live in sums by the year 2020.

Urban Community Development

Need of Community Development Programmes

Dr. K. Suneetha, Mr. V. Yellappa,
Mr. G. Raveendra

Introduction

India's urban population is second largest in the world after china. Barring China, America and Russia in numerical terms India's urban population is higher than the total urban population of all countries of the world. The U.N. has stated that we are living in the urban century. By 2030 more than 70 per cent of the world will be urbanized. As per 2001 census the slum population of India was 42.6 million which constitute 15.0 of the total urban population of the country. The Planning Commission of India estimated that the slum population will be increased to 93 million by 2011. Increasing levels of urbanization are caused by natural growth of the urban population and migration of the rural population towards cities. Over the past half century a great rural-to-urban population shift has occurred and the process of urbanization is set to continue well into the 21st century. There is a strong positive link between national levels of human development and urbanization levels. However the implications of rapid urban growth include increasing unemployment, environmental degradation, lack of urban services, overburdening of existing infrastructure and lack of access to land, finance and inadequate shelter.

Characteristics

The trend of urbanization in India is going rapidly. The urban population is characterized by lack of housing, shanty towns, pavement dwellers, lack of water and sanitation, filth and squalor housing and roads, low-income and poverty, delinquency and crime, illiteracy, neglect of children and women malnutrition, ill-health and gastro-intestinal and respiratory diseases etc.

According to William J. Cussion, the basic needs of urban/slum people are shelter improvement, environmental sanitation, pure water, health care and nutrition, education and proper recreation. The urban community development was thought of as a field and the process has been undertaken as slum improvement programmes, which touches the periphery of urban problems.

According to Oxford Dictionary of Geography "Slum is an area of poor housing, often characterized by multi-occupation and overcrowding. Schools are poor, items sold in local shops are relatively expensive and sanitation inadequate. Slum population often exhibits high concentration of drug abusers, alcoholics, criminals and vandals." The characteristics and problems associated with slum vary from place to place. Slums are usually characterized by urban decay, high rates of poverty, illiteracy and unemployment. They are commonly seen as breeding grounds for social problems such as crime, drug addiction, high rates of mental illness and suicide. In many poor countries they exhibit high rates of disease due to unsanitary conditions, malnutrition and lack of business activity such as leather work, cottage industries etc. Rural depopulation with thousands arriving daily into the cities makes slum clearance an uphill struggle. In many slums, especially in poor countries, many live in very narrow alleys that do not allow vehicles (like ambulance and fire fighting trucks) to pass. The lack of services such as routine garbage collection allows rubbish to accumulate in huge quantities. Additionally, informal settlements often face the brunt of natural and man-made disasters, such as landslides, as well as earthquakes and tropical storms.

Many slum dwellers employ themselves in the informal economy. This can include street vending, drug dealing, domestic work, and prostitution. In some slums people even recycle trash of different kinds for a living, selling either the odd usable goods or stripping broken goods for part or raw materials. AUNEX expert group has created an operational definition of slum as an area that combines to various extents the following characteristics—inadequate access to safe water; inadequate access to sanitation and other infrastructure; poor structural quality of housing, overcrowding and insecure residential, to status these one might add the low socio-economic status of its residents. The huge population of cities and slums leads to many transport problems like traffic jams, accidents etc. India although has enormous resources of water but it still suffers from urban water supply problem. Urban India also needs 200 million additional water connections, about 30 to 50 per cent households do not have sewerage connections, 250 million people will be in need of sanitation facilities, more than half the residents of Indian slums do not have access to toilets. The sustainability of urban development in India has to be seen in the context of shelter and slums, basic urban services, financing urban development and governance and planning.

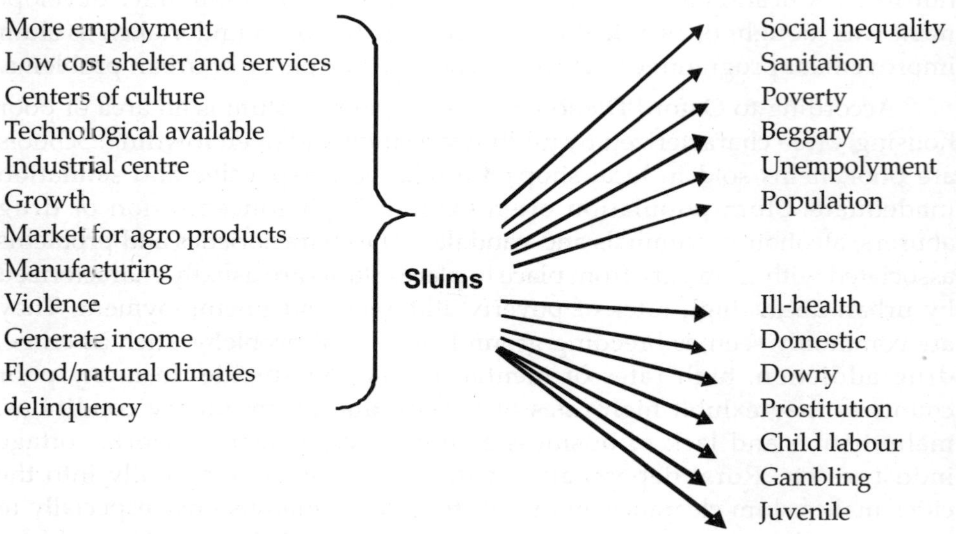

Causes of Slums

With the help of this conceptual framework the researcher want to explain what are the causes which leads to develop more number of slums and consequences of slums, impact on urban life. How these slums leads to unhealthy development of urban center/life. Unemployment and/or poor remuneration for the employed can be one of the main compelling factors to take shelter in slums. Slums often come into existence in the vicinity of the places and organizations providing employment opportunities to the lower strata of the workforce. This saves vital man-hours as well as the transportation cost from the settlement to the place of work. Further these slums develop as cultural centers, place for market goods, low cost manufacturing units with limited technology applications will be done for income generation. In some cases land once owned by people, which was providing them shelter and livelihood, is taken by the government for social and economic activities or for allocation to private enterprises. These residents are neither provided adequate compensation for their lands nor given alternative land which could make resettlement feasible. Hence, they are made landless due to alleged corruption and lack of ethical and moral values (*dharma*) amongst officials and politicians. However, the situation of slums varies from city to city depending upon overall population, employment potential, and the cost of living in the particular city. The unhealthy conditions in the slums will lead to more social problems which lead to social inequality.

Programmes

Urban community development (UCD) programmes were started in 1950s. Urban community development programme envisaged a process of social transformation in urban areas through which the people organized themselves in community. The urban community pilot projects were started in Delhi (1958), Ahmadabad (1962), Baroda (1965) and Calcutta (1966) to create civic consciousness, awareness about internal, external resources, improving living standards of people, and improving democratic institution etc. The programme Urban Basic Services intended for UNICEF aims at networking services of different agencies build the capacity of urban poor through self-help to avail the existing social, civic, and welfare services. Delhi urban community project drew attention of the planners, implementers, social scientists, evaluators and social worker. The institutions of *Vikas Mandal* (local development committee) established and by the community organizer to help the people in utilizing the civic services. The recent UCD programmes such as DWCUA, MEPMA, VAMBAY, AUWSP, SJSRY, NHHP, NSDP, MDM, and ICDS are focusing on development of urban poor.

Shelter-Related Programmes

National housing and habitat policy (1998)

International year of shelter for the homeless by the UN broad objectives of the policy are:

(i) Creation of surpluses in the housing stock with shelter options to the citizens, especially the vulnerable groups including the poor.

(ii) More employment for skilled and unskilled persons in rural and urban areas.

(iii) To empower the Panchayat Raj institutions and cooperative to mobilize resources.

Valmiki-ambedkar awasyojana

Introduced in 2001-02 is to meet a long-standing gap in programmes for slum dwellers, provision of shelter or upgrading of existing shelter of people living below the poverty line in urban slums, 20 per cent of total allocation under VAMBAY will be provided for sanitation and community toilets will be built for the urban poor and slum dwellers who will make a monthly contribution of about Rs. 20 per family, provision of water is also included in the scheme.

National slum development programme

The National Slum Development Programme initiated in 1997 as a scheme of special central assistance to the state government for slum improvement. The monitoring of the programme at the central level requires strengthening.

Nutrition and health-related programmes

The programmes of nutrition have been significantly expanded from the Seventh Five-Year Plan onwards. Special nutrition programmes such as the Mid-Day Meal (MDM) schematics. The interventions envisaged in the Tenth Five-Year Plan are:

(i) Adequate availability of foodstuff.

(ii) Prevention of under nutrition through nutrition education.

(iii) Operationalizing universal screening of all pregnant women, infants, pre-school and school children's for under-nutrition.

(iv) Promotion of appropriate dietary intake and lifestyle.

Employment–Oriented Programmes

Self-employment programme per urban poor (SEPUP)

In 1986 the government of India started the Self-Employment programme for urban poor by earmarking a slum of Rs. 200 crore as credit to be distributed to poor urban entrepreneurs whose income did not exceed Rs. 600 per month. The list of economic activities for which loans are available contains thirty-five items including hawking on hand carts, laundering, welding, cycle rickshaw operations, shoemaking and hairdressing.

Swarnajayanti shahari rozgar yojana (SJSRY)

The special scheme of urban self-employment under the SJSRY extends assistance to the urban poor living below the poverty line, with special attention to women and persons to SCs and STs to set up gainful self-employment ventures. The positive aspects of the SJSRY is that it contains the two basic requirements of any programme of poverty alleviation namely, community involvement and empowerment, and employment generation. The main components of this programme are identification of the non-government organization, self–help and credit activities, training for livelihood, credit and subsidy for economic activities, housing and sanitation, environmental improvement, wage employment etc.

In this context a study has been to carried in Nellore city, the study entitled "Urban Community Development: Need of Community Development Programmes" with few objectives such as:

(i) Perception of slum dwellers regarding social problems.

(ii) To know the respondents knowledge about community development programmes.

(iii) To study the available facilities in the urban slum area.

Hypothesis

(i) Association between level of knowledge and utilization of welfare programmes.

(ii) Perception of slum dwellers and their level of education are associated.

Study Area

Nellore district comprises three revenue divisions and three municipalities and one corporations. The Nellore municipal corporation comprises of total population 26, 60,000, among them males are 1,1000,34, females are 1,9000,31. The number of urban villages in Nellore municipal Corporation are 32 among them 3 are notified and 29 are not notified. Most of the slums in Nellore municipal corporation are very squalor and lack of proper seepage and drainage facilities. The hygienic conditions available and health services are very scare. In spite of various slum improvement, urban development programmes implemented by UCD authorities, MEPMA etc. The conditions of slums are alarming for the purpose of study the researcher identified eight slums namely Zakir Hussain Nagar, Survepalli Katta, Barmasalagunta, Gandhi Nagar, Vengalrao Nagar, Kotamitta, Vikuntapuram, Ummareddy Gunta.

Sampling

A descriptive research design was utilized to obtain qualitative and quantitative data to meet the aims and objectives of the research study. The universe of the sample comprises of the slums which are located in NMC (Nellore Municipal Corporation) area. The researcher by using simple random sampling method has chosen eight slums (Lottery method) among the slums in NMC. The total population of these slums is 12,019, from each slum 50 houses are selected purposively based on availability of individuals who are capable of expressing their perception regarding the problems they are facing in the slums and also available amenities and information about community development programmes.

Tools used in the Study

The researcher used a pre-tested interview schedule to collect the information regarding socio-economic and demographic details, living arrangements, information regarding respondent's view of their life at slums, and also available amenities and information about community development programmes. The interview schedule is divided into five parts. Part one consists 20 questions pertaining to socio-economic and demographic information of slum dwellers. Part two consists 11 questions to elucidate information pertaining to health status of respondents and part three consists 9 questions to elicit information regarding respondent's views on their lives at slums. Part four comprises 7 questions to measure the perception of respondent on social problems prevailing in the slums. Part five comprises 8 questions to elicit information regarding respondents awareness about available amenities and information about community development programmes.

Method of Data Collection

First the researcher met the key informers like ward members, teachers, anganwadi workers etc. In the study they welcomed them about the purpose of the study and sought their cooperation. Later they introduced the researcher to community people. The researcher also interacted with community people and explained the purpose and objectives of the study. Then researcher asked the cooperation of the public in data collection. The researcher fixed convenient time and place for interview and conducted interview in mother tongue, i.e., Telugu.

Results and Analysis

The data collected was coded and entered in SPSS 11.5. Later tabulated based on frequencies, means were calculated. Further 't' test ANOVA, Chi-square tests were carried out where ever essential to test the hypothesis. Later the results were discussed and inferences were drawn based on the results.

A little above four-fifths, i.e. 82.7 per cent of respondents are males and 17.3 per cent are females. A majority 90.3 per cent of the respondents are married. Nearly three fifths, i.e. 57.0 per cent of the respondents are illiterates. The results revealed that a little above two-fifths, i.e. 43.3 per cent of respondents belong to scheduled caste, and 30.0 per cent of the respondents are from backward caste. A majority, i.e. 89.7 per cent respondents are living in nuclear families and four-fifths, i.e. 80.0 per cent of the respondents are having 1-2 children. A majority 85.3 per cent of the respondents work as labourers. A little below three-fifths, i.e. 57.3 per cent of the respondents are living in own house and a little above two-fifths, i.e. 42.0 per cent respondents are living in *kuccha* houses. 96.7 per cent of the respondents are not having any other sources of income and nearly three-fourths of the respondents, i.e. 73.67 per cent are having loan for an amount of Rs. 3001-5000. Regarding the respondents monthly expenditure nearly two-fiths, i.e. 36 per cent of the respondents expences on food are Rs. 1000-1500, followed by 30 per cent of respondents expences on food are Rs. 1501-2000. Nearly half, i.e. 45.67 per cent of the respondents educational expenses are nil. 96.7 per cent of the respondents are not investing their money on any developmental activity. 96.0 per cent of the respondents spent less than Rs. 100 for recreation (cable connection) expenses. The results reveal that 82.7 per cent of the respondents are having habits of pan, gutka, smoking and alcohol etc. and as per gambling 60.0 per cent of the respondents are not having the habit of gambling.

Further the results regarding the living conditionwise distribution of the respondents. Nearly three-fourths, i.e. 71.7 per cent of the respondents are comfortable in living in slums and 28.3 per cent of the respondents are not comfortable in living in the slums. 93.0 per cent of the respondents are facing problems such as congested houses, improper roads, transport and hospital servises. (Fig. 21.1) and less 7.0 per cent of the respondents are comfortable in living in the slums. Study also reveals that 61.3 per cent of the respondents are facing problems due to unhygienic environment and followed by 20.3 per cent of the respondents are facing unsafe water and 18.3 per cent of the respondents are facing mosquitoes problem in the slums. Most of the respondents express that poverty (192), alcoholism (77) and gambling (22) etc. are more prevalent social problems in slums (Fig.21.2).

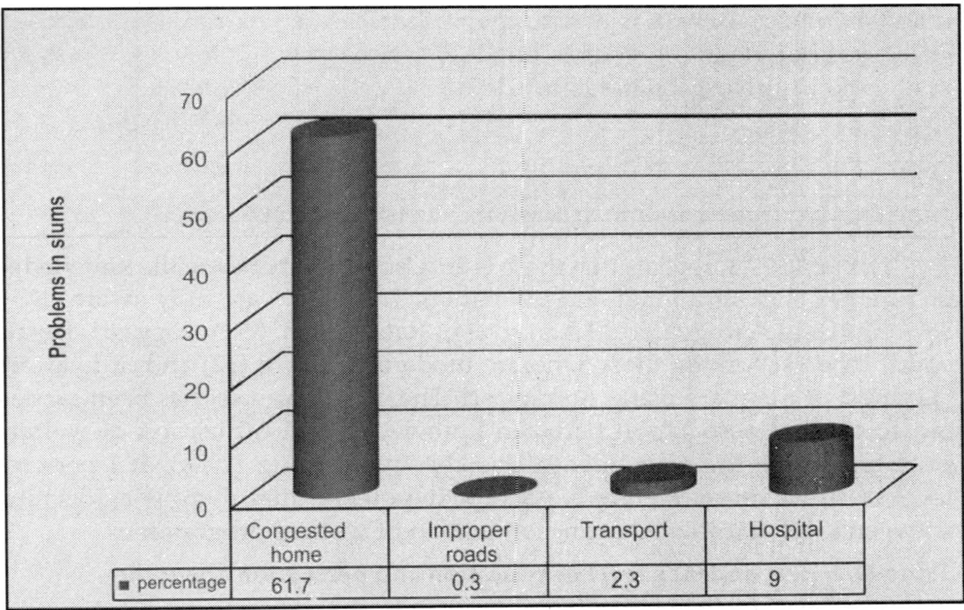

Fig. 21.1: Problems Facted by Respondents

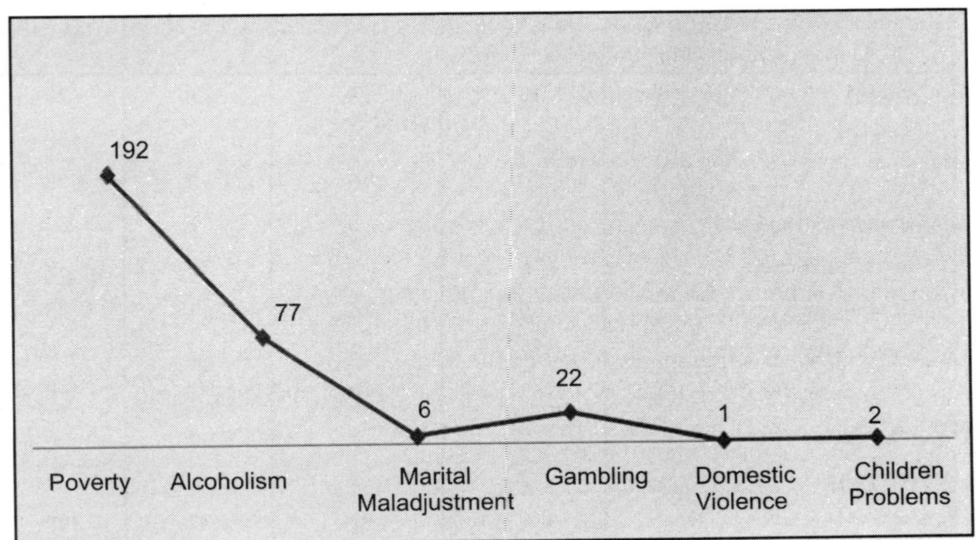

Fig. 21.2: Respondents Perception on Social Problems in Slums

Table 21 .1: Level of awareness and utilization of welfare programmes by the respondents

Utilization	Level of awareness			Total
	Fully aware	Some what aware	Little aware	
Aarogyasri	88	26	19	133
Aarogyasri, Pavala Vaddi	35	24	7	66
Aarogyasri, Ration card	39	21	3	63
Aarogyasri, Pavala Vaddi, 108 services, Ration card	14	21	3	38
Total	**176**	**92**	**32**	**300**
Df: 6, Chi-Square value = 22.498. Sig @ 0.01%				

The table 21.1, reveals that there is an association between the knowledge on number of programmes and utilization. Those who are fully aware (176), 88 were using Aarogyasri; 39 Aarogyasri, Ration card; 35 Aarogyasri, Pavala vaddi schems. Among those who are moderatly aware (92) and little aware (32) most of them are using Aarogyasri. The chi-square test has been carried out to findout association between knowledge and utilization of welfare programmes by the respondents. The chi-square value 22.498, at 1 per cent level of significance. Hence, we accept hypothesis that there is association between level of knowledge and utilization of welfare programmes.

Table 21.2: Respondent's level of education and perception about the problems faced by the respondents

Perception on Problems faced by the respondents	Level of Education			Total
	Illiterate	Primary education	Moderate education	
Poverty	53	18	8	79
Unemployment	17	15	3	35
Ill health	20	16	2	38
Domestic violence	26	5	6	37
Marital problems	6	3	0	9
Alcoholism	39	24	1	73
Child labour	2	3	1	6
Elder abuse	7	0	1	8
Juvenile delinquency	4	1	1	6
Gambling	2	7	0	9
Total	**176**	**92**	**32**	**300**
Df: 6, Chi-Square value: 22.498, Sig @ 1% level				

The table 21.2 reveals that there is association between level of education and their opinion on social problems. The respondents who are illiterates stated they were having more problems such as poverty, alcoholism, domestic violence, ill-health, unemployment etc. when compared to primary and moderate educated respondents. This may be due to those who are having education may minimize their problems with their awareness. Chi Square test has been carried out to know association between level of education and problems faced by the respondents. The Chi Square value is 22.498, significant at 1 per cent level, so we accept the hypothesis that there is association between level of education and problems faced by the respondents.

Conclusion

The slum dwellers are faced with insecurity of tenure, lack of basic services, especially water and sanitation, unsafe building structure, over-crowding, limited access to credit and formal job markets. Normally slums exist on polluted land. They suffer from water-borne disease. It is also believed that slums are places of high level of crimes. This is not universally true. Poverty is the main reason for slums. At the same time slums also provide low cost accommodation to poor migrants and necessary support. In the light of the above discussion it is evident that the Indian urban slum dwellers are living in poor conditions. Hence, in the study an attempt is made to throw light on the problems and conditions of urban slums and available amenities. The results revealed that a majority of respondents are males, married and living in nuclear families, most of them are illiterates, belongs to scheduled caste/backward caste and work as labourers. Majority of the respondents are facing problems such as congested houses, improper roads, transport and hospital servises, and unhygienic environment. Most of the respondents express that poverty, alcoholism and gambling etc. are more prevalent social problems in slums. The results reveals that there is association between level of knowledge and utilization of welfare programmes and there is association between level of education and problems faced by the respondents. Most of them expressed that there is a need to create awareness on UCD programmes and their effective implementation through strategies of community development such as self-help, community participation, felt needs, local leadership, technical assistance, etc.

References

1. Chatterjee, "Urban Community Development in India", in Wadia, A.R. (Ed.), *History and Philosophy of Social Work in India*, Allied Publishers, Bombay.
2. Chowdhry, Paul, D. (1993), *Hand Book of Social Welfare*, Atma Ram and Sons, Delhi.
3. Clinard, Marshall B., 1966, *Slums and Community Development*, The Free Press, New York.

4. Gans, Herbert J. (1962), *The Urban Villages: Group and Class in the Life of Italian, American*, The Free Press, New York.

5. Panditharatna, B.L. (1993), "Contemporary Urbanization of Sri Lanka; Impact on the Quality of Urban Environment" in Bidyut Mohanty, *Urbanization in Developing Countries*, pp. 54- 55.

6. Patel and Dubey (2010), "Slum and Urban Growth", Urban Social Work, New Delhi pp. 105- 106.

7. Patel and Dubey (2010), "Social Problems of Urban Settings", Urban Social Work, New Delhi, pp. 14-15.

8. Prasad, Ravindra (1993),"Urban Basic Programmes in India: A SWOT Analysis", in Bidyut Mohanty, *Urbanization in Developing Countries*, New Delhi, pp. 305, 306.

9. Thudipara Z, Jacob (2007), *Urban Community Development*, Rawat Publications, Jaipur.

Role of Community Participation in Urban Development

Dr. N. Rajani,
Mrs. Karima Ferhana

Introduction

Community participation has created a new dimension to the way practitioners and academics view urban development in today's cities. The purpose of this brief paper is to focus on what we mean by community participation, at what stages it may be implemented and its importance in urban services.

Why Community Participation is Important?

Community participation is important because it provides the commitment from the communities themselves. Community participation as an approach can eventually provide effectiveness, efficacy and empowerment. Although sustainable community participation and management alone cannot guarantee success, it can play a vital role in creating both an effective and efficient water and/or sanitation project.

Methodology

This paper is divided into different sections, namely what is meant by community participation (a brief literature review), stages where community participation can occur, the importance of community participation in urban areas, incentives and disincentives for community participation, pre-conditions for successful community participation and finally a summary note on community participation in urban development projects.

What is Meant by Community Participation?

In simple terms 'community participation' refers to the involvement of people in community development projects (UNCHS, 1991; Sheng, 1992;

Korten, 1987; Garilao, 1987). Since social, economic, educational and other conditions differ from one community to another, the form and degree of people's involvement in development activities also vary. This makes it difficult to define community participation precisely. However, since it implies action by the people to solve their own problems, it can be understood in terms of activities performed by the communities in their own development projects.

There is a wide range of types of community participation. At one end of the scale there may be merely some community participation in an agency designed and executed project. At the other, is full community planning, implementation and management of a project with no agency involvement?

Different Forms of Community Involvement

The following is a list of different forms of community involvement which may include certain members or beneficiaries in the community.

- Community leaders consulted by Agency
- Whole community consulted by Agency
- Financial contribution
- Material contribution
- Labor and skill contribution
- Operation and maintenance contribution
- Project management
- Women's representation in decision-making
- Involvement in health education or campaigns
- Providing specialized community workers such as health educators

Stages where 'Community Participation' can Occur in the Project Cycle

Community participation can take place at any one of numerous stages in a development project cycle, namely:

Needs assessment: Expressing opinions about desirable improvement, prioritizing goals and negotiating with agencies.

Planning: Formulating objectives, setting goals, criticizing plans.

Mobilizing: Raising awareness in the community about needs, establishing or actuating organizational structures within the community.

Training: Participating in formal or informal training activities to enhance communication, construction, maintenance and financial management skills.

Implementing: Engaging in administration, supervision or other management activities; contributing directly to the actual work of construction or maintenance with labour and materials; store-keeping; contributing cash towards costs, paying for services or membership fees of community organizations; deciding rules.

Monitoring and evaluation: Participating in the appraisal of work done, recognising improvements that can be made and redefining needs.

Role of NGOs or CBOs in Urban Services

Experiences in many developing countries during and since the International Drinking Water Supply and Sanitation Decade (1981-1990) demonstrate that even the best run water, sanitation or solid waste management schemes cannot successfully be implemented, operated and maintained without the full involvement and commitment of the users (IRC, 1993). Involvement and commitment of the users are usually funneled through the assistance of Non-Governmental and Community-Based Organizations. Overall, Non-Governmental Organizations (NGOs) and Community-Based Organizations (CBOs) have a growing importance and a new role as development organizations. One of the main reasons why NGOs have developed is because the public sector has not been able to adequately deliver services to meet the needs of the population. This is especially true for the low income areas. As a result NGOs have become major partners of the public sector in an effort to address local needs.

Why Should Community Participate?

The following is a list of some of the important reasons (Narayan, 1996) why community participation is one of the essential criteria for successful development projects:

- more will be accomplished;
- services can be provided more cheaply;
- there is an intrinsic value in participation;
- there is a catalyst for further development and a sense of responsibility is encouraged;
- there is a guarantee that a felt need is involved;
- ensures that 'things are done the right way';
- valuable indigenous knowledge is used;
- people are freed from dependence on others' skills; and
- people are more conscious of the causes of their poverty and what they can do about it.
- projects are more likely to be self-sustaining;
- increased involvement of women; and
- it is more likely that health benefits will be maximized.

Disincentives for Community Participation

The following are some of the main disincentives for individuals and/or community to be involved in community participation. Some of these reasons include:

- An unfair distribution of work amongst members of the community. Some members in the community may feel that they are asked to take on extra work tasks that provide them little financial/social or other incentives;
- A highly individualistic, movement oriented society;
- Individuals may not feel a sense of community and thereby question the purpose of their involvement in a development project;
- The feeling that the government should provide the facilities. The community may feel that the development project is simply another way of exploiting people.

Pre-Conditions for Successful Community Participation in Urban Areas

For community participation to be successful it is suggested that certain pre-conditions must be met. The pre-conditions that are cited below are not exclusive but rather reflect some of the major criteria that can make a development project successful through the use of community participation.

- There must be a community demand for an improved system. The people must want to solve 'their' problem.
- The information required for individuals or communities to make informed decision must be available. Information campaigns will often be necessary to 'market' desirable water supply, sanitation and solid waste management services. Examples should be built in the locality for inspection by those who are likely to be 'customers' in the future.
- Technologies and levels of service must be compatible with the community's needs and capacity to finance, manage and maintain them. This concept refers to providing appropriate technology that can be sustained by the community.
- The community must understand its options and be willing to take responsibility for the system. It must be clear from the start how the system will be paid for by the community and/or with the assistance of an outside agency.
- The community must be empowered to make decisions to control the system. The issue of community leadership training, committee training and skills training is an essential part of 'empowering' the community as a whole.
- The community should have the institutional capacity to manage the development and operation of the system and the solution must be within their means. The community should have the human resources to manage these institutions.

- There should be a policy framework to permit and support community management. The government must frame its legislation so that community development committees and co-operatives are legal.
- Effective external support services for the community must be available from governments, donors, NGOs or private sector. The people must have faith in these supporting programme personnel. There needs to be good co-ordination between these external groups.
- The challenge of community management must be simple enough at first so that people can participate, yet become increasingly complex so that they can grow in their ability to deal with problems and feel an increasing sense of accomplishment. This idea refers to the importance of creating early recognizable success so as to create enthusiasm for the rest of the project.

Summary and Conclusion

In this brief paper we have listed some of the main reasons why community participation has and can continue to work effectively in water, sanitation and solid waste management projects at the neighbourhood level. As cities continue to grow, there is a need to look at available resources including residents who can assist in implementing, developing and undertaking neighbourhood projects.

If local governments want to focus on providing both effective and efficient urban services they have to focus more on community participation for the provision of urban services. Such operations are, however, only successful when they have the cooperation of Non-Governmental and Community-Based Organizations. These organizations play a key role since they work directly with citizens in neighbourhoods and can assist most effectively in the implementation of the schemes. However, when local governments decide to cooperate with these organizations in order to obtain the participation of citizens, they have to face the dilemma of sharing some of their responsibility and power. This will require that local governments perceive their roles in a more democratic way, so that Non-Governmental and Community-Based Organizations and citizens can become partners in more effective urban services for the city as a whole.

References

1. Garilao, E., 1987, "Indigenous NGOs as Strategic Institutions: Managing the Relationship with Government and Resource Agencies", *World Development*, 15, pp. 113-121.
2. IRC, 1993, "Community Management Today—The Role of Communities in the Management of Improved Water Supply Stems, Occasional paper 20. The Hague.
3. Korten, D., 1987, "Third Generation NGO Strategies: A Key to People-Centered Development", *World Development*, 15, pp. 147-150.

4. Narayan, D., 1996, "Toward Participatory Research", World Bank Technical Paper Number 307, World Bank, Washington D.C.

5. Sheng, Y.K., 1992, "Community Participation in Low-income housing projects: problems and prospects", *Community Development Journal*, 25, (1), pp. 56-65.

Urban Financial Reforms – A Glance

Dr. A. Samanthakamani

In many nations, the Urban-Rural relationships has remained unbalanced in terms of population growth and income distribution. Urban development is a process of economic growth, depends on financial reforms to some extent. The urban policies in India till 1990s, focused on master plans, integrated development and environmental improvement of slums and provision of basic service. It was the National Commission on Urbanization (1988) which recognized the economic role and significance of the cities and towns in the national development process. But, the current urban reforms in India have a close linkage with the macro-economic policy reforms of the Government of India initiated during 1991. The economic reforms in the first phase included the components like opening up of the economy to foreign institutional investors and imports of technology and consumer goods. Simultaneously, the policy of economic liberalization was initiated while relaxing several administrative controls, which were aimed at encouraging privatization even in the sectors like infrastructure and basic services, which were earlier, the domain of public sector. The Rakesh Mohan Committee Report of 1996 suggested privatization and commercialization of all infrastructure development including urban. In fact, the committee had a profound impact on the urban infrastructure policy. This is echoed in the Ninth Five Year Plan, which strongly recommended adoption of a commercial and market approach to infrastructure planning, development and management.

The Ninth Plan suggested for private sector involvement in the projects like city beautification, solid waste management including commercialization of recycling of solid waste, housing land development and commercial complexes. Cost recovery was emphasized in the development of basic urban infrastructure. The Tenth Five Year Plan (2002-07) while commending the ongoing reforms, desired that the pace of movement be fast tracked—stressing the ongoing or first generation reforms like restructuring of property tax, internal revenue mobilization initiatives, accessing the capital market through municipal bonds, accrual accounting system, asset management, improved financial information system through computerization and public-private partnerships, the plan also emphasized the need for providing supportive administrative mechanisms to speed up the pace and stabilize the process to take up the second generation reforms.

The legal base for urban reforms was provided in the form of 74th Constitution Amendment Act (CAA) 1992. The 74th CAA envisions an empowered municipal governing system for ULBs in terms of resources, powers and expertise while providing an institutional backing to the urban reforms in India. The Government of India initiated to provide urban financial reforms and financial institutional mechanisms in the form of SFCs and integrating them with the central FC. Several reforms in the financial management sector followed this amendment in the ULBs across the country.

URBAN FINANCIAL REFORMS IN SOUTH INDIA

State level initiatives are underway to take forward the national urban reform agenda in India. Some are promoted by the international financial agencies like World Bank and ADB and some are structured into the Central and State government schemes.

The World Bank is supporting urban reforms in Andhra Pradesh while the ADB is supporting reforms in Karnataka and Kerala. The DFID (UK) and USAID are rendering financial assistance to the governments in the developing countries under their respective international assistance programs. The DFID is supporting municipal reforms in Andhra Pradesh while the USAID is promoting financial reforms in Tamilnadu. These apart each state has initiated reforms independent of the external project.

ANDHRA PRADESH

Andhra Pradesh has a long history of urban reforms beginning with the community development initiatives of 1970s in Hyderabad. The state has also experimented with direct election to the chairperson/mayor of ULBs and successfully implemented the reservations for weaker sections and women even before the 74th CAA was passed by the Parliament in 1992. Restructuring of property tax on plinth area basis and a comprehensive reform agenda under the Andhra Pradesh Urban Services for the Poor (APUSP) and Andhra Pradesh Urban Reforms and Municipal Services Project (APURMSP) are the main statewide financial reform initiatives in Andhra Pradesh.

Restructuring of the Property Tax on Plinth area Basis

Andhra Pradesh introduced the plinth area-based property tax in all the municipalities successfully back way in 1993. The reform was introduced with a legal backing by an amendment to the Andhra Pradesh Municipalities Act. Restructuring of the property tax assessment on plinth area basis in the municipalities could be considered a very progressive step especially, when the other states were still deliberating on its introduction. The property tax reform was one of the successful experiments in Andhra Pradesh and Patna generated national level discussion and many other states have adopted or inclined to adopt the plinth area system of property tax. Its relatively trouble-free implementation, people's acceptance and the support it received from the judiciary are noteworthy in this context. The reform generated additional revenues to the tune of Rs. 20 crore initially in 1993 when it was implemented and the revenue increased over the years. In spite of government interference putting a ceiling on the overall tax increase due to tax payers' pressures, the new system is being implemented in all the ULBs in the state and revision was also made during 2001-02 based on the plinth area.

With its widespread acceptability across the state, the Municipal Corporation of Hyderabad; which did not implement the area-based model till today, is now in the process of remodeling the property tax system on area basis and zoning as is being practiced in the other municipal bodies in the state.

The scale and pace of the urban reform movement increased in the state with the entry of international financial agencies and external aid. In Andhra Pradesh, two important internationally-funded projects that have statewide coverage are under implementation. One is Andhra Pradesh Urban Services for the Poor (APUSP), a poverty focused project assisted by the DFID and the other one is Andhra Pradesh Urban Reforms and Municipal Service Project (APURMSP) with financial support of the World Bank. Several reforms in municipal governance and urban development are being implemented under these schemes in ULBs in the state.

Andhra Pradesh Urban Services for the Poor

Slum–development projects in Andhra Pradesh, especially the former ODA (UK) supported projects in Hyderabad, Visakhapatnam and Vijayawada cities have a long history and gained international recognition. In fact, the success of these projects which promoted peoples participation and community development as the core elements in slum development, promoted the DFID (renamed department of ODA, UK) to extend the experiment into other class-I (C-I), cities in the state with town-wide focus on poverty alleviation and governance reform.

The significant aspect of financial assistance under APUSP is that the entire financial assistance of Rs. 745 crore comes as a grant. The project initially covered 32 Class-I towns and later it was extended to 10 more Class-I towns as per the 2001 census. The project has three complimentary components, viz., improving municipal performance through reforms (C-I), improving environmental infrastructure for the poor (C-2), and strengthening of civil society organizations (C-3). The C-I component focuses entirely on municipal reforms aimed at improving the performance capacity of the municipal bodies. Major areas of reform identified that have financial implications are improved revenue mobilization; updating accounts and adult; introduction of accrual based accounting system: improved asset management; and up-to-date poverty data for planning.

Financial performance improvement is one of the critical areas of the reform agenda under APUSP. Revenue improvement action plan and introduction of the accrual based double entry accounting system are the two major financial reforms initiated under the project. The ULBs are to prepare a revenue improvement action plan considering various revenue raising methods including tax and non-tax income. Expertise in the form of Municipal Accounting and Financial Associates (MAFAs) is drafted to help the ULBs in the change-over from the existing cash-based single entry accounting to the accrual-based double entry accounting system. Though the APUSP project focuses on urban poor, the reform component covers a wider canvas of institutional strengthening.

Andhra Pradesh Urban Reforms and Municipal Services Project

This is another major urban reform-oriented World Bank financed project. The APURMSP is being implemented in AP since 2004. A whole town approach is adopted in the scheme focusing on legal and institutional reforms, municipal capacity enhancement, infrastructure investment support for core areas of solid waste management and sanitation, water supply, drainage, roads and street lighting, project management and technical assistance. The project aims at comprehensive municipal governance reforms, enhanced accountability and financial soundness of the ULBs and improved quality of life in urban areas. The project covers all the ULBs in the state but it is not automatic inclusion in the scheme. Certain financial requirements viz., an operating surplus, up-to-date accounts and audit, property tax collection above 75 per cent, a reform action plan and council's willingness are stipulated to access the financial assistance by the ULBs.

The total project outlay is Rs. 1,350 crore trust headed by the chief secretary was formed to manage the funds, and AP Urban Finance and Infrastructure Development Corporation is administering it. The funding allocation is 70 per cent on town-wide infrastructure and 30 per cent on infrastructure in poor settlements. Of total project cost 70 per cent will be in the form of loan repayable in 20 years with a moratorium of five years and the local body has to bear 10 per cent of the cost. The remaining grant part of the funding will be available to slum development projects, solid waste management and few others.

The important feature of the APURMSP is that the ULBs must prepare a comprehensive Municipal Reforms Action Plan consisting of Financial/Revenue Improvement Action Plan (FIAP) and Institutional Development Action Plan (IDAP) to avail the financial assistance. The major reform areas suggested are: financial management, revenue improvement, financial viability, systems improvement, strengthening of self-help groups, services to the poor and participate consultancy process.

Other Reforms

E-procurement, computerization and PPP are the other reforms being attempted in the ULBs. Computerization of property tax, accounts and birth and death certification is in progress especially, in the corporations and APUSP towns. E-governance initiatives in the area of property tax, tenders, etc., are being successfully implemented in corporations like Hyderabad, Visakhapatnam, Vijayawada and Guntur and some other progressive ULBs. PPP initiatives are being made at the ULB level with active support from the state government. Fund your city scheme in Hyderabad and privatization of street lighting in Visakhapatnam are stand out examples in this respect. Both these initiative have demonstrated financial benefits to the ULBs. Sanitation is one major area where PPP initiatives are more prominent in the ULBs. The PPP method in urban sanitation is found beneficial to both, ULBs as well as communities. If the ULBs could reduce expenditure on sanitation front, communities are satisfied because they are getting clean environment, increasing acceptability of the PPP model of rendering urban services like sanitation by the urban communities as well as the local politicians shows the changing perception of urban governance.

E-procurement is one of the financial reforms that is being adopted in most of the departments in Andhra Pradesh. The commissioner of a municipality invites bids for a specific work to be executed giving details like description of the work period etc. The intending bidders would be required to enroll themselves on the 'e' procurement market place. The tenders should be in the prescribed form on e-procurement and the applications can be downloaded at free of cost from the website. The bids received online will be opened by the commissioner or his nominee at his office on the date and time mentioned.

The commissioner will follow the prescribed procedure in the finalization of the tenders. The e-procurement method is being adopted in the state to overcome the problems like contractors forming a ring to keep the rates low, and other political influences associated with personal contacts and this reform is being followed in respect of municipal works too.

Infrastructure Development Enabling Act, 2001

The government of Andhra Pradesh has been giving top priority for infrastructure development through PPP approach. Several mega infrastructure development projects are being taken-up in recent years, especially in the major cities like Hyderabad and Visakhapatnam and providing a legal base and administrative support is essential to implement big infrastructure projects. This act is made to facilitate PPP in the infrastructure development and its objectives are to conceptualize and identify the infrastructure projects to advise the government or any other government agency to initiate infrastructure projects in core areas. It covers sectors like roads, bridges, and by-passes, health, land reclamation, water supply and treatment, waste management, public markets, public buildings and etc. The aovernment constituted Infrastructure Authority in September, 2002 to administer the Act. The authority is chaired by either chief secretary or other equivalent experienced person and this initiative of government of AP is a good example for promoting mega infrastructure projects in the PPP model. Though the authority is established, it is still in the formative stage in terms of activities and staff support.

KARNATAKA

Karnataka has been playing a significant role in advancing the urban financial reform movement in the country. The state was way ahead in implementing the restructure devolution formula for the local bodies as recommended by the first State Finance Commission. In fact, the state pioneered the concept of global sharing of state revenues with the local bodies in India along with Tamilnadu. Single transfer in terms of a percentage share of the state's gross revenues was suggested in place of the existing multiple transfer method, which is hidden with complex administration problems. The government readily accepted and implemented the formula of global sharing as recommended by the first SFC from 1997-98 onwards. The state financial devolution has now become simple, transparent and rationalized.

A state level-financing agency called the Karnataka Urban Infrastructure Development Finance Corporation (KUIDFC) was established in 1993 with 100 per cent shareholding by the state government. The KUIDFC has been playing model role in the Bangalore Mega City Project sponsored by the Government of India; ADB projects in Mysore, Tumkur, Ramanagaram and Chennapatnam, World Bank in the northern region of the state. Karnataka has been receiving assistance from ADB since 1996 and it is provided US $132 million to decentralize urban growth from the Bangalore, Mysore, Tumkur, Chennapatnam and Ramanagaram cities. The project period was five years commencing from 1996 in continuation, the ADB also funded another project covering ten coastal towns with Mangalore as the nodal city. The project aims to develop these town socially, economically and environmentally by covering aspects like water supply, sanitation, underground drainage, solid water management, roads, housing and poverty alleviation. An interesting feature of this project is that it is proposed on the lines of self-sustaining without any subsidies. It is reported that the Karnataka Government had given assurances to this effect to avail the loan.

Several other reform are being carried out in the state—prominent of these are enactment of the new Karnataka Rent Act, privatization of urban infrastructure and services and introduction of the self-assessment scheme for property tax in all the ULBs.

Enhancement of the Karnataka Rent Act

Economic Administration Reforms Commission and the National Commission on Urbanization have recommended reforming the rent legislations in a way that balances the interests of both landlords and the tenant also stimulates future construction. The Government of India have formulated a model rent control law and recommended to the state governments to undertake amendments to existing rent control laws or enact new laws on the basis of the model law.

Privatization Policy

The state had announced the privatization policy in 1997 with the main objective of encouraging private sector participation in the infrastructure development including urban infrastructure and later this policy was further refined and made operational by the Infrastructure Development Corporation of Karnataka. As per the new draft policy, the key priority of the government is progressive elimination of subsidies and cross-subsidies so that the prices for services are commensurate with the real costs of provision.

Nirmala Nagar Project

Nirmala Nagar Project launched by the Government of Karnataka aims to make cities deliver and change the way people look at these institutions and greater accountability and citizens participation are pivotal to the program. The projects like urban Stree-Shakthi for poverty alleviation, urban cleanliness (solid waste management), access to toilets for urban poor, promotion of rain water harvesting, property tax reforms with GIS, computerization and implementation of fund based accounting services are being implemented through the program.

Introduction of Capital Value-Based Self-Assessment Scheme of Property Tax

The government of Karnataka had changed the assessment of property tax in ULBs from rental value to capital value-based on the plinth area and also introduced self-assessment scheme in all the ULBs. This is considered one of the significant steps to improve internal revenues of the ULBs. All the ULBs have changed over to the system of capital value in the state.

Computerization

Improving urban administration through computerization and increasing transparency and efficiency is also recognized as priority in Karnataka. Computerization is being taken up in phases like: Public grievance, property tax and birth and death registers are being computerized first. Ward works, payrolls and water supply billing will be computerized in the next phase. The e-governments foundation is supporting these reforms especially, property tax, GIS and fund-based accounting in the Nirmala Nagar Project. The computerization project is estimated to cost Rs. 21 crore and it is being supported by the ADB. Further, 57 websites have been launched covering all the Nirmala Nagar Project towns. All the project towns are provided with IT specialists who are being trained on the software developed for its application. A centralized data centre is also being developed. The maps produced through the physical surveys and the property tax information and other MIS generated through GIS surveys are being computerized.

Fund-Based Accounting

At the city level, the Bangalore Mahanagara Palike (BMP) had introduced fund-based accounting system in 2001-2002. It allows the ULBs to prepare their budget based on different funds established for different purposes as against the present method of following a single fund for all transactions.

Bangalore Agenda Task Force (BATF)

The Bangalore Agenda Task Force (2000) is an innovative institution constituted, under the chairmanship of the Chief Minister, to develop Bangalore as a model city through private-public partnership approach. Broadly, the BATF proceeded with the following self-made objectives:

- Make Bangalore a world class city with infrastructure and civic services comparable to international standards,
- Upgrade and enhance the managerial and administrative capabilities of various civic and administrative stakeholders viz., Bangalore Mahanagara Palike, Bangalore Development Authority, Bangalore Water Supply and Sewerage Board, Bangalore Metropolitan Transport Corporation, Bangalore City Police, Karnataka Power Transmission Corporation Limited and Bangalore Telecom.
- Enable provision of citizen-oriented, high-quality of life for individuals and communities.
- Augment financial resources and revenues of stakeholders to enable them to perform at world-class levels.

Mr. Nandan Nilekani, a young technocrat who became the chief executive officer (CEO) of Infosys in March 2002 and became the president, and managing director of the company headed the Bangalore agenda taskforce which was to look into problems faced by the state capital.

Karnataka Municipal Reforms Project

Karnataka Municipal Reforms Project is a World Bank assisted project which focuses on comprehensive and state-wide municipal reforms in conformity with the Government of India's reform agenda and the Tenth Plan urban reform objectives. It aims to invigorate the entire urban reform process in the state. The project is taken-up with the following specific objectives:

- Enhancing the capacity of the ULBs so that they discharge their responsibilities with greater sustainability and accountability in the spirit of the 74th CAA.
- Strengthening of the institutional and financial frameworks of the state level agencies and the ULBs.
- Improving the quality of urban infrastructure through mobilization of resources for investments.
- Improving the road system in Bangalore and sanitary conditions in eight ULBs surrounding Bangalore while ensuring financial viability and sustainability.

The project has four basic components: Institutional development component, municipal investment support component, Bangalore development component and project management component and this entire project is estimated to cost US $298.

KERALA

Kerala is considered the pioneer in the decentralized governance in the post-74th Constitution amendment period in India. Some of the important measures taken in Kerala are: enactment and making operational a new Municipality Act covering municipalities and corporations; demarcation of the functions of the ULBs; transfer of development functions along with resources in addition to the existing traditional functions, devolution of the third of state plan funds under different sectors to the local bodies—rural and urban on united basis and active peoples participation in decentralized planning process; and institutionalizing the decentralized governance with a back-up of appropriate laws and organizational structures. The successful partnership approach of decentralized governance involving the officials, non-officials and the people is lauded at national and international levels.

The state has done a pioneering work on the decentralized planning and implemented the provision of the District Planning Committee as provided by the 74th Constitution Amendment Act. In fact, the district planning system as aimed by the 74th CAA is being implemented in letter and spirit only in Kerala in entire South India and it may be in entire India. The district planning committees are functioning effectively and they are being guided by several working groups and technical committees. The decentralized planning in

Kerala is inextricably interwoven into the district development planning process. The government has issued detailed guidelines and organized a series of training and orientation programs to official and non-official functionaries. Another significant feature is about 35 per cent of the state plan budget is allocated to the rural and urban local bodies in the state. Accessing these plan funds is conditional to preparation of plans by the rural and urban local institutions adopting the procedures laid down in the guidelines. These plans of the local institutions are screened at the district level by the DPC and they are consolidated as district development plan.

A large number of technical experts, both working and retired, are associated with these technical advisory committees at different levels to ensure that the process and guidelines are meticulously followed. Another significant feature is active involvement of Ward committees and Ward Sabhas in the corporations and municipalities in the preparation of town level plans before their consolidation at the municipal level. In addition, as the town development plan also includes a list of beneficiaries, the representatives of community based and civil society organizations are actively involved in the Ward Sabha meetings. For detailed discussion and wider participation of civil society, the Ward Sabha meetings are split into working groups dealing with specific subjects like education, health, agriculture, sanitation, etc. This facilitates the active involvement of people's representatives, officials, experts and members of the community, particularly the poor.

From 2004 onwards, all approvals given by the district planning committees are being computerized and local governmentwise proceedings are issued by the member-secretary on behalf of the DPC. It is observed that this measure has certain advantages, a clear database on projects approved, a document for verification by local governments, treasuries and auditors, a tool of financial discipline as the amounts approved by DPC cannot be exceeded without prior permission of the DPC while bills are presented; an incentive to improve the costing of the projects; and an accountability tool preventing unauthorized change of projects.

During the last decade or so there has been increased flow of funds from the state to the local bodies. In the process, state devolution has, taken a wide spectrum in Kerala and the local bodies receive state revenues for mainly three main purposes viz., to augment their own resources to meet their traditional functions, to maintain the services and institutions transferred and to extend, and develop those services and institutions. As the institutional capacity building has not taken place according to the expectations, the local bodies could not absorb this increased low of funds. For instance, the state government withdrew the provision of carrying over unspent money to the extent of 25 per cent during 2003-04 for its own compulsions but it shows that the local bodies could not incur allocated funds under plan and resulted in the reduction of the plan size from Rs. 1900 crore to Rs. 1200 crore during that year. Further, the local bodies received nine per cent (about Rs. 531.11 crore— 205.32 crore general purpose grant and Rs. 325.79 crore maintenance grant) of the state tax revenues as per the recommendations of the second SFC only during 2004-05. The local bodies could not incur expenditure to the extent of allocation during the first year of 2nd SFC. The reasons cited are delay in the release of funds and the consequential delays in the planning and execution of the schemes.

A critical look at the affairs in Kerala reveal that there has been increased flow of funds from the state to the local bodies which has put tremendous pressure on the state finances leading to treasury restriction and cut-backs. At the other end, the participatory planning is said to be not working on the desired lines with initial enthusiasm. Over emphasis on personal benefits rather than on development of the town raises doubts over the purpose of people's participation, individual benefit or community development. This predicament appears to be common in all the development and welfare schemes and functional link between the departments of transferred functions and the local bodies is abysmally missing. There is a feeling that the working groups of officials, non-officials and NGOs, constituted for vetting the plan proposals are not working well resultantly, except poverty reduction investments, other economic development works are not progressing well and local bodies are suffering from lack of accountability and weak local resource mobilization. In recent years, through the Kerala information mission and the attention of the state appears to be shifting to make local bodies more effective in terms of their internal resources, utilization of available resource and financial accountability and the recommendations of the third SFC are pointers towards this direction.

Perspective

The international and national urban reforms thinking is reflected in the state level reforms, but the pace, scale and intensity of the reforms differed from state to state. International funding agencies viz., World Bank and DFID in Andhra Pradesh, ADB in Karnataka and Kerala, have been playing key role in the reform process. The state governments are struggling to strike a balance between the conditions of the international financial agencies and the local political and social issues and problems. The fall-out of privatization and commercial strategies having critical socio-political ramifications are yet to be tackled effectively. There is a criticism that the privatization and commercialization reforms, being pro-rich and elite focused are further widening the gap between rich and poor in urban areas. The enclaves of poor and rich and super-rich continue to grow especially, in the metro cities like Bangalore, and Hyderabad are taking aggressive stance of expansion in the shadow of its hype. The recent real estate boom and liberal land allocations and tax concessions to the private sector in these cities raised many questions having wider social and political implications.

The state level reform strategies bring out that Kerala is following a people centered approach through its decentralization plan. The approach is to devolve more functions and resources to the local bodies. The over emphasis on devolution had its own negative impact on the local resource mobilization and the local bodies are busy thinking on utilization of the revenues transferred under different mechanisms rather than thinking on the lines of self-reliance. The two international projects, APUSP and APURMSP have generated much urban reform thinking in AP through the ground-level realities are not matching the euphoria. However, there are indications that the local resource mobilization initiatives are strong in certain towns where the officials have taken the affairs seriously. The state has the distinction of making operational the restructured property system in all the municipal bodies based on the plinth area as back as 1993. The Bangalore Agenda Task Force, a PPP initiative played a critical role in Karnataka's urban reform process despite its accountability issue. The initiative led to several financial reforms at the state level like self-assessment scheme of property tax, fund-based accounting, GIS mapping and computerization. The introduction of self-assessment scheme on the capital value base in all the ULBs indicates the states commitment for streamlining the property tax administration. Its linking with e-governance and GIS is of special significance and if the project is implemented as designed, it can create good urban information system. On the accounting front, the fund based accounting is successfully working in Bangalore and in other Nirmala Nagar Project towns, it is progressing well.

The BATF experiment which could not sustain and the vigorous privatization strategies underway in cities like Bangalore and Hyderabad raises several issues and fears relating to accountability undermining the representative democratic process of governance at the local level. These issues need to be properly addressed if the reform momentum has to be sustained and another requirement that should receive prior attention is capacity building at the ULB level, which is awfully bad particularly, in the small and medium towns. Much of the reform thinking has been seen at the state level and in metro cities to a certain extent and large number of smaller towns and cities are yet to catch up. Ultimately, sustainability of the urban reform movement in the country depends lot on this so far neglected urban segment.

Urbanization: Reforms in Urban Local Bodies in India

Dr. I.S. Kishore, Dr. Reddi Bhaskara Reddy,
Dr. S. Anil Kumar Reddy

India is having its second largest urban population in the world; about 286 million populations are living in urban areas according to 2001 census. Urbanization has been considered as a problem in India and the urban local bodies has always struggled to solve the problems. With rapidly increasing population in the urban areas, urbanization has emerged as one of the most serious challenges before the urban local government.

Urban local governments occupy a prominent place in the administrative system of urban areas. India has seen the rise and fall of many urban centers of political, cultural and commercial significance in the earlier days. After Independence, Constitution of India made specific provisions for the establishment of Panchayati Raj Institutions. But no specific provisions are laid down for the establishment and development of these bodies. The 74th Constitution Amendment Act, 1993 sought to improve and strengthen urban governance and management of services. The institutional arrangement for urban local governments and service delivery mainly comprises the Constitutional provisions, State laws and different Constitutional bodies.

There are many reasons for limited improvement in functioning of urban local bodies in spite of 74th Constitution Amendment Act. For effective functioning of these bodies, there is need of constitutional amendments. The main objective of this paper is to evaluate administrative reforms in the field of ULBs after independence in India and also makes certain recommendations in terms of constitutional amendments as well as administrative actions in realm of urbanization.

ULBS—ADMINISTRATIVE REFORMS

ULBs in India have a history of three centuries. As a consequence of inadequate constitutional provisions for Urban Local Self governance, for efficiency and quality in the governance there were constitutional reforms in this system that makes urban governance unstable. Urban Local Self governance laws in India are very old and often do not enable ULBs to implement reforms. In course of time ULS governments did not achieve success due to several loopholes like apathy of the bureaucrats, political manipulations, interference by the local and state political leaders, delay in the release of financial resources, lack of popular enthusiasm and many more reasons. Here an attempt is made to discuss some of the administrative reforms in ULS governance in India after the Independence.

Years—1950s and 1960s

Throughout the 1950s and 1960s, the industrialization of the country moved ahead, cities grew of their own impetus, and the growing problems of congestion, poor housing and pollution went generally unnoticed. During this period, the role of ULBs remained almost unchanged from the time of Lord Ripon, viz. the management of local functions and services by municipal committees, to be entrusted with adequate financial resources. Thus, the ULBs provided basic infrastructure and services, and were empowered to levy and collect taxes to finance these services. As a corollary, it was the property owners and traders who became the major financiers of municipalities, and arrogated to themselves the right of first use of their services. Indian cities thus began their journey towards the exclusion of the poor from civic decision-making.

Years—1970s

By the early 1970s, the more industrialized states in western India became aware of the problems of congestion, and industries were given incentives to set up their operations somewhere in the hinterland. These schemes failed largely because of the lack of adequate social and physical infrastructure in these distant places. Instead, what happened was that the erstwhile industrial belts of the primate cities grew large enough to claim independent corporate status, and we have the unprecedented situation of full-fledged Municipal Corporations in these industrial townships, benefiting from the industrial development in their area through taxes, while the 'mother' city has been reduced to a dormitory town for the commuting workforce. The 1970s weakened local governments in two ways: financially, by transferring several of their key (and revenue earning) functions to statutory boards; and politically, by giving state governments the control and discretion in local affairs.

Years—1980s

The 1981 census brought home to the powers the urban reality of India and the inevitability of urbanization with all its accompanying challenges. During this decade, one of the major initiatives of the Government of India was setting up of the first National Commission on Urbanization (NCU) in 1985 under the Chairmanship of an eminent architect and town planner, with able urban administrators and academics as its members. For the first time since Independence, someone stood back and looked at what had become of a nation's dreams and just how far we had wandered away from our tryst with destiny, since that fateful midnight hour of 15 August 1947.

The Commission basically adopted a holistic approach to development, wherein our national choices could make cities either the repository of rural flotsam, or the generators of economic momentum for entire regions; and collectively, the engines of national growth. Its recommendations were far more detailed and covered everything from urban land, municipal administration and services, housing, employment and urban poverty to urban form, design and conservation. The Commission submitted its Report in 1988. It was very well received, and to be fair, the government of the day did incorporate its broader approach in framing the 74th Amendment to the Constitution in 1992 and launching an urban poverty alleviation scheme called the Nehru Rozgar Yojana. The fault, if any, lay not in the recommendations of the NCU but the way in which they were implemented. The fact remains however that the Commission, once and for all, changed the syntax of urban debate in India, and therein lies its success.

Years—1990s

In 1990s one of the great revolution in ULS governance in India is bringing up of the 74th Constitutional Amendment Act (CAA). It was approved by the Parliament in December 1992. The Act came into force on June 1st, 1993.

The 74th Constitutional Amendment Act, 1993

Answering the call for action given by the National Commission on Urbanisation, the Government of India promulgated the Constitution (Seventy-fourth Amendment) Act, in 1992. Outlining its reasons and objectives, the CAA states that, "...a review of the working of the urban local bodies has shown that in many states they have become weak and ineffective on account of a variety of reasons, including the failure to hold regular and periodical elections, prolonged supersessions, inadequate representation of weaker sections, lack of financial resources and inadequate devolution of powers and responsibilities upon them". It was felt that the powers and functions of Municipalities had gradually declined and been taken over by other authorities, and Urban Local Bodies were left with few or no resources. Even when there were some efforts at local planning, the poor were seldom involved and the delivery of municipal services was far from equitable.

The 74th CAA is aimed precisely at strengthening the third tier of government in urban areas, to enable their holistic development through efficient administration, effective delivery, decentralised planning and participatory decision-making. It aims to empower urban local bodies by the devolution of functions, planning responsibilities, a new system of fiscal transfers and the empowerment of women and weaker sections of society. By providing the much needed institutional capabilities to urban local governments, it is hoped that they will be better equipped to deal with urbanisation and urban growth.

The 74th Amendment proposes to strengthen ULBs in terms of their structure, composition, financial resources, functions and powers. Besides restoring to ULBs the traditional functions that were taken away by specific authorities, it makes them responsible for the preparation of economic plans and social justice; regulation of land use and construction; water supply, public health and the environment; slum improvement and upgradation; and urban poverty alleviation. The Amendment also aims to enhance people's participation through decentralised and consultative decision-making, greater transparency, stronger finances and a more rigorous democratic process.

Years—2000s

The Good Urban Governance Campaign (GUGC)

During the current decade, the first major initiative of the Government of India was the Good Urban Governance Campaign. In Sept 2001, this was undertaken in partnership with the United Nations Centre for Human Settlements. The objectives of the GUGC were three-fold. The campaign sought to trigger a debate and raise awareness about the normative principles of good urban governance in the country. It also wanted to share experiences about good urban governance across states and cities. These deliberations were designed to lead to the actual implementation of recommendations. The campaign discussions identified six key issues that were central to good urban governance. These were urban decentralization, municipal finance, urban environment, integration of the poor and marginalized, transparency and civic engagement, and municipal management and capacity building.

Model Municipal Law

In October 2003, Government of India recommended a Model Municipal Law (MML) to the states for adoption. The basic objectives of the MML are to implement in totality the provisions of the 74th Constitution Amendment for empowerment of the urban local bodies administratively and financially, such that they are equipped to perform their functions. It intends to enable the introduction of reforms with particular reference to allowing and promoting private sector participation, innovative methods of revenue generation and sound financial management, and incorporate tools such as transparency and accountability and wider civic participation that would strengthen good urban governance in municipal bodies of the country. The need of a Model Municipal Law to replace the current set of Municipal Laws was felt for several reasons. Most of the controls exercised by state governments on municipal bodies run counter to the spirit of local empowerment. Any attempt at financial innovation by municipal bodies or in the introduction of private sector participation in municipal services is hampered in the spirit of the Amendment Act, the functions of ULBs should match the functions suggested in the 12th Schedule. The provisions of the Law must allow a maximum of private sector participation, financial innovation and reforms and the provisions of the Law must encourage civic engagement and transparency and tools for good governance. The MML proposes a unified law for three levels of ULBs. Its most radical recommendation is an Empowered Standing Committee as the municipal executive comprising the Mayor/ Chairperson/President and a select number of other councillors. The Model Law provides for a State-level Municipal Establishment Audit Commission that will, at five yearly intervals, review the status of the Establishment Schedules of various Municipalities in the State. The Commission would fix norms and standards of manpower for different tasks performed at various levels of the municipalities.

Jawaharlal Nehru National Urban Renewal Mission (JNNURM)

By the dawn of the new millennium, the ground has already been laid for a major central government intervention, which was to take the shape of the JNNURM in 2005.

The government is now viewing the urbanisation process as an alternative strategy to eradicate rural poverty. Growth rate of population in the cities in the country is much higher than the general growth rate of population in the country and there is a need to strengthen the cities and towns to be able to brace up to the challenges ahead. The government of India, in December 2005, launched an ambitious programme called Jawaharlal Nehru National Urban Renewal Mission (JNNURM), for renewal of Indian cities on sustainable basis. 63 cities have been chosen under the Mission. There are also two sub-missions. First sub-mission aims at strengthening the urban infrastructure like water supply, sewerage, traffic flow, decongestion, scientific solid waste management, proper storm water drainage, preservation of heritage etc. Second sub-mission is aimed at providing basic services to the urban poor, including proper housing at affordable rates and upgradation of slums to ensure that all the slum areas in the mission cities are provided with the same level of facilities as are available to the better areas in the mission cities.

Private-Public Partnership (PPP)

The Ministry of Urban Development has designed Private-Public Partnership (PPP) guidelines to sensitise state governments and urban local bodies to the policy and procedural issues that need to be addressed so as to reform urban water supply and sewerage issues. The PPP guidelines recommend that a clearly articulated state urban water supply and sanitation sector (WSS) policy is needed. The guidelines have focused on improving the management and accountability of water distribution as the first priority for most towns and cities. Separating operational and management (O & M) responsibility from policy-making and regulation is also identified as an important step for better accountability. The guidelines recognise that a crucial element of success in sector reform involving the private sector is an appropriate legal framework. The regulatory framework should clearly delineate state and local-level regulatory roles. Because independent regulators are costly to set up and have limited success in reforming or regulating public sector operators, a Reform Facilitation Team could initially drive the reform agenda and create the platform for effective regulation.

The guidelines recognise that prospects for PPP success will be greatly influenced by: creating a project steering committee; employing an experienced and reputable adviser; developing and executing a public consultation programme; putting in place appropriate safeguards for current government employees; pre-qualifying prospective private partners who have relevant operating experience and financial strength. Other important steps include finalizing core terms and conditions of the contract through sharing of information with pre-qualified firms; securing state or even sovereign guarantees to mitigate risks; finalising tender documents; attempting to make selection of the winning bidder based on a single criterion; opening bids in public with clearly established procedures for technical and financial evaluation; restricting post-bid negotiations to non-core issues; and closing the transaction after prompt completion of any 'conditions precedent', which may have been included in the tender.

National Urban Information System

To meet the requirement of base maps for towns and cities, a pilot scheme for preparing large-scale urban maps using aerial photography for 52 towns was started during the Eighth Five Year Plan. The project envisaged development of technical capabilities of the town planning organizations at central and state level so as to enable updating of the maps in a revision cycle. The work of aerial photography and mapping was carried out by the National Remote Sensing Agency (NRSA). The Town Country and Planning Organization (TCPO) in collaboration with the concerned State Town Planning Departments is undertaking interpretation of aerial photographs and collection of other secondary data/information to generate thematic maps and graphic data base for the development of GIS and processing of information for use as multi-purpose maps. In view of the developments in information technology it is now imperative that the country moves up to exploit the available technologies in order to enhance the efficiency in both planning and management of urban settlements. In this context, the National Urban Information System Scheme (NUIS) has been prepared. It comprises broadly two major components with independent but related objectives, strategies and budget under a single umbrella: *(a)* Urban Spatial Information System Scheme (USIS); and *(b)* National Urban Databank and Indicators. The National Urban Databank and Indicators component will further comprise of housing and household statistics and urban observatories.

Conclusion

Urbanisation is one of the hot topic being discussed on various platforms not only in India but also throughout the world. It has been considered as problem in India as the ULGs in the country have always struggled to solve the problems that were posed due to urbanization. In India there were continuous reforms in the ULBs to tune the changing scenario in the country as recommended by different committees and commissions at an appropriate time. Still the functioning of the ULGs is not up to the expectations in spite of efforts made by the central and state governments due to many reasons. There is need to bring yet another constitutional amendment to the present Act for proper, effective and efficient manner throughout the country in a similar manner.

References

1. 74th Amendment Act, Government of India, 1992.
2. Chetan Vaidya, *Urban Issues, Reforms and Way Forward in India,* Ministry of Finance, Government of India, 2006.
3. "Decentralisation and Good Urban Governance in Southeast Asia", Workshop on Urbanisation in Southeast Asian Countries: Cities as Engines of Development, Singapore, March, 2010.
4. Human Development Resource Centre, "Decentralisation in India Challenges and Opportunities", UNDP, New Delhi, 2000.
5. Maheshwari, S.R. *Local Government in India,* Orient Longmans, Delhi, 1971, p. 17.
6. Report of the Royal Commission on Decentralisation in India, 1909, Vol. I, p. 282.
7. Sharma, V.N. "Our Nagar Mahapalikas: Major Steps towards Better Civic Rule", *Northern Patrika* (Supplement), February 1, 1960.
8. www.indiastudychannei.com
9. www.buzzle.com

Urban Local Government Institutions in India

Dr. C. Janardhan Reddy, Mr. K.V. Sunil Kumar, Mr. M.C. Sidda Reddy

The term Local Government has two words, 'Local' and Government. The term 'Local' relates to specific portions of the country defined by Locality, implying a definite area and the population living therein. The 'Local' institutions are concerned with the needs and problems of the area thus defined. The second word 'government' refers first to its representative character as it has to form part of the constitutional structure of the country, and in the second place to the 'autonomy' it possesses. The local authorities are the same flesh and blood as the sovereign, but to a limited extent. Each council is elected (directly or indirectly) by the people of an area, and it is answerable to that local electorate, just as the sovereign is ultimately responsible to the national electorate. Thus, local government becomes an integral part of democracy.

Local government is the regulation in particular localities, of matters of primarily of local importance by locally elected bodies raising the money necessary for their activities, by the imposition of local taxes and generally subordinate to the central/state government. Although the local authorities are elected bodies, they have to operate within the framework of the Constitution of the country and the law under which they are created.

From political point of view, local government is called 'democracy on the doorstep'. It contributes to the social and political education of the citizen. It is educative for the electors, who are called upon to do their voting in relation to issues that are readily comprehensible to them; and for the councilors, who can gain experience in the act of responsible leadership. Thus, it has both political and educational value. The democratic value of liberty, equality and fraternity become real in the self-governing community.

Modern local government has, in addition, to play a vital role in the economic development of the country, whether it is the town planning, housing activity, and trade or poverty alleviation. It should be used as a positive instrument in this direction. The economic value of local authorities is being increasingly recognized.

This paper is to focus origin and development of the urban local Government Institutions in India. Also an attempt is made to present the structure, powers and functions of urban local bodies.

URBAN LOCAL GOVERNMENT INSTITUTIONS

In the Constitution of India initially there was no provision for the establishment of local self governing institutions in urban India, though it did make reference, in one of the Directive Principles, about the establishment of Village Panchayats in rural India. Lacuna was rectified by the Constitution (74th Amendment) Act, 1992, which provided for the establishment and management of urban local self government in India. Urban Local Self Government in India has its roots in prehistoric times. On the basis of historical records, excavations and archaeological investigations, it is believed that some form of local self-government did exist in the remote past. In the Vedas and in the writings of Manu, Kautilya and also in the records of some travelers like Magasthnese, the origin of local self-government can be traced back to the Buddhist period.

The *Ramayana* and the *Mahabharata* also point to the existence of several forms of local self-government such as *Paura* (guild), *Nigama, Pauga* and *Gana,* performing various administrative and legislative functions and raising levies from different sources.

Local government continued during the succeeding period of Hindu rule in the form of town committees, which were known as *Goshthis* and *Mahajan Samitees.* The representative character of these *samitees* was respected by the rulers. These Mahajans sometimes delegated their functions to their representative or to *Panchakulars* (committees of five) who used to collect revenue of behalf on the state. In addition to *Panchkulas, Talara,* an officer of the state, supervised local administration and policing with the help of the elected representative.

In the Mauryan period followed by the Gupta era and subsequently in the medieval period, the system of local self-government continued to be more or less the same. However, the system of local self-government was quite in the Mughal period. The Mughals were fond of building new cities and maintaining them. Those cities were, by and large, centers of trade and industry. Surat, Patna and Ahmedabad, for example, happened to be provincial capitals and offered a rich market. Whatever urban administration was there, it was autocratic in form. The City *Kotwal,* appointed by the

Emperor, was the key-centre of municipal administration. He was responsible for maintenance of houses, roads, levy and collection of local taxes, tolls, transit duties etc. The markets were controlled by him. He kept a check on weights and measures and a vigil on the local prices. These are basically municipal functions, which were performed by him in addition to his foremost duty of maintaining law and order. Thus, in *kotwal* of the Muslim period, offices of the modern Municipal Commissioner and the City Magistrate were combined. However, the foundation of modern system of urban government was laid by the British Government.

Madras (Chennai) was the first city to have a local government established under a Charter, dated December 30, 1678, issued by Company. The Municipal Corporation, which came into existence on September 29, 1688, was to consist of Mayor, 12 Alderman and 60 to 120 Burgesses. The company declared in the Charter that I wanted to encourage people of all nations and all sects of religion residing within the limits of the corporation and that the Alderman should be form among the heads and chiefs of all respective castes. The Burgesses were also to be both from Europeans and Indians. The Mayorship was confined to the Englishmen.

With the renewal of Charter of the East India Company by the British Parliament in 1973, a new attempt was made to establish municipal organizations in the presidency towns. It empowered the Governor General-in-Council to appoint Justices of Peace from among the servants of East India Company and other British inhabitants for the Mayor's Courts. The Justices, beside judicial duties, were required to provide for scavenging, police, and repair of street, etc.

Lord Mayo's Resolution of 1870 made arrangements for strengthening the municipal institutions and increasing the association of Indians in these bodies. However, it was Lord Ripon's Resolution of 1882 that was hailed as the Magna Carta of local government and got Lord Ripon the title of the "Father of local self-government in India". He advocated the establishment of a network of local self-governing institutions, financial decentralization, adoption of election as a means of constituting local bodies and the education of the official elements to not more than a third of the total membership. In 1907, a Royal Commission on decentralization was established, which examined the reasons behind the failure of the local self-governing bodies. It was found that the failure was due to strict official control, excessive narrow franchise, meagre resources, lack of education and shortage of committed persons.

According to the Government of India Act, 1919, the local self-government became a 'transferred' subject under the control of a responsible minister. The Act increased the taxation powers of local bodies, lowered the franchise, reduced the nominated members and extended the communal electorate to a large number. As a result, the overall responsibility for the functioning of local bodies passed from the hands of district officer to the elected chairman. The working of urban local bodies during 1921-37 was neither a complete failure nor an unqualified success. According to Simon Commission, which reviewed the working of the Government of India Act, 1919 in every province, a few local bodies have discharged their responsibilities with undoubted success and others have been equally conspicuous failures, the bulk lies between these two extremes. According to the Government of India Act, 1935, dyarchy was done away with and full provincial autonomy was introduced. On 1st April 1937 popular ministries were formed and local self-government got a new impetus. But in 1939, popular ministries resigned as a protest against making India a party to the Second World War without consulting them. As a result, local self-government again got a set back. After the War was over and elections for the Provincial Legislative Assemblies took place in 1946, the newly constituted ministries again took up the cause of local self-governing bodies.

India got its Independence in 1947 and a new enthusiasm set in motion. As a result, elections were held for various local self-governing bodies. The Five Year Plans also periodically highlighted the problems of the municipal bodies and the inabilities of these bodies to meet the growing demands of urbanization. The central government has, from time to time, showed its concern for the need to improve the urban bodies by appointing several commissions and committees. They made useful recommendations on streamlining urban development in India.

The sum total effect of the recommendations and suggestions of these bodies resulted in the enactment of the Constitution (74th Amendment) Act, 1992. It made statutory provisions for the establishment, empowerment and functioning of urban local self-governing institutions. The main provisions of this Act can be grouped under two categories—compulsory and voluntary. Some of the *compulsory* provisions are:

- constitution of Nagar Panchayats, Municipal Councils and Municipal Corporations;
- Reservation of seats in urban local bodies for Scheduled Castes/Scheduled Tribes in proportion to their population;
- Reservation of seats for women up to one-third seats;
- The State Election Commission, constituted with reference to conducting elections to the Panchayati Raj bodies, should also conduct elections to the urban local self-governing bodies;
- The State Finance Commission, constituted with reference to financial affairs of the Panchayati Raj bodies, should also look into the financial affairs of the local urban self-governing bodies;

- Tenure of urban local self-governing bodies fixed at five years, if dissolved earlier, fresh elections to be held within six months.

Voluntary provisions are:

- Giving voting rights to members of the Union and State Legislatures in these bodies;
- Providing reservation for Backward Classes;
- Giving financial powers in relation to taxes, duties, tolls and fees etc;
- Making the municipal bodies autonomous and devolution of powers to these bodies to perform some or all of the functions enumerated in the Twelfth Schedule added to the Constitution through the Constitution (74th Amendment] Act and/or to prepare plans for economic development.

Structure of Urban Bodies

The Constitution, as amended, provides for the establishment of Nagar Panchayats for transitional areas (that is to say, an area in transition from a rural area to an urban area), Municipal Councils for smaller urban areas and Municipal Corporations for larger urban areas. However, no municipality can be constituted in areas that come under the jurisdiction of an industrial establishment that provides or proposes to provide municipal services therein.

MUNICIPAL BODIES

All the seats in municipal bodies should be filled by persons chosen by direct election from the territorial constituencies in the municipal area. However, the Legislature of a State may, by law, provide for the representation in a municipal body of persons having special knowledge or experience of municipal administration, the members of Rajya Sabha, Lok Sabha and the members of Legislative Council and Legislative Assembly of the State, representing constituencies which comprise wholly or partly the municipal area and the chair persons of Wards Committees.

There should be Wards Committees, consisting of one or more Wards, within the territorial area of a municipal body having a population of three lakhs or more. The Legislature of a State may, by law, make provision with respect to the composition and the territorial area of a Wards Committee and the manner in which the seats in a Wards Committee should be filled.

However, the Legislature of a State can make provision for the constitution of other committees in addition to the Wards Committees. Seats should be reserved for the Scheduled Castes and the Scheduled Tribes in every municipal body in proportion to their population. Out of these reserved seats (for Scheduled Castes and Scheduled Tribes) one-third would be reserved for women belonging to these communities. Similarly, not less than one-third of the total number of seats to be filled by direct election in every municipal body should be reserved for women (including their reservation in the quota of Scheduled Castes and Scheduled Tribes). Similarly, the offices of chairpersons in the municipal bodies should be reserved for the Scheduled Castes, Scheduled Tribes and women in such manner as the Legislature of a State may, by law, provide. The Legislature of a State may also make provision for reservation of seats in municipal bodies or offices of chairpersons, for other Backward Classes.

A person who has attained the age of 21 years will be eligible to be elected as a member of a municipal body. The superintendence, direction and control of, the preparation of the electoral rolls for, and the conduct of all elections to municipal bodies should be vested in the State Election Commission, constituted with reference to holding elections for Panchayati Raj institutions.

The tenure of every municipal body should be five years. They can, however, be dissolved earlier after giving them reasonable opportunity of being heard. Their election of the new municipal body should be held before the expiry of its tenure or within six months of its dissolution, as the case may be.

The Legislature of a State may extend powers and authority of municipal bodies, if necessary, to enable them to function as institutions of self-government. It may authorize a municipal body to levy, collect and appropriate such taxes, duties, tolls, and fees as it thinks fit. It may also assign a share in those taxes, duties, tolls, and fees that are levied and collected by the State Government itself. It may also make provision for making grants-in-aid to municipal bodies from the Consolidated Fund of the State. It may also provide for constitution of such funds for crediting all money received by the municipal bodies and their withdrawal.

The Finance Commission, constituted with reference to Panchayati Raj Institutions, should also review the financial position of the municipal bodies and; make recommendations to the Governor, as to:

- the principles which should govern the distribution between the State and the municipal bodies of the net proceeds of the taxes, duties, tolls and fees leviable by the State;
- the determination of the taxes, duties, tolls and fees which may be assigned to or appropriated by the municipal bodies and the grants-in-aid to the municipal bodies from the Consolidated Fund of the State;
- the measures needed to improve the financial position of the municipal bodies.

Powers and Functions of Urban Local Bodies

The Constitutional Amendment Act (CAA 74) mandates compulsory reconstitution of municipal bodies within a stipulated time frame, thus ensuring continuity of local representatives. The twelfth schedule of the Constitutional Amendment Act (CAA 74) has listed 18 functions and responsibilities to local bodies. These are:

1. Urban planning, including town planning;
2. Regulation of land use and construction of buildings;
3. Planning for economic and social development;
4. Roads and bridges;
5. Water supply for domestic, industrial, and commercial purposes;
6. Public health, sanitation, conservancy, and solid waste management;
7. Fire services;
8. Urban forestry, protection of the environment, and promotion of ecological aspects;
9. Safeguarding the interests of weaker sections of society, including the handicapped and mentally retarded;
10. Slum improvement and upgradation;
11. Urban poverty alleviation;
12. Provision of urban amenities and facilities such as parks, gardens, and playgrounds;
13. Promotion of cultural, educational and aesthetic aspects;
14. Burials and burial grounds; cremation grounds and electric crematoria;
15. Cattle pounds, prevention of cruelty to animals;
16. Vital statistics, including registration of births and deaths;
17. Public amenities including street lighting, parking lots, bus-stop, and public conveniences;
18. Regulation of slaughterhouses and tanneries.

References

1. Mahaeshwari, S.R., *Local Government in India,* Orient Longmans, Delhi, 1971, p. 17.
2. *Memoranda Submitted to the Indian Statutory Commission by the Govt. of India,* Vol. V, 1930, p. 1064.
3. *Report of the Royal Commission on Decentralization in India,* 1909, Vol. I, p. 282.
4. *Report of the Indian Statutory Commission,* Vol. I, chapter 4, para 349.
5. *Report of the Local Self-Government,* vide Notification No. 11/6/XI-457, Municipal Department, dated March 24, 1938), Part II, Para II, Para XI, p. 3.
6. 74th Amendment Act, Government of India, 1992.
7. Mohanty P.K., "Reforming Municipal Finances: Some Suggestions in the Context of India's Decentralization Initiative", *Urban India,* January–June 1995.

Urbanization: Challenges to Decentralization of Powers in India

Dr. C.L. Chenna Reddy,
Dr. P.B. Reddy

Liberalization and globalization in India heralded rapid economic growth which also contributed to increase in the level of urbanization from 26 per cent in 1991 to 28 per cent in 2001 and is further expected to increase to 30 per cent by 2011 and 38 per cent by 2026. Rapid urbanization in India is inevitable and has been duly recognized. The increasing urban population has given rise in the number of urban poor and slums, causing pressure on urban land, basic services and infrastructure. This is posing a challenge to promote inclusive, sustainable and equitable and pro-poor cities. Urbanization has been considered as a problem in India since a long time and the Urban Local Governments in the country have always struggled to solve the problems. But in recent years the perception has changed. The cities and major towns are contributing more than 65 per cent of the GDP in the recent years; the government has begun to look at the urban areas as engines of growth. With rapidly increasing population in the urban areas, urbanisation has emerged as one of the most serious challenges before the administrators, planners and executives in India.

Urbanisation is posing many challenges to the Public Administration particularly in decentralisation of powers in India. It is one of the most concerning factors for legislators and bureaucrats though they are striving a lot for smooth and effective functioning of different institutions in Urban Local Self Governance. In an attempt to improve efficiency and service quality, many of Urban Local Self Governances in India initiated decentralisation of powers as per the 74th Constitutional Amendment Act, 1993, wherein the burden of service delivery is shifted to grassroot level of governments. To be effective, decentralisation requires increased capability and administrative capacity on the part of the Urban Local Self Governance. It also requires significant administrative changes on part of the local governments. Due to lack of requisite decentralisation of powers to local bodies, with long legacies of socialism and central planning like India, policy-makers and their donor partners face difficult challenges in such systems of government. There is more pressing need for the development of local government. The main objective of this paper is to discuss some of the challenges posed by urbanization to Urban Local Bodies and also to focus on the present situation of decentralisation of powers to ULBs in India especially after 74th Constitutional Amendment Act came into force on June 1st, 1993.

Challenges of Urbanisation

Problem of urbanization is manifestation of lopsided urbanization, faulty urban planning, urbanisation with poor economic base and without having functional categories. Hence India's urbanisation is followed by some basic challenges. They are as follows:

Infrastructure

There are serious gaps in the availability of infrastructure facilities in urban areas. Roads are getting congested with more and more new vehicles getting registered every day and parking has become a serious problem in most urban areas.

Population explosion

It has been observed that industrialization and urbanization leads to an increase in the population of the region at a very fast pace. The population growth results in a situation where the facilities provided by the government are to be shared among many people. This can further give rise to inequitable distribution of wealth and resources. Providing the huge population with essential resources becomes a big challenge due to population explosion. It also puts a tremendous strain on the finances and policy-makers of the country.

Poverty

Most of these cities using capital intensive technologies cannot generate employment for these distressed rural poor. So there is transfer of rural poverty to urban poverty. Poverty induced migration of illiterate and unskilled labourer occurs in class I cities addressing urban involution and urban decay.

Drinking water

According to 2001 census only 65.4 per cent of the households in the cities and towns had access to drinking water within their premises. Remaining households either had the water supply source outside their premises or away from their houses.

Housing

Scarcity of space for the construction of houses and buildings results in deforestation which causes several environmental problems. The problem of slums in urban cities is becoming more and more difficult to tackle due to the issue of displacement that the huge population residing in these slums will face.

Lighting

More than 12 per cent of the households in the urban areas did not have an electric source of lighting and had to depend on other sources like kerosene.

Education facilities

In the urban areas education is also a key challenge, particularly for the poor. While the affluent and upper middle classes normally have best of educational facilities available to them in the cities, the poorer sections find it hard to have access even to basic educational facilities.

Health care facilities

As per the report of a Taskforce appointed by the government of India to advise on health scenario in the urban slums, it was pointed out that 6 out of 10 children in slum areas are delivered at home. Further, more than half of India's urban poor children are underweight and the state of under-nutrition in urban areas is worse than in the rural areas. Reach and utilisation of essential preventive health services by the urban poor is generally found to be very low and about 60 per cent of the children below one year of age are not fully immunized. Only 4 per cent couples use birth spacing methods.

Wastage management

Solid waste management is also a serious problem in the country, particularly in the cities. Safe disposal of the solid waste in a scientific manner is a major issue in Indian cities and towns. With over 350 million people living in urban areas and generating millions of tones of garbage every day, without proper arrangements for safe disposal of the garbage serious problem of water contamination and environment pollution is on the anvil. The problem is worst in the areas inhabited by the poor and in the slums.

Environmental pollution and degradation

The increased number of vehicles on the roads and industrial wastes are the main sources of air pollution. Urbanization also leads to a rise in the noise pollution levels. Contamination of sea, river and lake water due to various human activities are also a serious issue resulting out of fast urbanization. Land pollution is also a matter of great concern. These types of pollution can cause adverse effects on the health and well being of people.

Increase in crime

Surveys conducted suggest that the crime rate is much higher in urban cities as compared to backward regions. The rise in the number of crimes is due to the need to earn wealth which results in people resorting to unfair means. The common man in the urban areas suffers the most because of the rise in criminal activities.

Decentralisation of Responsibilities

The 74th Constitutional Amendment Act (CAA)

The 74th Constitutional Amendment Act of India is seen as a landmark in the history of decentralised governance in India. The main objective of this Amendment is to empower the people to take on increasing responsibilities of local self-governance through municipalities. The 74th CAA provides for a broad structure of municipalities for organising urban governance with an accountable, responsive and decentralised system enabling participation of citizens in urban governance.

Considerable headway has been made since the enactment of the 74th CAA where many states have devolved functions and powers to local authorities. State Finance Commissions have been constituted and have made recommendations for resource allocations to ULBs. Administrative and democratic decentralisation have been made mandatory, and consequently, most states have made arrangements for periodic elections to these bodies and have also indicated 18 subjects over which local authorities would have a say. But there are large differences between states in the degree to which this Amendment have been implemented.

Critique on 74th CAA

It is nearing two decades since the Constitution was amended and during this duration, several steps have been taken towards achieving the objectives of these Amendments particularly in decentralisation of powers. Still much have to be done not on paper but in spirit to actively face the challenges posed by the urbanization for effective and efficient administration in Urban Local Bodies in India.

Challenges

1. *Adequate Devolution of Resources, Authority and Responsibility:* Fiscal decentralisation, an essential precondition for adequate devolution of authority, powers, responsibilities, has not made much headway.
2. Similarly, more attention is needed to create conditions for more synergy in the operations of the central and state governments, while strengthening the capacity of local governance institutions to progressively overcome the challenges posed by poverty and social inequalities.

3. Failure to hold regular and periodical elections, prolonged supersessions, inadequate representation of weaker sections, lack of financial resources and inadequate devolution of powers and responsibilities upon them.
4. It was felt that the powers and functions of municipalities had gradually declined and been taken over by other authorities, and Urban Local Bodies were left with few or no resources.
5. Even when there were some efforts at local planning, the poor were seldom involved and the delivery of municipal services was far from equitable.
6. The XII Schedule is not mandated and it is up to the state governments to decide as to which of the XII Schedule functions may be devolved to the ULBs. Most States, have amended their Acts to include part or in some cases all of these. Studies suggest that only marginal changes that were regarded as mandatory have been carried out. A comparison of the atate legislations' with central Act reveal that few state governments have availed of the opportunity presented by the 74th Constitutional Amendment to clarify municipal functions listed as 'obligatory' and 'discretionary' and avoids overlapping institutional functiona and geographic jurisdictions.
7. In almost all states with the exception of West Bengal and Kerala, political decentralisation has not been backed by enough financial devolution. Thus, ULBs have to depend upon the state government's political and bureaucratic lobbies to access funds. Also, there is still very significant dependence in terms of permission seeking for even relatively simple matters. This further reinforces the lack of financial devolution.
8. In most of the states, Mayors do not have executive powers as they are vested with the Commissioners.

Measures

The 74th CAA proposes to strengthen ULBs in terms of their structure, composition, financial resources, functions and powers. Besides restoring to ULBs the traditional functions that were taken away by specific authorities, makes them responsible for the preparation of economic plans and social justice; regulation of land use and construction; water supply, public health and the environment; slum improvement and upgradation and urban poverty alleviation. In this context, the Ninth Plan Document mentions support to State Finance Commissions and support to District Planning as two critical areas for strengthening these institutions. In the light of the emphasis placed upon decentralisation in India's national plans, international cooperation must seek to identify areas of intervention that help lend more substance and credibility to Urban Local Bodies. There is a need for interventions that help counter skepticism and promote local democracy, which is consistent with the objectives of sustainable human development. By providing the much needed institutional capabilities to urban local governments, it is hoped that they will be better equipped to deal with urbanization and urban growth.

Conclusion

Challenges of urbanization can be dealt with through efficient government policies and proper implementation. It is important for all nations of the world to come together and discuss ways to solve these problems completely. There is need to transfer additional functions to ULBs so that they can be able to face challenges posed by urbanization. There is need to build credibility of ULGs through improved administration and dissemination and networking of ULGs is crucial. Constitutional amendments are required to achieve objectives of decentralization to face the urbanization's challenges. It is need of the hour to integrate different urban development and related programmes at local, state and national level to develop sustainable urban development. To make the politico administrative system more responsive to the needs and aspirations of citizens, to move the public decision-making process closer to the people, better urban governance decentralization of powers are very essential.

References

1. Registrar General, 'Census of India, 2001, India', New Delhi, 25th July, 2001.
2. Human Development Resource Centre, *'Decentralisation in India Challenges and Opportunities'*, UNDP, New Delhi, 2000.
3. Kranthi Kiran, *'Urbanisation—A Challenge to India'*, http://www.india study channel.com.
4. Chetan vaidya, *'Urban Issues, Reforms and Way Forward in India'*, Ministry of Finance, Government of India, 2006.
5. "Decentralisation and Good Urban Governance in Southeast Asia", Workshop on Urbanisation in Southeast Asian Countries: Cities as Engines of Development, Singapore, March, 2010.

A Study on Vulnerability Assessment for Balasahyoga Families in Urban Areas

Dr. P. Ganesh,
Dr. T. Chandrasekarayya

Introduction

In India, it has been estimated that 5.1 million people living with HIV infection. The response to the AIDS epidemic in India is yet to take a serious look at the issue of children affected by and vulnerable to HIV/AIDS due to their invisibility, and voicelessness. Policy and programming initiatives to address the needs of children affected by and vulnerable to HIV/AIDS have fallen short at all levels. As per 2001 census, there are 400 million children in India under the age of 18 years (Registrar General of India, 2001). The number of orphans in India by all causes is estimated to be 35 million (UNICEF, 2004) and the estimate of destitute children is 44 million (Catalysts for Social Action, 2004). Some of these children might have lost their parent(s) due to AIDS and others might be highly vulnerable to acquiring HIV infection. Media reports citied that more than one million children in India under the age of 15 have lost one or both parents to HIV/AIDS (*The Guardian*, March 23, 2005). Children below 14 years constitute 4.3 per cent of the cumulative AIDS cases reported in India as on July 2005. Another projection made by the Design Team of the third phase of the National AIDS Control Programme (NACP) estimates 170,698 children infected with HIV in 2006 (Thomas, 2006). In every child who comes into the world, the hopes and dreams of the human race are born anew. Children are the flag bearers of our common future— a future that is in our hands as never before. For the world has the knowledge, the resources and the legal imperatives to give every child the best possible start in life, in a family environment that offers the love, the care and the nurturing that children need to grow, to learn and to develop to the fullest. In this context "Balasahyoga" is a program where comprehensive Care, Support and Treatment (CST) services are provided to the HIV infected and affected children and their families with the objective of improving their quality of life. After proving one year services, a study was conducted on vulnerability assessment for Balasahyoga families in urban areas of Kadapa district, Andhra Pradesh. This study is immensely useful to policy and programming initiatives to address the needs of children affected by and vulnerable to HIV/AIDS. Keeping in view this study aims to ascertain the vulnerability status of the HIV infected and affected families after providing one year services on Care, Support and Treatment through Balasahyoga program. It also aimed to link different stakeholders with different kinds of services/schemes that needs for these families.

Objectives of the study

1. To assess the level of resilience in the HIV infected and affected families after completed one year of CST services.
2. Mapping the marginalized families in the intervention areas and the depth of issues as well to extend the comprehensive services including social entitlements.

Methodology

The study was carried out in four urban regions in the district, i.e Kadapa, Rajampeta, Rayachoti and Jammalamadugu using stratified sampling. Cluster sampling procedure was followed for the selection of households from different pockets of the regions. The sampling unit for the study was HIV infected and affected families registered in Balasahyoga program before one year to the study date. Parent headed, Widow headed, Grandparent headed, Child headed and Discordant couple families took part in the study. Thus a total of 127 families were selected and data were collected. A structured interview schedule has been developed exclusively for the present study comprising all categories. The data were collected by the Field Supervisors, Counselors and Family Case Managers using interview schedule by interviewing each of the selected individual at their home.

Data analysis

The collected data were analyzed using computer. Three point scales is used for scoring the answer for each parameter. When the results scored for all HHs the lowest score is recorded as 33 and the highest score is recorded as 48. These scores were divided in three categories giving equal probability i.e grade 'A' is 48 – 43, grade 'B' is 42 - 38 and grade 'C' is 37 - 33. Grade 'A' is considered as highly resilient families, Grade 'B' is considered as resilient and Grade 'C' is considered as vulnerable families. The Univariate, Bivariate analysis was carried out using Excel format.

Results

The results of the study are discussed here under:

Table 27.1: Distribution of families by vulnerability status in all domains

Vulnerable index	Number of Families	Per cent
Highly Resilient	33	26
Resilient	69	54
Vulnerable	25	20
Total	127	100

The analysis in table 27.1 shows that little more than half (54%) of the families are resilient in all domains of their life. One-forth (26%) of the families are highly resilient and 20 per cent of the families are under vulnerable condition.

Table 27.2: Distribution of families by domain and vulnerability status

Domain	Vulnerable index			Total
	Highly Resilient	Resilient	Vulnerable	
Health	70 (55%)	57 (45%)	—	127
Psychosocial support	14 (13%)	84 (66%)	29 (23%)	127
Nutrition	22 (17%)	76 (60%)	29 (23%)	127
Education	71 (56%)	13 (10%)	43 (34%)	127
Safety net	0	27 (21%)	100 (79%)	127

Table 27.2 provides vulnerability status of the families by all domains of their life. More than half (55%) of the families are highly resilient in health domain. 66 per cent of the families are resilient in psychosocial domain and 60 per cent in nutrition and only 27 per cent are resilient in food security/ safety net.

Table 27.3: Distribution of families by type of family and vulnerability status

Type of Family	Vulnerable index			Total
	Highly Resilient	Resilient	Vulnerable	
Parent headed	24 (67)	38 (55)	10 (45)	72 (57)
Widow headed	4 (11)	17 (25)	10 (45)	31 (24)
Grandparent headed	8 (22)	13 (19)	0	21 (17)
Child headed	0	1 (1)	2 (9)	3 (2)
Total	36 (100)	69 (100)	22 (100)	127 (100)
Total %	28%	54%	17%	

Note: Percentages are shown in the brackets.

Table 27.3 furnishes information on vulnerability status of the families by type of family. More than two-thirds (67%) of the families are highly resilient in parent headed HHs following Grandparent headed HH (22%), least scored in Widow headed HHs (11%) and none of the Child headed family is scored under high resilient.

Table 27.4: Distribution of families by discordant couple and vulnerability status

Type of family	Vulnerable index			Total
	Highly Resilient	Resilient	Vulnerable	Total
Discordant Couple	3 (18)	13 (76)	1 (6)	17 (100)

Table 27.4 provides vulnerability status of the discordant couple families. Little more than three-fourth (76%) of the families are scored as resilient, followed by 18 per cent highly resilient and 6 per cent families are scored vulnerable.

Table 27.5: Distribution of families by social Status (caste) and vulnerability Status

Social Status	Vulnerable index			Total
	Highly Resilient	Resilient	Vulnerable	Total
FC	17 (47)	21 (30)	5 (23)	43 (34)
BC	10 (28)	34 (49)	11 (50)	55 (43)
SC	6 (17)	11 (16)	5 (23)	22 (17)
ST	3 (8)	3 (4)	1 (5)	7 (6)
Total	36 (100)	69 (100)	22 (100)	127 (100)
Total %	28%	54%	17%	

Table 27.5 provides vulnerability status of the families by social status (caste). Nearly half of the families are observed as highly resilient in Forward Caste, followed by 28 per cent in Backward Caste, 17 per cent in Scheduled Caste and least (8%) in Scheduled Tribe. Half (50%) of the vulnerable families are observed in Backward Caste than FC and SC.

Table 27.6: Distribution of families by economic status and area of residence

Type of Family	Area			
	Highly Resilient	Resilient	Vulnerable	
	Urban	Semi Urban	Urban Hinterland	Total
BPL families	27%	18%	55%	100%
Non-BPL families	44%	9%	47%	100%
Total	43%	9%	48%	100%
Total (No.)	54	12	61	127

Table 27.6 provides vulnerability status of the families by Economic status and area of their residence. More than half (55%) of the BPL (Below Poverty Line) families are living in urban hinterland with vulnerable condition, than urban (27%) and followed to semi urban (18%).

Table 27.7: Distribution of families by area of residence and vulnerability status in health

Health	Area				
	Urban	Semi -Urban	Urban Hinterland	Total	%
Highly Resilient	30 (43)	7 (10)	33 (47)	70	55%
Resilient	24 (42)	5 (9)	28 (49)	57	45%
Vulnerable	0	0	0	0	0
Total	54	12	61	127	100%
	43%	9%	48%	100%	

Table 27.7 provides vulnerability status of the families in health by area of residence. Nearly half (47%) of the families are observed as highly resilient in urban hinterland in health, followed to (43%) in urban and least (10%) in semi-urban areas. None of the vulnerable families are scored in any area in health domain.

Table 29.8: Distribution of families by type of family and vulnerability status in health

Health	Type of Family					
	Parent Headed	Widow Headed	Grandparent Headed	Child Headed	Total	%
Highly resilient	51 (73)	8 (11)	10 (10)	1 (1.5)	70	33
Resilient	21 (37)	23 (40)	11 (19)	2 (4)	57	67
Vulnerable	0	0	0	0	0	0
Total	72	31	21	3	127	100
	57%	24%	17%	2%	100%	

Table 27.8 provides vulnerability status of the families in health by type of family. Nearly three-fourth (47%) of the families are observed as highly resilient in health among parent headed families, mere (11%) in widow headed, 10 per cent in grand parent headed and worst (1.5%) among child headed families. None of the vulnerable families are scored among all types of families in health domain.

Table 27.9: Distribution of families by social status and vulnerability status in health

Health	Social Status					
	FC	BC	SC	ST	Total	%
Highly resilient	25 (36)	29 (41)	12 (17)	4 (6)	70	57
Resilient	18 (32)	26 (46)	10 (17)	3 (5)	57	43
Vulnerable	0	0	0	0	0	0
Total	43	55	22	7	127	100
%	34%	43%	17%	6%	100%	

Table 27.9 provides vulnerability status of the families in health by social status (caste). Little more than two-fifths (41%) among Backward Caste families scored as highly resilient in health, followed by 36 per cent Forward Caste, 17 per cent among Scheduled Caste and mere 6 per cent among Scheduled Tribe. None of the vulnerable families are scored among all caste groups in health domain.

Recommendations and Conclusion

On the whole only 25 per cent of the families stands on resilient in all the domains such as health, nutrition, Psychosocial, education and safety net, the following services are recommended to improve the quality of life of these families.

- The existing health facilities at regional level should be strengthened in conducting early infant diagnosis (EID), Pre-ART screening, opportunity Infections (OI) treatment including TB, registration for ART services and follow-up the medicine adherence.
- Home-based counseling to be provided by ICTC and ARTC counselors and NGO out reach workers (ORW) to HIV infected and affected families on improved water handling and sanitation practices; personal and domestic hygiene.
- Extensive needs-based counselling services to be provided basing on age, stage of illness. Identified discordant couple should be provided home-based counselling on safe sex practices.
- Life skills education to be provided at ward level to children aged 6-18 years.
- Periodic nutritional assessments to be done for children aged 0-5 years and 6-14 years and categories them as severely acute malnourished (SAM) or moderately acute malnourished (MAM) and normal. Based on this they should be provided nutrition and dietary counseling, including breast-feeding, infant feeding, demonstrations, and linkages to existing food programs for supplementary nutrition: ICDS, Mid-Day meal and double ration could be provided through ICDS to children who falls under SAM and MAM.
- The ORWs of the government and private needs to support and monitor the school enrolment and retention of the children living in HIV infected and affected families.
- Linkages with universal primary education program for formal and non-formal education. Orphan children should be joined Residential Bridge Schools (RBS) and follow-up their care and support.
- Food security assessments to be done for all HIV infected and affected households and food security interventions to be provided to highly food insecure households.

- Government and local NGOs should make sure by visiting the door steps that all HIV/AIDS infected and affected families are availed all eligible and available welfare schemes.

References

1. Catalysts for Social Action, 2004: A Research Paper Covering Adoption Agencies in Mumbai and Pune', www.csa.org.in/adoptionwhitepaperd.htm accessed November 21.
2. Registrar General of India, 2001: Census of India, 2001, New Delhi.
3. Thomas, Kurien, 2006: Projections on HIV Epidemic in India- Preparatory Document for NACP-III Project Implementation Plan, NACO, New Delhi.
4. UNICEF, 2004: "Children on the Brink—A Joint Report on New Orphan Estimates and Framework for Action", UNAIDS, UNICEF and USAID, New York.

Social Work Interventions in Urban Health Setting

Dr. D. Sai Sujatha,
Mrs. V.T. Hinduja

Introduction

Social workers provide interventions to individuals, families and groups in order to assist them with their needs and issues. Health interventions are intended to aid clients in alleviating problems impeding their well-being. The interventions used by social workers are those that are identified as potentially helpful on the basis of the social worker's ongoing assessment of the client. Health intervention trials represent a shift in health research from investigations that focus primarily on the individual to those that focus on larger groups and communities.

Social workers will play a more significant role in providing health and mental health services and in shaping the changes needed to make the managed care more responsive to client needs of diverse urban situations. Small ailments such as a 'runny nose' or headache can affect ones mood and subsequently, interaction with other people. Major illnesses can be depressing and disabling (Miller, 1983; Holosko and Taylor, 1989; Germain, 1984). Lack of financial means and poor access to medical and health services can be major barriers to recovery for some people (Miller, 1983; Oen, 1991). Social work in health care requires multilateral intervention at different focuses of change (Miller and Rehr, 1983; Carlton,1984).

The National Association of Social Workers (NASW) has identified a number of specialty practice areas where social workers work that influence the types of interventions selected for use with clients. Areas of practice include aging, alcohol, tobacco and other drugs, children, adolescents and young adults, child welfare, health, mental health, private practice, school social work, social and economic justice and peace. Interventions can include: psychotherapy (individual, couples, families, group), counseling to aid with loss and adjustment, case management, crisis intervention, brief therapy, relaxation training, anger management and stress management.

Social work has created a professional repertoire consisting of theoretical explanations (and a conceptual grasp of the various realities—patients, health care providers, and their institutions). Practice principles, models of intervention, strategies, and techniques. The needs of patients and of organizations have guided the development of the various models of practice. 'Some of these provide general approaches and tools for psychosocial assessment and interventions. Others are site problem, and population specific. Still others focus on the major social work functions such as case management, inter-disciplinary collaboration liaison' (D hooper, 1994, p. 50). Still others aimed at improving social workers' effectiveness and efficiency. Professional accountability and autonomy.

The social work profession not only values diversity in its clients it also value diversity within its own group. Therefore, this paper focuses on the need for social work intervention with individuals, families, groups and communities.

Social Work in Health Setting

Social workers work in many different types of settings, including hospitals, mental health facilities, child welfare centers, guidance clinics, schools, substance abuse programs and prisons/correctional facilities. These program and service areas vary on the type of problems that clients bring to a particular setting, representing specializations in social work.

Doctors and planners in despite the financial difficulties stated general objectives of medical social service in the manual of procedures for medical social service of the Social Welfare Department (SWD, 1987) are much more comprehensively directed to the social and emotional needs of patients and their families. These objectives are:

1. To assist patients and their families with the social and emotional problems involved in illness situations;
2. To enable them to make the best use of medical and rehabilitative services in the community;
3. To contribute to the total rehabilitation (physical, mental and social) of individuals and their re-integration in to society; and
4. To strive for the promotion of health of patients, their families and the community.

Role of Social Work in Health Setting

Social work practices are the direct approach to fulfill the needs of individuals, families, groups and communities. Social work tries to provide the best services as much as possible within the available resources for the same. The social worker provides interventions in various settings in terms of primary health care, health education, psychosocial counseling, mental health interventions, and family counseling, drug and alcohol counseling, recreation, employment services, parenting education, and childcare and placement services by medical and psychiatric social workers with the help of government and non-governmental organizations.

According to Jacobs and Lurie (1984) the social workers become an indispensable part of the home care team. They are able to provide counseling, assist the patient with concrete financial, housing, and medical equipment problems, advocate for the patient with welfare and health care system, Medicaid, support the patient in compliance with the treatment regimes, help the patient understand and deal with strained family relationships and help the patient be reconciled to chronic illness. Indeed in the absence of good social work care, the home care service can be an exercise in the application of medical technology, while the patient remain miserable, kept alive physically but in turmoil and suffering emotionally.

Social work in home care, by providing services in the home, returns to the origins of the profession, to that subtle, artful blending of support, counseling and advocacy which social workers do best.

Garner adds that other commonly needed social worker roles and functions include:

1. Helping the clients and/or families cope with their losses, including anticipated ones;
2. Promoting medical compliance;
3. Psychosocial counseling as needed;
4. Advocating on behalf of the clients or families; and
5. Discharge planning when clients no longer need the home health agency (HHA) services or when they need another level of service, such as a nursing home, hospital, or rehabilitation center. (1995,1632).

To meet these needs social worker will follow the certain social work methods such as social case work, social group work, community organization, social welfare administration, social action and social research.

Need of Social Work Intervention and Health

The need for social work health intervention arises when the resources available to an individual, family or community are insufficient and lack of knowledge about the disease, reasons for disease and illness and prognosis are major concerns of the caregiver and barriers to look after the patent. Therapeutic alliance is important to provide interventions and trust need to be established with the patient.

Most social workers are currently expected to cover a huge span of approaches. This may not be appropriate in the future. Different strands can be identified, which, while not exclusive of each other, form the primary focus individual social workers' interventions.

The social worker plays different roles to provide health interventions on the areas; given in table 28.1.

Table 28.1: Health issues and areas of intervention for different types of social workers

Social workers	Health issues	Modes of intervention
Community workers	Poverty, unemployment, malnutrition, environmental deprivation and hazards, pollution	Advocacy, volunteer, mobilization, self help empowerment, networking
Industrial social workers	Industrial health and safety, occupational hazards	Adjustment to industrial injury and death, advocacy, legislative reform
Family service workers	Family break down due to health crisis, illness and disability, domestic violence	Counseling, bereavement, caregiver support, community care
Medical social workers	Psychological issues arising in acute hospitals, specialist clinics, methadone clinics, homes and institutions	Counseling, case management, financial and marital assistance, fee waiving discharge planning: patients' advocacy
Mental health workers, psychiatric social workers and rehabilitation workers	Stress, mental retardation, psychiatric crisis, suicide	Mental health promotion, rehabilitation, social skills and life skills training, community rehabilitation
Youth workers and school social workers	Physical and sexual abuse, high risk behavior, substance abuse, attempted suicide	Rebuilding of self adjustment to crisis, sex education and family planning, behavior modification
Health promoters especially workers in the field of service for the elderly	Chronic illness, pain, mental health and self-care issues	Prevention and early identification of health issues in elderly social service centers and community centers
Social planners	Social apathy, lack of health knowledge and awareness, gaps in service delivery, low consumer participation	Research, problem identifi-cation, continuity of care, effective resource allocation, management and organizational reform, policy change, patients rights

Source: Cecilia Lai, Wan Chan, 1996.

Skills of Social Worker in Health Intervention

Clients perceive social workers as symbols of authority with power to influence their lives. Clients often bring with them a fund of past experiences with professionals or stereotypes of helping professionals passed on by friends or family. Thus, the first sessions are partly efforts to explore the realities of the situation. A structure is needed to free the client to accept the offer of help. The crucial skills involved in the beginning phase of practice include—

1. Clarifying the purpose of intervention,
2. Clarifying the workers role,
3. Reaching for the clients feedback, and
4. Exploring issues of authority.

Contracting is never completed in the first session, it is a ongoing process, and the common ground between the clients felt needs and the agencies, services will evolve and change over time. With regard to resistant and mandated clients it is important that the worker bring up the obstacles that make the clients ability to accept help. Mutual expectations need to be defined and are part of the contracting process.

Social Worker—Health Policy

Review of the literature defining need in social policy already exists. There is agreement between policy-makers and people using service that an outcomes approach is a basis on which user centered services, must be accessible, available and affordable to all categories of people to utilize the health services. It shows that the role of social worker in health and policy planning is essential.

Conclusion

Social workers must also take into account how the diversity of client populations affects practice, models of practice need to be adapted to culturally sensitive variations introduced by knowledgeable and responsive social workers.

References

1. C., F. Chan, A. Chang, P. Chow, J. Leung, 1996 (a), *Therapeutic Group in Medical Settings*, Resource Paper Series No. 25. Hongkong; Department of Social Work and Social Administration, University of Hongkong.
2. Jacobs and Lurie (1984); Lois A. Fort Cowls, *Social Work in the Health Field* A Care Perspective (second edition).
3. Miller, J. F. 1983, *Coping with Chronic illness: Overcoming Powerlessness*, Philadelphia.
4. NASW Social Work Speciality Areas

5. R Miller, and H. Rehr (eds). 1983, *Social Work Issues in Healthcare,* New Jersey: Prentice, Hall.

6. Social Welfare Department, 1987 "Manual of Procedures for Medical Social Service of the Social Welfare Department" (amended edition.) Unpublished Manual of Procedures.

7. T .O. Carlton, 1984, *Clinical Social Work in Health Settings: A Guide to Professional Practice with Exemplars,* New York: Springer Publishing.

Family Life Education and Human Life Cycles

Dr. A. kusuma,
Mr. B. Eresha

Introduction

A child is born and nurtured in a family. During the process of his growth he passes through various phases before he reaches adulthood viz., infancy, childhood and adolescence. The first and the last are periods of rapid growth. During adolescence the growing boy or girl passes through physiological, psychological and emotional changes and prepares himself or herself for adult roles, namely social and economic responsibilities. This phase starts around at 10 years age for girls and continues through teens, while for boys it starts a year to two later and continues till 20 or 21 years of age. This change and growth may continue even later but is not so rapid.

Attitude towards sex and sexuality are formed quite early in life. Children learn more from observing and hearing to what goes on at home and their immediate circle. Even a small child learns that discussion or questions about genitals or sex is a taboo at home and good boys and girls do not ask such questions. When they reach adolescence and need information about their own sexuality, they feel embarrassed in asking questions and even, if they to ask, parents are usually unable to answer them. Therefore, while on the one hand there is a need for counseling and information regarding human sexuality for the young people, there is no proper channel available for imparting the information. Whatever information they get is from their friends who themselves do not have correct information or mass media like television and films which again give more importance to sex appeal than scientific information. Books and magazines are another source of information. But they hardly get information from two most desirable sources, namely, school and parents.

The first signs of adolescence are the physiological changes when there is a sudden growth and they gain height rapidly. This is followed by other changes like menstruation for girls and cracking of voice for boys. This is followed by psychological and emotional changes when boys and girls like to group together with the members of their own sex but are curious about the opposite sex. They get emotionally involved very easily and develop very strong bonds of friendship.

But if they are unable to get the emotional support or an object for and worship, they may feel lost and will be prepared to do anything for someone otherwise undesirable but prepared to give them this support. They pass through phases of emotional stress and strain and may appear to be moody, enjoying one moment. Boys may start spending most of the time outside the home while girls may start bolting their doors and spend hours in their bathrooms or behind closed doors.

Parents also at times feel at loss as how to behave with them. A boy of 11 or 12 years age may crave for the show of affection by mother in private but resent being even called by his pet name in front of his friends. A girl may help the mother or do some major chores at home if she is in mood but resents if she is asked or expected to do the same thing. Since they gain height, parents may expect them to take responsibilities and do certain jobs but when they discuss some family affairs or take certain decisions they are asked not to interferes since they are still considered as children. In India where early marriage is still quite prevalent, the consent of bride and the groom, particularly of the former, is many times not considered necessary as they are considered as children. This is true perhaps of other countries also wherever arranged marriages are prevalent.

Because of lack of understanding, sometimes a generation gap (more an upper-class urban phenomenon) emerges. Youth at this age are supposed to be idealists while the elders are realists. Therefore for better understanding and harmonious relationships it is necessary that both try to understand each other. Since the elders have already gone through the adolescence phase it is all the more obligatory on their part to try to understand their children and help them in understanding themselves.

Definition

Family life education is an educational process designed to assist young people in their physical, social, emotional and moral development in the socio-cultural context of family and society.

Need and Resources in Family Life Education

(a) Teenage pregnançy is not desirable as it leads to high infant mortality rate (IMR) and maternal mortality rate (MMR).

(*b*) The institution of family has for centuries nurtured the young and fulfilled most of their needs of socialization, security and sex. But due to external pressure and internal erosion that very institution is in danger today.

Until and unless some real alternatives is found to this institution, the families need to be revitalized which is possible only when each member of the family is conscious of its importance and his own roles and responsibilities in keeping the family together.

(*c*) Today about seventy per cent of Indians population live in the rural areas but by the turn of the century half of the population will live in the urban areas. And a majority of those migrating from rural to urban areas would be young people between the age of 15 to 24 years (20 to 40%). These will be separated from their families and will be without any mornings in the cities. The support of extended family and tradition would not be there and therefore they need help, information, guidance, counseling and reassurance, before leaving home and, after landing in the city.

(*d*) Due to better nutrition, girls in both developed and developing countries are physically maturing earlier. Hence, young people need information about their own body, personal hygiene and re-productive biology. Many parents are not in a position to satisfy the needs of their children. Hence sex education has to be given by the teachers of the organizations working with adolescents.

Need and Resourcess in a Family

S. No.	*Needs*		*Resourcess*
1.	Physical	:	(Food, shelter, water, air clothes) – money,
2.	Biological	:	(Sex)–marriage,
3.	Emotional	:	Love, affection, belongingness,
4.	Psychological	:	Sharing, caring, joy, recreation, togetherneses,
5.	Social	:	Group activities friends, pear groups inmates, social gathering, employment relatives, education.

Objectives

The overall go of family life education is to help youth to understand themselves and lead to their optimum growth and happiness. The objectives of family life education are:

1. To help young people to understand and cope up with their needs during growing up and accept changes—physical, psychological, social as natural process.

Maslow's Need Hierarchy

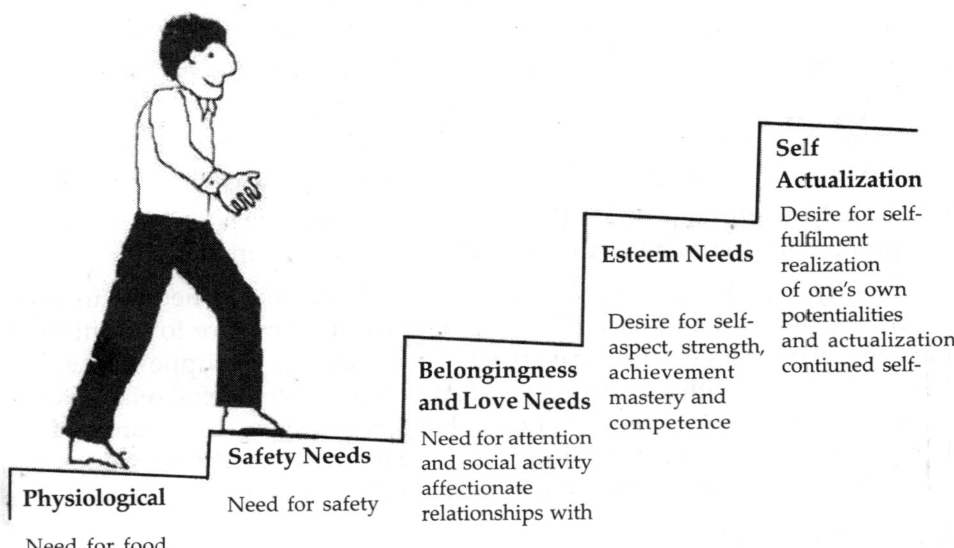

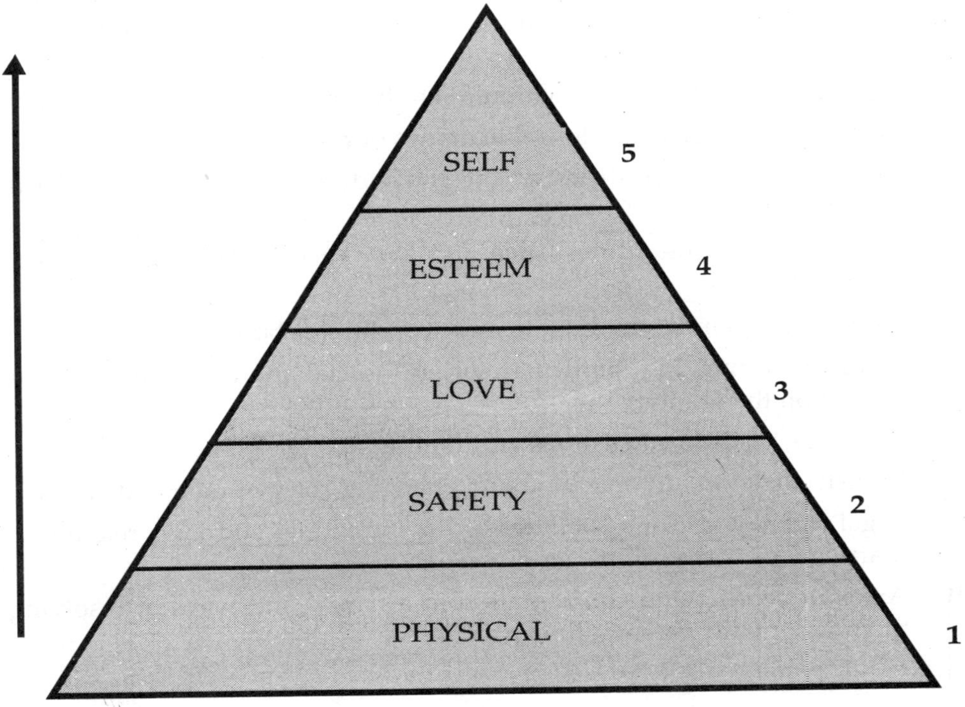

SELF 5

ESTEEM 4

LOVE 3

SAFETY 2

PHYSICAL 1

2. To help the youth (and also their family members) to accept change (external), adjust and develop rational attitudes towards healthy interpersonal relationships within the family and with the community.
3. To prepare youth for marriage, responsible parenthood and other adult roles.
4. To identify such values which have proved conducive for the growth, sustenance of family, society and retain and inculate them.
5. To help youth appreciate their roles at various stages of life cycle and prepare for the same in the context of their family and society.

Family Life Education is a way of assisting young people in their emotional, physical and social development as they prepare for adulthood, marriage, parenthood and a career (earning a living). It supports them as they learn to cope with the challenges of adult life, with personal relationships and with taking part in community life. It helps young people to understand themselves and the world in which they live to clarify their own values and to use information effectively to take responsible decisions.

Scope and Content

Scope of Family Life Education is extensive it includes all that is relevant to home and family living.

Marriage, making a home, budgeting, starting a family, childcare, recreation, parent-child relationships, changing roles and row this effects family life.

1. Interpersonal relationship within a family, peer group and community.
2. Basic human needs and desirable modes of fulfilling them.
3. Roles and responsibilities of the individual in the family and the community.
4. Education for the adolescence and guidance to parents wherever necessary.
5. Home management, budgeting and worklife for both boys and girls.
6. Status of women in a particular society—social and economic—and its impact on the family.
7. Religious, traditional customs and family.
8. Industrialization, urbanization and changing roles of men and women.
9. Legal rights and responsibilities of the individual and laws relating to marriage, property rights, employment, welfare etc.
10. Areas of conflict and confrontation in a family and ways of resolving them in a family or community.

Family Life Education is meant for stimulating and guiding self-development for satisfactory and successful family living. Therefore, this can be offered at any stage of education and is useful even for very small children. Though there are many common problems of the adolescence, there is a lot of variation from country to country and even within the country between different communities and regions. There will also be variation between urban and rural youth, educated and out-of-school youth, boys and girls etc. As such, though for certain aspects, some common topics can be identified, yet each has to be structured keeping in mind the specific needs and knowledge about the status of the target group. At the end of such a course, a student should have learnt about the life cycle, puberty (adolescence) and accompanying biological and psychological change. A student should also have comprehension of his feelings and desires, about the anatomy and physiology of human reproductive system, socio-cultural norms of the society, adult roles and the needed preparation for adult life, career, marriage and parenthood.

Family Life Cycle Diagram

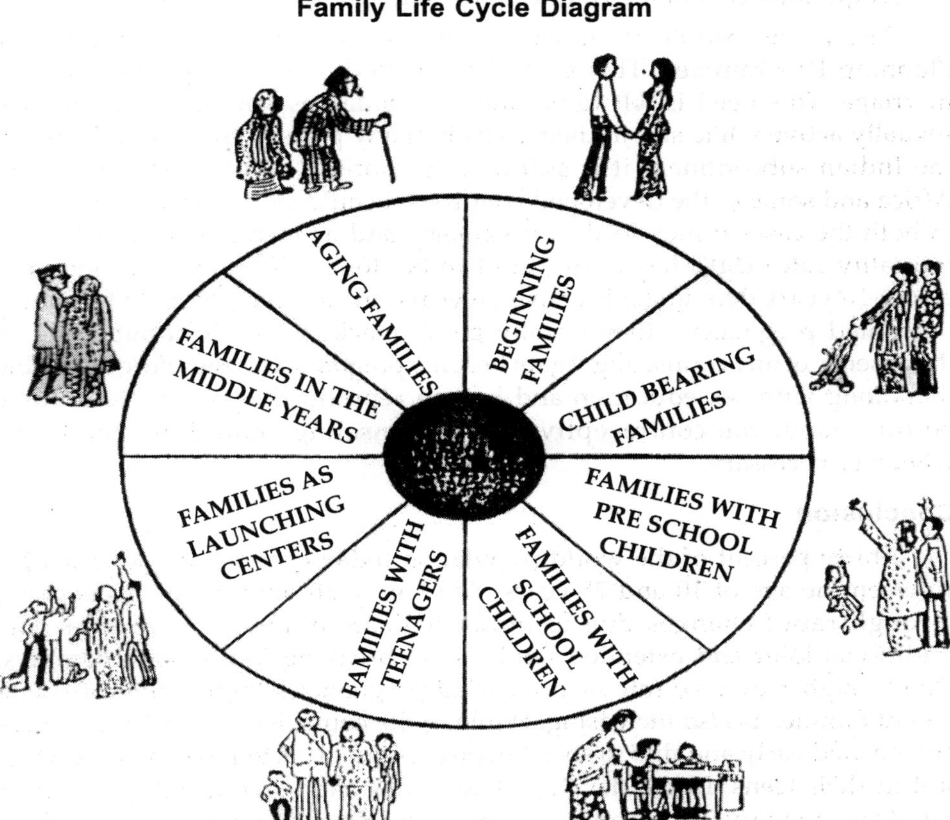

Family Life Education and Family Planning

Family Planning movement was started by pioneers like Margaret Sanger on Humanistic grounds. They felt that unplanned and undesired pregnancies cause a lot of suffering to the women and effected the children and the whole family.

In India like many other countries, family planning has been integrated with maternity, child health (MCH) and general health delivery system so as to improve the health status of the whole family. Thus the objective is the well-being of the family at micro-level and stabilizing the population at national or macro-level to maintain a balance between the resources and the populations. Youth of today who are between the age group of 15 and 25 years are entering the reproductive age group. They constitute 18.2 per cent of the India's population. With majority of them getting married before the age of 20 (particularly girls). This is social pressure on begetting a son at the earliest. According to family planning programme the age of wife is between 18 to 46 years. The present statistics shows that in the implementation of the programme the concentration is more on sterilization methods and hence the programme covers the couples in the age group of thirty and above.

The young people are given education about population and Family Planning Programmes. This should be treated as part of preparation for marriage. This need is felt to be universal today as young people become sexually active while still in their teens in many parts of the world. While in the Indian subcontinent it is still largely confined to married couples, in Africa and some of the developed countries it could be premarital. However, in both the cases it may lead to pregnancy and as mentioned earlier infant mortality rate (IMR) has been found to be double if the age of mother is below 18 years than if she is above 20 years. In case they want to terminate unwanted pregnancies they usually go to quacks which is harmful and in the absence of any counseling, again become pregnant. It is therefore advisable that along with sex education and human reproductive system youth may be told about the contraceptives and counseling should also be given wherever necessary.

Conclusion

Thirty percent of the world population today consists of young people between the age of 10 and 25 years. The family all over the world is going through rapid changes due to industrialization and urbanization. The traditional joint and extended families are breaking into nuclear families. Due to higher divorce rate or premarital pregnancies the number of single parent families is also increasing. While in the countries like India teenagers are married early and due to social pressures are expected to bear sons while still in their teens. In the developed countries and some of the developing countries premarital sex and pregnancies are on the increase. This leads to the problems like high IMR, maternal mortality. Ill-health of mother and child, discontinuation of education. Stigm associated with premarital pregnancy and hence the need to guard against young girls falling a prey to abortion by quacks. Therefore, a graded family life education including sex education should be provided to young people while still in their schools. The course should include some information on family planning where the culture permits.

It is also necessary to provide counseling centres for youth preferably linked to school and college where feasible, as well as family and marriage guidance centre which can provide responsible and personalized guidance to youth in regard to individual problems. Peer group counseling needs to be developed so that young people with inclination to serve the community may be trained in sex education, sexuality/family life education, to help other young people to understand their own growth and development as well as how to make responsible decisions in regard to their own fertility.

Family Life Education that takes place in communities is a unique type of education. The business of outreach of family life education involves taking family science principles and practices to the general public—individuals, couples, parents, whole families—in varied educational settings outside the traditional classroom. Some outreach family life educators are employed as field agents or as university campus- based specialists within the Cooperative Extension System. Others may work in social work of other human service agency contexts or as media representatives. Those with an entrepreneurial spirit may develop their own family life education business and market their programs nationally. Still others may hold traditional university positions that include some outreach expectations.

References

1. *Population Education for Quality of Life*, M.M. Mascarenhas.
2. *Family Life Education*, UNESCO Principal Regional Office for Asia and the Pacific, Bangkok–1988.
3. *Family Welfare Programme in India*, Poonam Sharma.
4. *Family Life Education*, Jagannath Mohanth, Susandhya Mohanth.
5. *Family Life Education*, Mrs. Sarala Mukhi.
6. Understanding Family Life Education and its Implications for Young People by Smt. Mamatha Lakshmamma.

INDEX